RESURRECTION AND I

MW01070137

Far more than a discrete proposition, the resurrection of Jesus entails an imaginative world to be inhabited and cultivated-a world that would transform our moral stances by reframing the horizons and desires that shape and often distort our views of transcendence, self and neighbor, and death. Sarah Bachelard's Resurrection and Moral Imagination *powerfully evokes such a world, yet does so by showing how the distinctive features of Christian imagination open up to and are deepened by sustained conversation across philosophical and theological boundaries. While skillfully conducting this conversation, Bachelard's own keen insights provide the reader with a rich sense of the Christian's resurrection ethic as a wisdom ethic.*

Brian Robinette, Boston College, USA

More than any other book I have read, Resurrection and Moral Imagination *brings the kind of moral philosophy first developed in the English-speaking world by Iris Murdoch, into critical dialogue with theology. In prose of enviable simplicity, with sensitivity, depth and sometimes startling originality, Bachelard explores the ways each needs the other.*

Raimond Gaita, University of Melbourne, Australia

Innovative, lucid and sensitive, this is a genuinely fresh look at what is distinctive about the Christian moral vision, worked out in conversation with a variety of sympathetic but more secular voices, including Rai Gaita and Iris Murdoch. Sarah Bachelard is a really significant new voice in theological ethics.

Rowan Williams, Magdalene College, Cambridge, UK

Moral life gathers its shape, force and meaning in relation to an underlying sense of reality, imaginatively conceived. Significant contemporary writing in philosophy appeals to the concept of 'transcendence' to explore what is deepest in our moral experience, but leaves this notion theologically unspecified. This book reflects on the appeal to transcendence in ethics with reference to the Resurrection of Jesus. Bachelard argues that the Resurrection reveals that the ultimate reality in which human life is held is gracious, forgiving and reconciling, a Goodness that is 'for us'. Faith in this testimony transforms the possibilities of moral life, both conceptually and in practice. It invites our participation in a goodness experienced non-dualistically as grace, and so profoundly affects the formation of the moral self, the practice of moral judgement and the shape of moral concepts. From this perspective, contemporary philosophical discussion about 'transcendence' in moral thought is cast in a new light, and debates about the continuity between theological and secular ethics gain a thoroughly new dimension. Bachelard demonstrates that placing the Resurrection at the heart of our ethical reflection resonates with the deepest currents of our lived moral experience and transfigures our approach to moral life and thought.

Transcending Boundaries in Philosophy and Theology

Series editors:
Martin Warner, University of Warwick
Kevin Vanhoozer, Wheaton College and Graduate School

Transcending Boundaries in Philosophy and Theology is an interdisciplinary series exploring new opportunities in the dialogue between philosophy and theology that go beyond more traditional 'faith and reason' debates and take account of the contemporary reshaping of intellectual boundaries. For much of the modern era, the relation of philosophy and theology has been conceived in terms of antagonism or subordination, but recent intellectual developments hold out considerable potential for a renewed dialogue in which philosophy and theology have common cause for revisioning their respective identities, reconceiving their relationship, and combining their resources. This series explores constructively for the 21st century the resources available for engaging with those forms of enquiry, experience and sensibility that theology has historically sought to address. Drawing together new writing and research from leading international scholars in the field, this high profile research series offers an important contribution to contemporary research across the interdisciplinary perspectives relating theology and philosophy.

Also in this series

Resurrection and Moral Imagination

SARAH BACHELARD
Australian Catholic University, Canberra

LONDON AND NEW YORK

First published 2014 by Ashgate Publishing

Published 2016 by Routledge
2 Park Square, Milton Park, Abingdon, Oxon OX14 4RN
711 Third Avenue, New York, NY 10017, USA

First issued in paperback 2017

Routledge is an imprint of the Taylor & Francis Group, an informa business

British Library Cataloguing in Publication Data
A catalogue record for this book is available from the British Library

Library of Congress has cataloged the printed edition as follows:
Bachelard, Sarah.
 Resurrection and moral imagination / by Sarah Bachelard
    pages cm. – (Transcending boundaries in philosophy and theology)
 Includes bibliographical references and index.
 ISBN 978-1-4094-0637-2 (hardcover)
1. Jesus Christ–Resurrection. 2. Transcendence (Philosophy)
3. Ethics. I. Title.
 BT482.B33 2013
 241–dc23

                                                                            2013013627

ISBN 13: 978-1-138-50369-4 (pbk)
ISBN 13: 978-1-4094-0637-2 (hbk)

For Neil
anam cara

Contents

Acknowledgements

My first thanks go to Martin Warner and Kevin Vanhoozer for their invitation to contribute to the series Transcending Boundaries in Philosophy and Theology. I am particularly grateful to Martin Warner for his very helpful comments on successive drafts, and his sustained encouragement and support for the project. Sarah Lloyd, David Shervington and staff in the publication team at Ashgate have been patient and helpful, and have offered prompt editorial support and advice.

I began research for this book while on study leave in Central Australia, where I was wonderfully befriended by Keith Castle and Stella Hayes at 'Whitegums'. Their hospitality helped me to engage the meaning of resurrection in the desert context, which was at that time for me personal as well as geographical, and I wish to record my gratitude for their kindness. I am grateful to St Mark's National Theological Centre for initial support for that period of leave and particularly to my former colleagues, Scott Cowdell and Heather Thomson, for their continued friendship and solidarity. Kaye Malins and Susan Phillips offered me access to library resources and rescue from many an overdue notice, and I thank them for their gentle encouragement. I particularly thank Scott Cowdell and Andrew Gleeson for their prompt, careful reading of the final draft and generous encouragement of my endeavour.

The Australian Catholic University appointed me to an honorary research fellowship, which came with the gift of an office and a place to write. I am very grateful to the ACU School of Theology and particularly my colleagues Alan Cadwallader and Raymond Canning for their support. Kerrie Hide has been a deep source of hope and faith in a difficult journey and I thank her for her wisdom, discernment and love. I want also to acknowledge the friendship, trust and support of Andrew Bachelard, Michael Bachelard, Nikolai Blaskow, Susan Bridge, Vicky Brock, Ian Chaplin, Julie Demicoli, Sue Dunbar, Greg Ezzy, Graeme Garrett, Gail Hagon, Sarah Macneil, Anna Molan, Rebecca Newland, Susanna Pain, Sally Paxton, Meredith Sissons, and members of Benedictus Contemplative Church.

My mother, Sally, who readers will discover has helped me to see something of the nature of resurrection (Chapter 2), has provided a home for me and much else during the writing of the book and her love has sustained me in life. I cannot adequately acknowledge what she has given me, but I thank her with all my heart. Finally, to Neil, who has shared in a journey through chaos and unmaking, drawn deeply into the faith of resurrection from the inside out, my love and wondering gratitude for all that has been, all that is, and all that is to come.

Sarah Bachelard
Canberra, Australia
November 2013

Copyright Acknowledgements

Introduction

Fifteen years ago I would have been incredulous to learn that I would one day write a book in a series, Transcending Boundaries in Philosophy and Theology, and from a theological standpoint. At that time, I was immersed in doctoral work in moral philosophy, focused on the writing of Iris Murdoch, Raimond Gaita and Cora Diamond. In these thinkers I had found what seemed to be the necessary and sufficient bridge between my lived moral experience and a Christian tradition that I no longer found credible or attractive. They wrote from a lively sense of the depth and mystery of human life that I found woefully lacking in the analytic tradition of moral philosophy, and yet managed (as I thought) to find space for that mystery apart from orthodox religious confession. Then, twelve years ago, the unexpected happened and I found myself, astonished, bewildered and slightly terrified, being drawn back to Christian faith.

I begin with this autobiographical note because the boundary I seek to 'transcend' in this book is not only a disciplinary boundary but is also within me. I have stood on both sides of it and feel the power of each. On the one hand, I know what it means to have to *learn* to say the word 'God' in my own voice, and I know the fear of falling by religious means into untruth and false consolation. On the other hand, I know the experience of a rich and difficult-to-articulate reality that is transforming and life giving, and that for me to stop listening, responding to and entrusting myself to it would be to fall into unreality. I use the word 'God' because I find I cannot but name certain aspects of my experience by it.

For a long time Jesus was, for me, the tricky bit. How is it possible that a man dying over two thousand years ago in painful circumstances makes a difference to our life now? What does it mean to say that this same man is alive and that it is possible to encounter the 'risen Jesus'? And what difference does the proclaimed resurrection of this Jesus make to the possibilities of life in the world, particularly our moral life? *Resurrection and Moral Imagination* is my attempt to engage these questions. I do so in large part by way of a dialogue with the work of Gaita and Murdoch, whose explicit disavowal of faith commitment or theological elaboration of the moral domain still poses, in my view, among the deepest of the philosophical challenges to a Christian conception of ethics.

This means that the book has two sets of readers in mind. On the one hand, I seek to develop a theological conception of ethics sourced in the apostolic witness to the resurrection and the new life it promises. In a celebrated early essay, Iris Murdoch pointed out that our background picture of the world profoundly affects our moral lives. Moral differences arise not simply because we make different choices within a shared view of reality, or because we 'select different objects out of the same world'. Rather, she argued, many of our most profound moral differences are an expression of the fact that 'we see different worlds'.[1] She mentioned, for example, the difference between

> people whose fundamental moral belief is that we all live in the same empirical and rationally comprehensible world and that morality is the adoption of universal and openly defensible rules of conduct … [and] other people whose fundamental belief is that we live in a world whose mystery transcends us and that morality is the exploration of that mystery in so far as it concerns each individual.[2]

I shall argue that the resurrection of Jesus transformed the first disciples' picture of the world, not in an abstract or theoretical way but through their transformed *experience* of being alive, their undergoing of new possibilities in reality and of changes in their own subjectivity. If Jesus is raised from the dead, then, nothing is quite what it was thought to be: God and power, death and life, goodness and judgement, fear, forgiveness, love and human being – all are constellated in radically new ways around the person of the risen Christ. So, writes the apostle Paul,

> the love of Christ urges us on, because we are convinced that one has died for all; therefore all have died. And he died for all, so that those who live might live no longer for themselves, but for him who died and was raised for them. From now on, therefore, we regard no one from a human point of view; even though we once knew Christ from a human point of view, we know him no longer in that way. So if anyone is in Christ, there is a new creation: everything old has passed away; see, everything has become new! (2 Cor. 5.14–17)[3]

Despite the fact that resurrection has been oddly neglected as a source for theological ethics, my central thesis is that this transformation in reality and its possibilities profoundly affects the horizon against which moral life finds its shape, significance and meaning. And it is this horizon, the taken-for-granted background picture of reality, that I am calling our 'moral imagination'.

On the other hand, I seek to open a conversation in moral philosophy with those who sense that what goes deepest in our moral lives calls for some appeal

---

[1]   Iris Murdoch, 'Vision and Choice in Morality', *Proceedings of the Aristotelian Society*, supp. vol. 30 (1956): 32–58, p.41. See Cora Diamond's discussion of Murdoch's argument in '"We Are Perpetually Moralists": Iris Murdoch, Fact and Value', in Maria Antonaccio and William Schweiker (eds), *Iris Murdoch and the Search for Human Goodness* (Chicago, IL: University of Chicago Press, 1996), pp.79–109.

[2]   Murdoch, 'Vision and Choice in Morality', p.47. Murdoch's prime interest at this point was not to defend one or other basic 'picture', but to criticise analytic moral philosophy for its neglect of these differences and its assumption that its own procedure for analysing the moral field was morally neutral.

[3]   All biblical quotations are from the New Revised Standard Version.

to notions of transcendence or mystery, and yet who do not wish to connect that appeal to religious or Christian faith, at least not in any confessional sense.[4] In relation to this dimension of the book's argument, my central thesis is that theological elaboration of the appeal to transcendence made by Murdoch and Gaita is not only possible but necessary if the deepest of their insights into moral life and understanding are to be realised.

I begin Chapter 1, accordingly, with Gaita's and Murdoch's understanding that certain kinds of experience signify that there is more to moral reality than can be accounted for by ethical naturalism. They each point to encounters with goodness that seem of a different order – the 'absolute goodness' seen in certain deeds, the love of saints that makes visible the humanity of those whom we find it hard to recognise as fully our fellows. These encounters claim them in testimony, but, for a combination of epistemological, moral and personal reasons, both Gaita and Murdoch deny that this testimony calls for metaphysical underpinning or theological completion. I am sympathetic to aspects of their resistance to religious 'explanation' of these encounters. Nevertheless, I argue that the possibility of human beings becoming capable of the 'love of saints' and the concept of goodness with which such love is interdependent are more reliant upon Christian practice and belonging than they allow. If that is so, then the question is whether the possibility of that form of love and that concept of goodness can be kept alive, apart from relationship to the theological reality to which they are both testimony and response.

In Chapter 2 I begin, as it were, from the other end. Whereas the first chapter engages with philosophers arguing in non-theological terms for the significance of some appeal to transcendence in ethics, in this chapter I begin to explore the shape of transcendence in the light of specifically theological revelation, the story of the life, death and resurrection of Jesus Christ. I am interested in the shape of the reality that is, in Murdoch's terms, the 'proper background' to morals. I do not claim that *only* the Christian tradition can offer resources for articulating and elaborating our sense of the nature of transcendent reality. My aim is simply to explore what kind of elaboration *is* possible from the resources of this tradition, and the kind of difference it might make to our lived experience. This is the chapter in which I engage the question of the meaning of resurrection, considering its plausibility as

---

[4] Both Gaita and Murdoch, as well as others influenced by them, acknowledge the significance of Christian 'ideas' and practice in the conceptions of love, goodness and individuality to which they appeal, but claim that these conceptions can continue to nourish ethical understanding and practice apart from their roots in Christian life. As I have been completing this manuscript I have become aware of two recent collections by philosophers exploring the connections between ethics and religion, particularly with reference to the work of Raimond Gaita. They are: Christopher Cordner (ed.), *Philosophy, Ethics and a Common Humanity: Essays in Honour of Raimond Gaita* (London: Routledge, 2011), and Joseph Carlisle, James Carter and Daniel Whistler (eds), *Moral Powers, Fragile Beliefs: Essays in Moral and Religious Philosophy* (New York: Continuum, 2011).

history or event, and the question of how we are to receive the apostolic witness. I conclude this chapter by sketching the moral significance of the differences in the conception of reality made visible and humanly accessible by the resurrection, in comparison with the non-theological accounts of ethical transcendence offered by Murdoch and Gaita.

The next three chapters develop a theological ethics from the resurrection. Rather than focus on particular moral issues or problems, I explore the difference made by the resurrection to our imaginative sense of moral life as a whole, including the difference it makes to the content and significance of moral concepts, the practice of moral thinking and judgement, and the formation of the moral self.

In Chapter 3, I argue that the reconciliation wrought by the resurrection and its transformation of human subjectivity also transforms our understanding of goodness, law and the self. Most human moral systems, I argue, are dualistic. They define goodness over against badness, and are internally related to the construction of personal and group identities that are also defined over against others. With the resurrection of Jesus, as the Letter to the Ephesians expresses it, the 'dividing wall', the 'hostility between us' has been 'broken down' (Eph. 2.14) and this means that there emerges the possibility of human identity formation and of Goodness that are over against nothing at all. This is the Goodness of God that is grace, and in which human beings are invited to participate. In Chapter 4, I explore the ramifications of this possibility of Goodness for moral life. I argue that, when we are no longer concerned with defending or defining ourselves or our goodness over against others or against death, when we live with death and judgement behind, then moral life partakes of a new freedom. This gives rise to three distinctive marks of ethics sourced in resurrection: revelation, vulnerability and compassion. These marks do not function as rules for moral choice in specific circumstances or as law, but they constitute criteria for discerning the horizon, the underlying reality, from which our moral responsiveness and discourse proceeds.

A significant question for ethics sourced in resurrection is the relationship between human mortality and moral meaning. The facts of our mortality and finitude, the limit conditions of human life, seem connected in important ways with our sense of the seriousness of morality and the preciousness of our lives. How does the proclamation of resurrection life intersect with this conceptual conditioning of our moral life by mortality, in ways that are not falsifying and glib? And, on the other hand, how does the proclamation of resurrection life make visible the ways in which some of our moral concepts and forms of moral thinking are complicit with, in thrall to, death? Chapter 5 explores these questions in a way that, again, makes clearer the differences between a non-dogmatic appeal to transcendent reality and a conception of transcendence sourced in the resurrection. Finally, in Chapter 6 I turn to the question of the practice of resurrection ethics in the context of a secular age, the role of the church, and the possibilities of common or public moral discourse.

Earlier I quoted from the Letter to the Ephesians, which speaks of the peace made possible by Jesus' life, death and resurrection having broken down the 'dividing walls' between us. The writer of the letter was speaking about the walls between Jew and Gentile. The series of which this book is part seeks to break down another wall, that between philosophy and theology in a secular age. In this context, far from being 'our peace', Jesus may seem to be the problem, the occasion of division rather than its reconciliation. My hope is that this book suggests otherwise, both deepening theological appreciation of the centrality of resurrection for Christian moral life and contributing to a philosophical revaluation of the meaning of Christ for our common world.

Chapter 1

Transcendence in Ethics

The philosopher Raimond Gaita has written of an experience he had at seventeen while he was working as a ward assistant at a psychiatric hospital.[1] The patients at the hospital were judged to be incurable – some had been there over thirty years – and, Gaita says, 'they appeared to have irretrievably lost everything which gives meaning to our lives'.[2] They had long since ceased to receive visits from friends, wives, children and even parents; often they were treated brutishly by the psychiatrists and nurses. A small number of psychiatrists, however, worked devotedly to improve their conditions and they spoke 'against all appearances, of the inalienable *dignity* of even those patients'.[3] Gaita says that he admired these psychiatrists enormously.

One day a nun came to the ward and everything in her demeanour towards the patients,

> the way she spoke to them, her facial expressions, the inflexions of her body – contrasted with and showed up the behaviour of those noble psychiatrists. She showed that they were, despite their best efforts, condescending, as I too had been. She thereby revealed that even such patients were, as the psychiatrists and I had sincerely and generously professed, the equals of those who wanted to help them; but she also revealed that in our hearts we did not believe this.[4]

For Gaita, reflecting on this episode, what was astonishing about the nun's love for the patients was its power to reveal what their affliction had obscured, the power to reveal their full humanity and moral equality. Gaita insists that he cannot explain *how* the nun's love revealed the humanity of the patients, nor can he demonstrate that her love was *justified* by anything about them. What she revealed, he says, is essentially mysterious, and he is simply claimed in testimony by it. He goes on to say, 'there are philosophies that leave or create conceptual space for such mystery, and there are some which close that space. Most do not even see the need for it'.[5]

Raimond Gaita is one among a small number of contemporary moral philosophers who explore the limits of a wholly naturalistic ethic, one that leaves

---

[1] Raimond Gaita, *A Common Humanity: Thinking about Love and Truth & Justice* (Melbourne: Text Publishing, 1999), p.18.

[2] Gaita, *A Common Humanity*, p.17.

[3] Gaita, *A Common Humanity*, p.17.

[4] Gaita, *A Common Humanity*, pp.18–19.

[5] Gaita, *A Common Humanity*, p.19.

no room for mystery or goodness with a capital 'G'. For Gaita, his encounter with the nun's love showed that ethics answerable to what is morally deepest in human experience must open into the reality marked out by these concepts of mystery and absolute goodness. This is a view shared by Iris Murdoch, who, pre-eminently in the world of English-language philosophy, has insisted on and explored this relationship between morality and the transcendent good.[6] Significantly, however, although both Gaita and Murdoch believe that an adequate philosophical account of morality must acknowledge the irreducible and mysterious goodness that conditions its deepest manifestations, each wants to leave that mystery theologically unspecified. Murdoch speaks of the proper background to morals as a 'non-dogmatic mysticism';[7] Gaita speaks of 'absolute goodness' and 'ethical other-worldliness'.[8] While possessing a sensibility deeply influenced by the Christian tradition as well as Platonism, neither can make sense of a specifically Christian characterisation of the space of ethical transcendence.

In my judgement, Gaita's and Murdoch's explorations of moral reality and the moral life are among the deepest and most significant in contemporary philosophy. They are also, at one level, among the most congenial to theological ethics. For this very reason, however, their clear refusal of any theological articulation or development of their approach must be taken seriously by a theologian.[9] To what extent is their resistance to theological articulation of the space of ethical transcendence morally, philosophically and even theologically

---

[6]   Iris Murdoch, *The Sovereignty of Good* (London: Routledge, 1970). Moral philosophers influenced by Murdoch in this regard include Cora Diamond, Martha Nussbaum and Charles Taylor. See, for example, Charles Taylor, 'Iris Murdoch and Moral Philosophy', in Maria Antonaccio and William Schweiker (eds), *Iris Murdoch and the Search for Human Goodness* (Chicago, IL: University of Chicago Press, 1996), pp.3–28; Cora Diamond, '"We Are Perpetually Moralists": Iris Murdoch, Fact, and Value', in Antonaccio and Schweiker (eds), *Iris Murdoch and the Search for Human Goodness*, pp.79–109. Fergus Kerr examines the role played by conceptions of transcendence in the thinking of a number of contemporary philosophers, including Murdoch, in *Immortal Longings: Versions of Transcending Humanity* (London: SPCK, 1997). Essays in a recent collection in honour of Raimond Gaita explore the significance of goodness in ethics and in Gaita's thought: Christopher Cordner (ed.), *Philosophy, Ethics and a Common Humanity: Essays in Honour of Raimond Gaita* (London: Routledge, 2011).

[7]   Murdoch, *Sovereignty of Good*, p.74.

[8]   Raimond Gaita, *Good and Evil: An Absolute Conception*, second edition (London: Routledge, 2004), chapter 12.

[9]   The question of the congeniality or otherwise of Murdoch's moral philosophy for theological ethics is discussed in a number of the essays in Antonaccio and Schweiker (eds), *Iris Murdoch and the Search for Human Goodness*, and in Jennifer Spencer Goodyer, 'The Blank Face of Love: The Possibility of Goodness in the Literary and Philosophical Work of Iris Murdoch', *Modern Theology*, 25/2 (2009): 217–237. Mark Wynn explores this question in relation to Gaita's work in 'Saintliness and the Moral Life: Gaita as a Source for Christian Ethics', *Journal of Religious Ethics*, 31 (2003): 463–485.

important? Conversely, to what extent might this resistance cause us to miss something significant? In this chapter, I begin to explore these questions by considering in more detail how the appeal to absolute or transcendent goodness is necessary, on both Gaita's and Murdoch's view, for a proper understanding of ethics. Before I turn to this task, however, some brief remarks about the concept of transcendence are necessary.

The notion of 'transcendence' is philosophically tricky. It is defined largely by contrast with 'naturalism', and this may give rise to the charge that its definition is merely stipulative. Charles Taylor, for example, has argued that a wholly immanent or naturalistic account of reality struggles properly to do justice to the human experiences of creativity, ethics and art.[10] In response, William David Hart has criticised Charles Taylor's appeal to transcendence, where 'transcendence' means a 'superhuman' reality beyond a 'naturalistic ontology', because it illegitimately truncates the concept of nature. Such an appeal

> fails to acknowledge intermundane, 'this-worldly', and naturalistic forms of transcendence. As I construe it, 'naturalism' is … a metaphysically laden category that describes everything that is and the 'appearance' of everything that is: … that is, nature doing what it does and everything that follows that agency. On this view, no one quite knows what nature can do. The 'self-surpassing' capacities of nature continually surprise, mystify, and enchant. Nature is 'magical'.[11]

In other words, why shouldn't what appears to 'transcend' nature be conceived as part of the depth of nature itself?

Gaita himself seems to reflect something of this concern in more recent writing, distancing his argument from certain ways of speaking of 'transcendence' or at least from some of its cognate terms. Although in the second edition of *Good and Evil* he continues to draw a distinction between non-reductive naturalism and absolute goodness in ethics, he writes in the new preface that he now 'regrets' using the expressions 'ethical other-worldliness' and 'mystery'. They sound 'either too religious or too theoretically formidable'.[12] He thinks that he 'should have been content to characterize the wondrousness of saintly love – to mark its conceptual features, to locate it in a sympathetic conceptual space and to leave it at that'.[13]

---

[10] Charles Taylor, *A Secular Age* (Cambridge, MA: Harvard University Press, 2007), p.597.

[11] William David Hart, 'Naturalizing Christian Ethics: A Critique of Charles Taylor's *A Secular Age*', *Journal of Religious Ethics*, 40/1 (2012): 149–170, pp.153–154.

[12] Gaita, *Good and Evil*, p.xxx.

[13] Gaita, *Good and Evil*, p.xxxi. Stephen Mulhall has questioned the cogency of this disavowal, suggesting that Gaita's discussion of saintly love requires that it be characterised as necessarily rather than contingently mysterious, given the nature of the 'transfiguration wrought upon the nonreductively naturalistic conception of individuality by the work of saintly love': 'The Work of Saintly Love: The Religious Impulse in Gaita's Writing', in

Later in this chapter, I return to Gaita's discussion of whether particular metaphysical or ontological claims are implied by or require resolution for the appeal to transcendence in ethics to be considered illuminative of moral reality. For the moment I prescind from these questions, and simply draw on the concept of transcendence to gesture towards and explore certain phenomena in the moral field that seem qualitatively distinct.[14] Like Gaita and Murdoch, I invite the reader to recognise these phenomena without having to commit to any particular claims about their ontology or metaphysical implications. My interest at this stage is not primarily in ontology, but in our lived moral experience.

Appeal to Transcendence

For both Gaita and Murdoch, the refusal of much contemporary philosophy to think of ethics as opening into what they call absolute or transcendent goodness leads to impoverished accounts of the moral domain. It leads to blindness to certain aspects of reality, inability to account for the formation of moral selves capable of deep and truthful responsiveness to that reality, and a truncated or distorted set of moral concepts. In the case of Gaita's nun, for example, the mysterious power of her love to reveal the full humanity of the patients suggests that moral 'reality' is not straightforwardly accessible to anyone, not a matter of simple empirical experience. Moral reality has normative depth.[15] The nun's example shows that the revelation of this depth is dependent upon a certain kind of responsiveness and at the same time exposes the poverty of the concepts by which the psychiatrists were attempting the same moral work. That is, on Gaita's account, the nun revealed the relative poverty of the concept of dignity with which the psychiatrists attempted to secure the equality of the patients, as compared with her practice of unconditional love.[16]

Cordner (ed.), *Philosophy, Ethics and a Common Humanity*, pp.21–36, pp.31–32. Recently, in response to Mulhall, Gaita has acknowledged the justice of his criticism, conceding that when he retreated from the expression 'ethical other-worldliness' it 'was a mistake': Raimond Gaita, 'Morality, Metaphysics and Religion', in Joseph Carlisle, James Carter and Daniel Webster (eds), *Moral Powers, Fragile Beliefs: Essays in Moral and Religious Philosophy* (New York: Continuum, 2011), pp.3–28, p.27.

[14] Gaita, *Good and Evil*, pp.208–209. When he introduces the term 'absolute goodness', Gaita quotes the philosopher R.F. Holland, who notes that '90% of all ethical phenomena', 'every customary and mediocre goodness', can be accounted for without this transcendent conception. Yet what remains 'unaccounted for' by naturalistic understanding of the ethical domain is precisely what colours the whole: 'Even the old example of returning books to the library is caught up in it: "there could coexist, for at least some people in a society, a concern for truth of an altogether different character, in which not to falsify became a spiritual demeanour"'.

[15] See Murdoch, *Sovereignty of Good*, p.37.

[16] Gaita, *A Common Humanity*, p.18. I discuss this claim more fully in Chapter 5.

The appeal to transcendence arises, then, for both Gaita and Murdoch in response to certain kinds of experience. Gaita speaks of 'marking an encounter' with goodness, or with love whose purity is an occasion for wonder, or with remorse as a 'pained, bewildered realization of what it means ... to wrong someone';[17] Murdoch appeals often to 'our' awareness of what it is like to strive to be morally better, our sense of being answerable to a reality whose demand is absolute and whose authority cannot be denied.[18] They each note that, although there is an essentially mysterious quality to these experiences or encounters, they are not esoteric or disconnected from ordinary life. They 'reveal something universal',[19] something that is perfectly well, if unreflectively, understood by 'unselfish mothers of large families' and 'virtuous peasants'.[20] If we are to understand the true nature of morality and of goodness, then it is to these kinds of encounter that we must attend.

There are three features of these kinds of experience that are significant for Gaita and Murdoch, and which help to give content to the concept of transcendence at issue here. They are the experience of being answerable to a reality beyond oneself, the experience of some aspect of reality being revealed in a new way, and the experience of being in contact with a source of moral transformation. By exploring in more detail the nature and significance of these experiences, we shall be in a better position to consider what difference it makes to refuse theological articulation of this space of transcendence.

First, let us consider the experience of answerability. Moral philosophies are sometimes defined according to whether they are realist or non-realist, or realist or voluntarist. The distinction is between those philosophers who believe that moral value is in some sense 'out there', objective, existing independently of the valuing activity of the moral agent, and those who believe that moral value resides in the will or preference or rational choice of the moral agent. To speak of being answerable to a reality beyond the self is a form of realism. As Murdoch puts it somewhat trenchantly, 'The ordinary person does not, unless corrupted by philosophy, believe that he creates value by his choices. He thinks that some things really are better than others and that he is capable of getting it wrong'.[21]

Having said that, however, neither Gaita nor Murdoch is primarily interested in defending the philosophical position of moral 'realism'.[22] That is not the point of their appeal to the experience of answerability. Rather, they seek to explore the sense that a human life is answerable to a reality that transcends it on pain of untruthfulness. At issue is not a philosophical claim about the ontological status of

[17] Gaita, *Good and Evil*, p.xiv.

[18] Murdoch, *Sovereignty of Good*, p.62.

[19] Gaita, *Good and Evil*, p.xv.

[20] Murdoch, *Sovereignty of Good*, pp.53, 74.

[21] Murdoch, *Sovereignty of Good*, p.97.

[22] Gaita questions the grammar of the terms in which moral realism is philosophically advocated, and suggests that Murdoch's appeal to reality has a different grammar. *Good and Evil*, pp.190, 211.

moral value. Much more seriously, what is at issue is the possibility that one's *life* might be lived in illusion, that one might fail to be properly oriented towards the real. When that is the case, then moral perception or vision is necessarily distorted, and deep responsiveness to the reality of other people is impossible. So, there are two elements to this claim. One is that human life can be more or less attuned to reality. The second is that the reality in question is the good. Ultimately, on this view, the real and the good are identified.

What is the evidence for this complex claim? Murdoch begins with the assertion that 'human beings are naturally selfish' and that our consciousness, far from being 'a transparent glass' through which we view the world, is 'a cloud of more or less fantastic reverie designed to protect the psyche from pain'. We avoid reality by seeking consolation 'either through imagined inflation of self or through fictions of a theological nature'. Even our loving is 'more often than not an assertion of self'.[23] The obscure complex of psychic energy that comprises our selves, the 'fat relentless ego',[24] gets in the way of truthful perception of reality, such that to see the world as it is requires moral imagination and effort.[25] We can actually *see* this mechanism at work, Murdoch says, in the practice of art:

> Art presents the most comprehensible examples of the almost irresistible human tendency to seek consolation in fantasy and also of the effort to resist this and the vision of reality which comes with success. Success in fact is rare. Almost all art is a form of fantasy-consolation and few artists achieve the vision of the real.[26]

Indeed,

> Good art shows us how difficult it is to be objective by showing us how differently the world looks to an objective vision ... Art transcends selfish and obsessive limitations of personality and can enlarge the sensibility of its consumer. It is a kind of goodness by proxy.[27]

In the same way, Murdoch says, in the moral life we need to attend with increasing depth and truthfulness to what is there and this calls for growing freedom from the fantasy-ridden self whose fears and preoccupations veil reality. Faced with difficult moral questions, the 'love which brings the right answer is an exercise of justice and realism and really *looking*. The difficulty is to keep the attention fixed upon the real situation and to prevent it from returning surreptitiously to the self with consolations of self-pity, resentment, fantasy and despair ... It is a *task*

---

23   Murdoch, *Sovereignty of Good*, pp.78–79.
24   Murdoch, *Sovereignty of Good*, p.52.
25   Murdoch, *Sovereignty of Good*, p.37.
26   Murdoch, *Sovereignty of Good*, p.64.
27   Murdoch, *Sovereignty of Good*, pp.86–87.

to come to see the world as it is'.[28] That this is so, however, reveals the relation between 'virtue and reality'.[29] In other words, the identification of the real with the good is made known to us by the fact that it is through the exercise of the virtues that we come closer to reality. The moral life is capable of endless deepening because of the infinite depth of the reality to which it is answerable. We know its endlessness, its transcendence, because we sense the distance between the 'very good' and the idea of perfection that calls us to seek ever deeper attunement to 'the world as it really is'.[30]

Gaita likewise emphasises the task, the moral work that it is to respond truthfully to the world.[31] Whereas Murdoch explores the nature of this task with reference to the work of the artist and the ordinary effort required for us to respond justly to another,[32] Gaita points to the experience of being 'claimed in testimony' by certain encounters. Following R.F. Holland, he says that 'someone who speaks of absolute goodness does so under pressure – the pressure of … "marking an encounter"'.[33] The pressure to mark such an encounter, being claimed in testimony by it, is 'a kind of confession, in the sense in which we speak of a confession of faith. It expresses a requirement to be true to something'.[34] As his example of the nun shows, part of what is 'confessed', part of what he is called to be true to, is the reality made visible by love of a particular purity. So certain kinds of encounter with goodness claim a witness in testimony both to the reality of the goodness itself, and to the reality revealed in its light. Again, following Holland, Gaita insists that 'absolute goodness *is something*',[35] but also that the 'something' it is cannot be identified independently of what it reveals.

Here, then, is the second feature of the experiences that lead Murdoch and Gaita to appeal to transcendent goodness in ethics. There is the experience of being answerable to an infinite depth in reality on pain of dwelling in illusion, and there is the experience that, insofar as attention or openness to that depth is allowed to transform responsiveness, it has the power of revelation. So, Gaita says, the nun's love had the power to reveal what the patients' affliction had obscured, the power to reveal their full humanity and moral equality. Elsewhere he speaks of Mother Teresa's compassion, which, because it was without a trace of condescension, 'revealed – taught – what it is to be a human being because of

---

[28] Murdoch, *Sovereignty of Good*, p.91.

[29] Murdoch, *Sovereignty of Good*, p.91.

[30] Murdoch, *Sovereignty of Good*, p.93.

[31] He notes that the conception of 'the world' here 'is not independently intelligible from the ethical character of the task'. *Good and Evil*, p.212.

[32] Murdoch's famous example of a mother-in-law, M, engaged in the moral work of attempting to see her daughter-in-law, D, more justly invites us into this experience. *Sovereignty of Good*, pp.17–18.

[33] Gaita, *Good and Evil*, p.207.

[34] Gaita, *Good and Evil*, p.207.

[35] Gaita, *Good and Evil*, p.207.

the light it threw on the afflicted. The wonder which is in response to her is not a wonder at her, but a wonder *that human life could be as her love revealed it to be*'.[36] Murdoch too understands the good as necessarily transcendent because of what is revealed in its light:

> In its *light* we come to see that A, which superficially resembles B, is really better than B. And this can occur, indeed must occur, without our having the sovereign idea in any sense 'taped'. This is the true sense of the 'indefinability' of the good ... It always lies beyond, and it is from this beyond that it exercises its *authority*.[37]

Goodness is not itself directly visible or accessible, but its reality is known through its effect. That is the reality to which some are claimed in testimony in the wake of particular encounters.

The third feature of the appeal to transcendent goodness to which I want to draw attention is the understanding that there is the possibility of transformation in human life, which has the character of gift. This transformation is linked in some way with contemplation of, attention to, the good, which (at least according to Murdoch) may be understood as a source of energy. Gaita explores this aspect of the appeal to transcendence by comparing the moral work required to cultivate the virtues with the possibility of love like Mother Teresa's. He writes:

> We wonder at what we take to be instances of pure love, but it is not wonder at a feat which would excite our admiration. There are many kinds of wonder – wonder at a person's skill, wonder at a person's courage, wonder at the beauty of the world. Great talent, great courage and great resilience excite our admiration partly because they are at the limit of an empirically conditioned sense of human powers. The purity of love is, however, of a different order, as is the humility which is inseparable from it. They strike us not as achievements, but as gifts. It is quite natural to speak of feats of courage, but we can only speak satirically of feats of love and humility.[38]

And a little later, he says:

> Some people love better than others, and in relation to the requirement to love better than we do, there is much that may properly be described as the development of certain powers and capacities. A certain dimension of the requirement to love better is analogous to the requirement to be more courageous ... But with certain kinds of love we are judged under a conception of perfection, and we call that perfection purity ... The salient points are that pure love is not an achievement

---

[36]   Gaita, *Good and Evil*, p.205.
[37]   Murdoch, *Sovereignty of Good*, p.62.
[38]   Gaita, *Good and Evil*, pp.202–203.

and that our sense of its value is not of it as something at the furthest limits of what is humanly achievable.[39]

Gaita's point here is that the love displayed by the nun in his story and by Mother Teresa is sourced in a different place than our ordinary efforts at moral improvement. There is something qualitatively different about love of that purity, about love that has this power of revelation, and it has the form of gift rather than achievement. Her love was not a virtue that Mother Teresa possessed, but a light that she shed on those around her – indeed, he says, 'there is a sense in which she disappeared from consideration'.[40] It is this qualitative difference that seeks expression by appeal to the concepts of transcendence, of absolute goodness.

Gaita does not explore how the gift of this capacity to love might be received; he simply registers its presence. Murdoch notes that prayer has traditionally opened people to this 'good energy', this energy of the good that transforms the selfish and illusion-ridden individual.[41] She suggests that a 'non-dogmatic' version of such prayer remains essential for the moral life:

> I think there is a place both inside and outside religion for a sort of contemplation of the Good, not just by dedicated experts but by ordinary people: an attention which is not just the planning of particular good actions but an attempt to look right away from self towards a distant transcendent perfection, a source of uncontaminated energy, a source of *new* and quite undreamt of virtue ... This is the true mysticism, a kind of undogmatic prayer which is real and important, though perhaps also difficult and easily corrupted.[42]

The 'religious' overtones of the three features of the appeal to transcendence I have discussed are clear. They involve the experience of life as answerable to a reality beyond itself on pain of untruthfulness, the sense that the world we live in is revealed more perspicuously in its light, and the sense that this reality is a source of transformation in human life. Obedience, revelation, transformation. Why, then, do Murdoch and Gaita resist theological articulation of their appeal to transcendence?

Non-dogmatic Mysticism

There are epistemological, moral and personal reasons intertwined in Gaita's and Murdoch's arguments at this point. In what follows, I seek to engage with each. First, for Gaita, the appeal to transcendence must not be understood as an attempt to provide a religious justification or foundation for ethics. Ethics, he believes, does

---

[39]   Gaita, *Good and Evil*, pp.203–204.
[40]   Gaita, *Good and Evil*, p.205.
[41]   For example, see Murdoch, *Sovereignty of Good*, p.83.
[42]   Murdoch, *Sovereignty of Good*, pp.101–102.

not need any such justification. Whatever the nun may have said about the sources of her responsiveness does not prove the truth of a religious faith or doctrine.[43] Gaita does not deny that the nun herself almost certainly believed that the patients were all God's children and equally loved by Him,[44] and that her response to them was shaped by 'virtues of character, imagination and sensibility, given content and form by the disciplines of her vocation'.[45] Nevertheless, he insists,

> as someone who was witness to the nun's love and is claimed in fidelity to it, I have no understanding of what it revealed independently of the quality of her love ... I can only say that the quality of her love proved that [the patients] are rightly the objects of our non-condescending treatment ... But if someone were now to ask me what informs my sense that they are *rightly* the objects of such treatment, I can appeal only to the purity of her love. For me, the purity of the love proved the reality of what it revealed.[46]

In other words, Gaita is arguing, rightly I think, that someone who holds merely to the propositional truth that 'we are all God's children' is no more capable of revealing the humanity of the psychiatric patients than someone who asserts their inalienable dignity. Each may sincerely wish to believe in their hearts what they say, but sincere profession of belief is not enough. Likewise, Gaita is right to trust the reality revealed by the nun's love, independently of any discursive religious explanation or justification for how such a thing could be. Yet, I wonder whether more can be said.

The nun's love was shaped and nourished at least in part, let us say, by the picture and the experience of reality expressed by saying that we are all God's children. It is true that merely saying those words, without their being alive, inhabited by and inhabiting her life, would prove nothing. The question, however, is whether the kind of love she displayed would have been possible without the shaping pressure of those words or words like them, and the felt experience to which they testify.[47] And if we judge the life and love shaped by those words to be deeply truthful, deeply revelatory of reality, then might we not think that there is something true and real in her experience to be explored? Can we assume that we can explore the ethical significance of her love, without taking seriously the matrix in which it arises? I wonder, then, if an appeal to non-dogmatic mysticism will limit our capacity to explore what is significant in the nun's example for ethics.

---

43   Gaita, *A Common Humanity*, p.21.
44   Gaita, *A Common Humanity*, p.21.
45   Gaita, *A Common Humanity*, p.20.
46   Gaita, *A Common Humanity*, p.21.
47   This is one of the themes in Stanley Hauerwas's discussion of Murdoch's moral philosophy in 'Murdochian Muddles: Can We Get Through Them If God Does Not Exist?', in Antonaccio and Schweiker (eds), *Iris Murdoch and the Search for Human Goodness*, pp.190–208.

Let me say a little more about this. Part of what is at issue, I suspect, is the difficulty of the words 'reality' and 'existence' in the context of ethics. Gaita rightly resists the assumption that recognising or responding to the moral 'reality' revealed by the nun's love is dependent upon believing in the metaphysical 'reality' of God. The assumption that what the nun revealed requires explanation or justification beyond itself is false, and the assumption that the posited existence of God might provide such underwriting is illusory. That, says Gaita, is because the 'reality' revealed by the nun cannot become 'an object for the speculative, discursive intelligence', but can be recognised only by someone claimed in testimony by it, by someone standing 'as [an] historical, individual, human being' who is 'not so much … report[ing] their experiences as data, but … find[ing] themselves in them and … speak[ing] authoritatively out of them'.[48] In other words, witnessing to the reality of goodness like this is a matter of finding one's own 'voice', speaking out of one's own encounter with it. Nothing is added to this testimony by attempting to underwrite it with metaphysical or religious propositions about the existence of God.

This argument, however, relies on two different ways of understanding 'reality'. Gaita, as we have seen, argues that the 'reality' of goodness cannot be known except as we ourselves are claimed in testimony by it – it is not something that we can know in theory, in the third-person, as an object of speculative intelligence. His objection to metaphysical or religious underwriting of this reality is that, insofar as the concept of God *is* deployed in theory, in the third person, as an object of speculative intelligence, then it neither explains nor underpins anything. So, he says, 'Because the reality of goodness is not a reality that could be unmysterious to an ideal epistemic being, it is not a notion of reality suitable for a religious (really a metaphysical) underwriting of absolute ethics'.[49]

I agree with this. Yet, as Gaita himself goes on to discuss, the 'reality' of God need not be conceived as something available to the 'discursive, speculative intelligence' any more than the reality of goodness need be conceived that way.[50] Philosophers sometimes speak as if to believe in God is to be able to assert 'that there exists a God with certain attributes'.[51] But, notes Gaita, it belongs to the grammar of serious religious speech that it be capable of deepening my life in certain ways, that it be concerned with what is spiritual.[52] It belongs to the grammar of serious religious speech that I am able to speak of God in my own voice. So I would say that recognising or testifying to the 'reality' of God necessarily involves being able to do such things (however gropingly or hesitantly) as to pray, or to say 'Thy will be done', or to see one's life as answerable to a

---

48   Gaita, *Good and Evil*, p.208.
49   Gaita, *Good and Evil*, p.215.
50   Mulhall has noted the equivocation in Gaita's argument at this point. 'The Work of Saintly Love', p.30.
51   Gaita, *Good and Evil*, p.218.
52   Gaita, *Good and Evil*, p.219.

calling. It is to offer one's heart to be known. As with the reality of goodness to which Gaita was claimed in testimony by his encounter with the nun, speaking of the reality of God is also a matter of being claimed in testimony, claimed in response. And, as with finding oneself claimed in testimony by an encounter with goodness, the condition of truthful religious testimony is the 'capacity, not so much to report [one's] experiences as data, but to find [oneself] in them and to speak authoritatively out of them'.[53]

Gaita is right to resist the view that the nun's love is only really what he thought it was if God exists; that if God does not exist, then the patients are not our equals, her love is not 'justified', and his sense of being claimed in testimony to its reality is illusory. In other words, he is right to deny that what he encountered in the nun is explained or justified only if he provides metaphysical underwriting for it. He can simply leave the encounter as it is – a part of our moral life that cannot be theorised away. Does, however, refusal to succumb to the pressure metaphysically to underwrite the reality of the goodness he encountered mean that we cannot explore how it was that the nun came to be capable of that kind of revelatory love? Does it mean that we cannot ask whether the 'reality' of God, known not to the discursive intelligence but encountered in prayer, discipleship, testimony and love, makes a difference to moral possibility and impossibility, to the very shape of the goodness to which Gaita bears witness?

I do not think Gaita would say we cannot make such an exploration, but simply that he cannot speak authoritatively out of that ground. For Gaita, as for Murdoch, it is not possible to speak in the 'first person', claimed in testimony by encounter with God. Murdoch speaks of the way in which it 'used' to be possible to believe that God exists,[54] and Gaita notes that, if the nun explained her responsiveness with reference to her love of Jesus, he 'need not even understand what that means, let alone "believe it", in order to respond as [he has] described'.[55] Part of the task of this book is to explore theologically the moral terrain sketched by Gaita and Murdoch, and that will necessarily involve reflection on what might be at stake in ethics as the possibility of serious religious speech 'goes dead' for large parts of our culture.

In addition to these epistemological and personal reasons for refusing theological articulation of the space of transcendence in ethics, Murdoch raises a distinct moral objection. The major problem, for Murdoch, of appealing to God in ethics is the problem of false consolation. As we have already noted, the tendency

[53]   Gaita, *Good and Evil*, p.208.

[54]   For example, Murdoch, *Sovereignty of Good*, pp.74, 79. Murdoch's 'unbelief' is discussed by various essays in Antonaccio and Schweiker (eds), *Iris Murdoch and the Search for Human Goodness*, and particularly by Taylor, 'Iris Murdoch and Moral Philosophy', and Hauerwas, 'Murdochian Muddles'.

[55]   This quotation comes from Gaita's discussion of Mother Theresa, in which he explores the same issues as those raised in connection with the example of the nun: *Good and Evil*, p.214.

to seek false consolation is, on Murdoch's view, a serial temptation for human beings and one of the primary ways in which we avoid being in touch with the real. Any attempt to conceive of value as unitary runs the danger of turning into false consolation: '"it all somehow must make sense", or "there is a best decision here"'.[56] This is true, Murdoch acknowledges, of her concept of the good as of God, but the notion of God as 'person' is particularly susceptible to corruption and fantasy. 'As soon as any idea is a consolation the tendency to falsify it becomes strong: hence the traditional problem of preventing the idea of God from degenerating in the believer's mind'.[57]

That much religious discourse does degenerate into glib or consoling fantasy may be readily admitted. Rowan Williams has noted that

> [t]he weightiest criticisms of Christian speech and practice amount to this: that Christian language actually fails to transform the world's meaning because it neglects or trivializes or evades aspects of the human. It is notoriously awkward about sexuality; it risks being unserious about death when it speaks too glibly and confidently about eternal life; it can disguise the abiding reality of unhealed and meaningless suffering. So it is that some of those most serious about the renewal of a moral discourse reject formal Christian commitment as something that would weaken or corrupt their imagination.[58]

Murdoch is, of course, aware that 'God' *need* not be conceived as a consoling super-person, and that religious speech and practice is in a constant process of its own purification through, among other things, the practice of silence, the refusal to represent God in language or image, the concern with idolatry.[59] She writes: 'The "true saint" believes in "God" but not as a super-person who satisfies all our ordinary desires "in the end". (There is no end, there is no reward)'.[60] Why, then, does she seem to insist that theological understanding of reality is always linked to falsity? 'No existing thing could be what we have meant by God. Any existing God would be less than God. An existent God would be an idol or a demon ... God does not and cannot exist'.[61]

Murdoch's position turns, I think, on her insistence that human life has no external purpose or *telos*. To believe that it does, to hold that there is any ultimate meaning, is to deny the deepest features of reality, which are that human life is

---

[56]   Murdoch, *Sovereignty of Good*, p.57.

[57]   Murdoch, *Sovereignty of Good*, p.57.

[58]   Rowan Williams, 'The Judgement of the World', in *On Christian Theology* (Oxford: Blackwell Publishers, 2000), pp.29–43, p.40.

[59]   Murdoch, for example, draws significantly on the work of Simone Weil, whose writing about God may be characterised as *essentially* concerned with the purification of idolatry.

[60]   Iris Murdoch, *Metaphysics as a Guide to Morals* (London: Penguin, 1993), p.106.

[61]   Murdoch, *Metaphysics*, p.508.

governed by chance, death and necessity.[62] Moreover, to prettify these features of reality, to refuse to attend to them and live nakedly in the face of them, is the very thing that makes goodness impossible. Since God does, seemingly, act as guarantor of some external purpose or meaning for human life, God as traditionally conceived is an enemy of true morality. That is why Murdoch thinks that when 'Bonhoeffer says that God wants us to live as if there were no God I suspect he is misusing words',[63] and why she approves of demythologising theologians who seek for 'a theology that can continue without God'.[64]

Let me consider in a little more detail what might be at stake here. I have already noted Murdoch's identification of the good with the real. To attend truthfully to reality calls for the ever-deepening exercise of virtue – of love, justice, compassion, honesty. The most difficult part of reality for us to face is our own mortality, the vulnerability of our lives to chance and necessity, and the ultimate vanity of all our plans and designs. Becoming good is internally related to our patient and faithful willingness to accept this reality, and is at the same time the condition of our seeing the world as it really is. Thus, says Murdoch,

> Goodness is connected with the acceptance of real death and real chance and real transience and only against the background of this acceptance, which is psychologically so difficult, can we understand the full extent of what virtue is like. The acceptance of death is an acceptance of our own nothingness which is an automatic spur to our concern with what is not ourselves.[65]

And again:

> The Good has nothing to do with purpose, indeed it excludes the idea of purpose. 'All is vanity' is the beginning and the end of ethics. The only genuine way to be good is to be good 'for nothing' in the midst of a scene where every 'natural' thing, including one's own mind, is subject to chance, that is, to necessity. That 'for nothing' is indeed the experienced correlate of the invisibility or non-representable blankness of the idea of Good itself.[66]

There is an austere beauty in this refusal of the consoling promise of ultimate purpose and in the pure, unrewarded love of the good, although, as Murdoch herself notes in relation to existentialism, there can be a subtle kind of 'consolation' in the refusal of consolation.[67] There is no argument that can be straightforwardly brought either for or against this picture of reality. Murdoch acknowledges that her claim

---

[62]   Murdoch, *Sovereignty of Good*, pp.79 and passim.
[63]   Murdoch, *Sovereignty of Good*, p.79.
[64]   Murdoch, *Metaphysics*, p.511.
[65]   Murdoch, *Sovereignty of Good*, p.103.
[66]   Murdoch, *Sovereignty of Good*, p.71.
[67]   Murdoch, *Sovereignty of Good*, p.82.

that human life has no external point or *telos* is simply an assertion, and cannot be argued for any more than can its opposite.[68] I shall not present a full response to Murdoch here, since it is part of the task of this book as a whole to suggest a different picture and to show the difference it makes to ethics. Let me suggest, however, the direction from which I think a theological response might be made.

Murdoch is concerned that too easy a proclamation that 'all will be well', too comfortable a religious story about human meaning and significance, leads to obliteration of the random, finite, pointless particularity of the world. It leads us to *dominate* the world rather than attend to it,[69] to refuse to acknowledge the reality of unredeemed suffering and tragedy:

> Any story which we tell about ourselves consoles us since it imposes pattern upon something which might otherwise seem intolerably chancy and incomplete. However, human life is chancy and incomplete. It is the role of tragedy, and also of comedy, and of painting to show us suffering without a thrill and death without a consolation ... All is vanity. The only thing which is of real importance is the ability to see it all clearly and respond to it justly which is inseparable from virtue.[70]

As my earlier quotation from Rowan Williams acknowledged, the charge that it seeks to dominate or falsify reality is well made against a great deal of Christian discourse. I wonder, however, if Murdoch's decision that '[a]ll is vanity' itself risks foreclosing attention to reality, and itself risks avoiding a certain kind of suffering, a certain invitation to openness and incompletion?

'All is vanity' expresses the experience of a world that is 'self-enclosed'.[71] There is nothing here to hope for.[72] Hope, of course, often appears as precisely the refusal to face reality to which Murdoch objects – 'maybe it won't be so bad after all'. The theological virtue of hope, however, is of a fundamentally different character to this kind of wishful optimism. It is the determination to hold open the space of possibility, the possibility of the new, in the face of all that contradicts it. It is hoping for what is not seen, as St Paul puts it (Rom. 8.24); trusting that love is stronger than death (Rom. 8.37–39). This is a vulnerable and open posture between presumption and despair,[73] and requires the disciplined exercise of

---

[68] Murdoch, *Sovereignty of Good*, p.79.

[69] Murdoch, *Sovereignty of Good*, p.82.

[70] Murdoch, *Sovereignty of Good*, p.87.

[71] Murdoch, *Sovereignty of Good*, p.79.

[72] Hauerwas notes that Murdoch's understanding of the 'pointlessness' of reality is connected to her use of the myth of the Demiurge, and her refusal of the doctrine of creation *ex nihilo* and its connection with hope. 'Murdochian Muddles', pp.201 ff.

[73] Jürgen Moltmann identifies these two as the corruptions of Christian hope. *Theology of Hope: On the Ground and Implications of a Christian Eschatology* (Minneapolis, MN: Fortress Press, 1993), p.23.

patience, attention and faith. Rather than refusing to face the truth of reality, it acknowledges that possibility and love are constitutive of reality and waits in faith for them. At times, this can be an infinitely more painful place to inhabit than the resigned stoicism that Murdoch seems to recommend. It does not (need not) deny the appalling pain and suffering of the present, and yet it refuses nevertheless to foreclose the reality of possibility, a responsive hope imaged in the Christian tradition in terms of faith in God's goodness and promise. This is clearly a stance, as is Murdoch's, of faith. Giving fuller testimony to it will be, as I noted earlier, a large part of the work of this book.

I have been exploring in this section some of the reasons for Gaita's and Murdoch's resistance to theological articulation of the transcendent good. They are reasons that need to be taken seriously, but I do not believe they demonstrate that theological elaboration of transcendence in ethics necessarily implies a faulty ontology of moral value or a falsely consoling picture of reality. In the final section of this chapter, I say why theological elaboration of this terrain is important and explore what is at risk in its refusal.

Transcendence, Goodness and God

Goodness with a capital 'G' is real. Gaita is claimed in testimony by his encounter with it. Murdoch encounters it too, in the love of saints and in great art, in the experience of the *distance* between our approximation of goodness and the idea of perfection that beckons us on. This reality can be affirmed, for both Gaita and Murdoch, independently of God. It can nourish our living and deepen our love for the world as 'God' used to, but without the mythological baggage that now seems literally in-credible to many in the contemporary Western world. Gaita is less concerned than Murdoch to argue that the concept of God *cannot* be retained. He merely writes as someone claimed in testimony by goodness, but who cannot speak in his own voice about God. Murdoch takes a stronger stance. Not only can God now not generally be believed, but we are probably better off without the concept. The good takes us morally to the same place as God, and with fewer risks. The '"Good" is not the old God in disguise, but rather what the old God symbolized'.[74]

What are the implications of disconnecting goodness from God, from Christian language and forms of life? There are two distinct though related issues. They concern the *content* of the concept of goodness, and the question of how such goodness becomes or remains realisable, a live possibility for human being.

Goodness is difficult to define and to see in itself.[75] That is part of its mystery. Murdoch says that 'the source of vision is not in the ordinary sense seen',[76] and

---

[74] Murdoch, *Metaphysics*, p.428.
[75] Murdoch, *Sovereignty of Good*, pp.74, 98–99.
[76] Murdoch, *Sovereignty of Good*, p.98.

Gaita, commenting on his reason for judging Mother Teresa's love to be especially pure, speaks of what is revealed in its light, its power to reveal the full humanity of the afflicted. He quotes Simone Weil, saying that 'if we wish to know how bright a torch is, then we do not look at the bulb: we look to see what it has the power to illuminate'.[77] What is it in someone's behaviour or demeanour that makes us wonder at its goodness? 'Other moral concepts (often those of the virtues) enter the description of those actions whose goodness is a matter for wonder',[78] but the goodness of those actions is not exhausted by their identification with other virtues. As Murdoch puts it, if we ask what 'courage' is or 'truth' is, the idea of the Good must enter our explanation: '"True courage is ...". And if we try to define Good as X we have to add that we mean of course a good X'.[79]

As the discussion so far clearly indicates, however, for both Murdoch and Gaita there is a relationship between absolute goodness and the love of saints; indeed, their concept of absolute goodness is conditioned by the love exhibited by these exemplars of the Christian tradition.[80] This may seem truer of Gaita's account than Murdoch's, since she declines finally to identify the concept of the good with love, arguing that love is that in us which draws us towards the good by which love itself is purified.[81] Drawing on Plato's picture of Love in the *Symposium* as being poor and needy, she writes, 'Love is the tension between the imperfect soul and the magnetic perfection which is conceived of as lying beyond it'.[82] Nevertheless, she also claims that, when it is even partially refined, love is the 'force that joins us to the Good and joins us to the world through the Good. Its existence is the unmistakable sign that we are spiritual creatures ... It is a reflection of the warmth and light of the sun'.[83]

This suggests that Murdoch's Platonism is Christianised and that, as for Gaita, the nature of the good, the 'sun', is revealed by what it makes possible, namely love of a certain purity, 'unselfish and just. The mother loving the retarded child or loving the tiresome elderly relation'.[84] Absolute goodness and pure, other-regarding, other-revealing love belong together. Such love, Mark Wynn notes, is unconditional, not premised on the empirical qualities or particular achievements

---

[77]   Gaita, *Good and Evil*, p.205.

[78]   Gaita, *Good and Evil*, p.210.

[79]   Murdoch, *Sovereignty of Good*, p.98.

[80]   Christopher Cordner has suggested that there is a 'recurrent ambivalence' in Gaita's thought about the equivalence between Socratic–Platonic and Christian conceptions of absolute goodness. Cordner argues, and I agree, that in fact the concept of goodness that most animates Gaita's thought has Christian rather than Platonic roots and this is shown by its interdependence with love: 'Gaita and Plato: Goodness, Love and Beauty', in *Philosophy, Ethics and a Common Humanity*, pp.49–67, pp.54–55. See Gaita's acknowledgement of this point in 'Morality, Metaphysics and Religion', p.27.

[81]   Murdoch, *Sovereignty of Good*, p.102.

[82]   Murdoch, *Sovereignty of Good*, p.103.

[83]   Murdoch, *Sovereignty of Good*, p.103.

[84]   Murdoch, *Sovereignty of Good*, p.103.

of its object, and non-possessive. It 'is surely an instance of (or perhaps simply identical with) what Christians have called neighbor love'.[85] My question is whether this kind of love and the concept of goodness with which it is interdependent can continue to exist indefinitely as possibilities for moral life once detached from this spiritual–linguistic tradition.[86]

Gaita acknowledges that the existence of forms of unconditional love 'depends upon certain practices and customs as much as it informs them'.[87] He speaks of unconditional parental love and the love of saints, noting that neither is 'universally an ideal amongst the peoples of the earth, and even in cultures such as ours where they are (or have been) celebrated, people's hold on them is often fragile'.[88]

What is an example of a different concept of goodness, one that is not interdependent in this way with unconditional, other-regarding love? Christopher Cordner points to Plato's *Symposium* where, as I have already noted, love is an expression of *lack*.[89] 'Love is always the Love of something, and ... that something is what [the lover] lacks'.[90] There is a relationship between love and the good, since what is loved is understood as something good. However, as Cordner notes,

> if and when that goal is achieved, he will lack no more, and therefore no longer love that good, because he will be perfect or complete with respect to it ... It is part of this picture of Plato's that human beings cannot in their earthly condition finally achieve perfection or completeness, so they will in fact continue to love, and so to seek, the good that they lack ... But it is a central element of Plato's vision, at least in the *Phaedrus* and the *Symposium*, that whatever or whoever *is* good does not love.[91]

A corollary of this is that we seek and love the good because of the lack in us, but love is not and cannot be an expression of our goodness. And part of what

---

    [85]   Mark Wynn, *Emotional Experience and Religious Understanding: Integrating Perception, Conception and Feeling* (Cambridge: Cambridge University Press, 2005), p.41.

    [86]   I do not claim that this kind of love is known only to the Christian tradition. Clearly the Jewish tradition is the root from which this Christian understanding grows, and there are at least comparable concepts in other spiritual traditions. My interest, however, is in the effect of the cultural loss of the spiritual and theological background to our moral concepts, which are largely derived from a Christian context.

    [87]   Gaita, *A Common Humanity*, p.22.

    [88]   Gaita, *A Common Humanity*, p.22.

    [89]   Christopher Cordner, 'Two Conceptions of Love in Philosophical Thought', *Sophia* 50 (2011): 315–329, p.316. See also his discussion in 'Gaita and Plato'.

    [90]   Plato, *Symposium* 200e, trans. M. Joyce, in E. Hamilton and H. Cairns (eds), *The Collected Dialogues of Plato* (Princeton, NJ: Princeton University Press, 1961), p.553, cited in Cordner, 'Two Conceptions of Love in Philosophical Thought', p.316.

    [91]   Cordner, 'Two Conceptions of Love in Philosophical Thought', p.316.

this means is that it makes no sense to say that the good (God) could love us.[92] The connection between love and transcendent goodness in the Christian tradition is very different although it is well to be aware that these conceptions have a complex history.[93] Cordner writes that, 'In the Christian picture, God loves out of fullness of being ... This conception of God is simply unintelligible on Plato's view of things, precisely because on Plato's view love never expresses "fullness" of being, but only a lack in the one loving'.[94] Furthermore, again on the Christian picture, insofar as human loving partakes of the creative power of God's love, it is likewise an expression of 'what is good and whole in us' rather than lack.[95]

Cordner's discussion alerts us to the fact that there is nothing necessary about understanding goodness as expressive of and informing love of a certain purity and wholeness. It is possible to live in a world that does not recognise goodness as interdependent with unconditional, other-regarding love. It is, however, precisely this kind of love that has the power to reveal, to attend to, the full humanity of another, including those others whose affliction renders their humanity invisible. So, as Gaita acknowledges, it is the love of saints that 'yields' to us a conception of individuals as infinitely precious, that yields to us our deepest sense of what a human being is. Gaita notes that the conception of individuals as infinitely precious was not unknown to the world 'before the love of saints' and he quotes from Homer's *Iliad* to illustrate the point. Nevertheless,

> The love of saints depends on, builds on and transforms that sense of individuality.
> It deepens the language of love, which nourishes and is nourished by our sense
> that human beings are irreplaceable and, because of that transformation, it
> compels some people to affirm that even those who suffer affliction so severe
> that they have irrecoverably lost everything that gives sense to our lives, and
> even the most radical evildoers, are fully our fellow human beings. As with the
> love it transforms, the love of saints plays a constitutive and revelatory role.[96]

---

[92]   Martin Warner likewise notes that Plato's conception of love in the *Symposium* means that 'it is only the lover, not the beloved, who is consumed by desire and, analogously, the unitary radiance which is ultimately the proper object of love cannot itself love'. 'Love and Transcendence', in Carlisle, Carter and Webster (eds), *Moral Powers, Fragile Beliefs: Essays in Moral and Religious Philosophy*, pp.157–183, p.165. Unlike Cordner, Warner suggests, however, that Plato's treatment of love in the *Phaedrus* presents a somewhat different picture, treating the truest form of *eros* as a reciprocal relation between lover and beloved, leading to the joint seeking of wisdom.

[93]   Warner brings out the extent to which the various Platonic accounts of love, expanded by Plotinus, have been incorporated into the complex history of Christian conceptions of the relationship between human and divine love. 'Love and Transcendence'.

[94]   Cordner, 'Two Conceptions of Love in Philosophical Thought', p.318. Cordner qualifies this remark slightly with reference to the *Lysis*, suggesting that here Plato 'spontaneously thinks of *philia* as a love emanating from the goodness of those who are friends'.

[95]   Cordner, 'Two Conceptions of Love in Philosophical Thought', p.319.

[96]   Gaita, *Good and Evil*, p.xxiv.

How is it that the language and practice of the love of saints yields our deepest sense of what a human being is? Its central feature is that it is love that makes room for the other, sees deeply the independent reality of the other, and wonders at the very fact of their being. Like the love of God, it has the power to nourish existence. Cordner discusses a number of examples of such love, including a reading of the parable of the Good Samaritan. What he emphasises is that the love he is concerned with, the unconditional love of saints, is not reducible to its practical expression nor its responsiveness to particular qualities or attributes of its recipient. 'Unconditional' just means that it is love for another as this very one who is. To be the object of such love is to be acknowledged at the deepest level of one's being:

> The man helped by the Samaritan will be pleased that he was carried to safety and that his wounds were tended. For that help he will likely be grateful. But if he was helped in a certain spirit, he may also be grateful for that, as something more and different, and indeed that 'something' may be what touches him most deeply.[97]

Cordner goes on to say that, in the circumstances, love for the wounded man could not be expressed by the Samaritan without actually helping him. Yet, love is more than this. In the same way that someone may have all their physical needs met or their rights honoured, and yet still experience being condescended to, or dismissed, or their deepest self neglected or unattended,[98] so the woundedness of the one helped by the Samaritan can only be fully tended if he experiences 'what is done in helping him as an affirmation of *him*',[99] this particular and irreplaceable human being. If he is tended in this way, then, even if he never sees the Samaritan again, this experience of being loved 'might even so remain a kind of beacon in his life, a source of continuing "nourishment of his soul", to use Simone Weil's phrase'.[100]

What makes possible this kind of love? Rather than being an expression of lack in the self, it seems to issue, as Cordner says, from 'fullness of being', from wholeness. It reflects a basic security that allows the lover to go out towards the beloved, to let go of self-concern so as to attend to the other. The Christian tradition understands this to be the dynamic of God's own being. God is nothing other than this energy of self-dispossessing love, whose love for humanity is the basis of our security and so our capacity for self-giving. The question is whether, in our

---

[97]   Cordner, 'Two Conceptions of Love in Philosophical Thought', p.323.

[98]   Cordner gives examples of someone coming from the unemployment office saying that while none of his rights had been violated, yet he felt humiliated by the 'spirit' in which he was treated; and of a child whose needs are tended by her parents but in a spirit of impatience rather than full presence. 'Two Conceptions of Love in Philosophical Thought', p.325.

[99]   Cordner, 'Two Conceptions of Love in Philosophical Thought', p.323.

[100]   Cordner, 'Two Conceptions of Love in Philosophical Thought', p.324.

culture, its continuance as a human possibility can be as readily disconnected from spiritual practice and theological articulation as the philosophers imply.

Murdoch and Gaita know that the quality of attention paid to others by saints, the love that reveals reality, involves dispossession of the self. Murdoch speaks of 'unselfing'; Gaita speaks of the way in which Mother Teresa 'disappears' – we are not conscious of her, but simply of what is revealed in the light of her gaze. This is the humility that is inseparable from her love. After centuries of Christian formation, there is a sense in which this kind of attention and the language and practices that sustain it just are available in our culture. Cordner speaks of Christian 'ideas', which, regardless of our theological commitments, can be seen as humanly important.[101] I agree that the routine practice of loving attention to another does not require explicit theological formulation or spiritual discipline.

And yet, we are concerned not simply with routine practice. It is not, Gaita suggests, routine practice that will continue to make the reality of others visible in a way that enables us to keep the afflicted fully among us. As Mark Wynn among others has noted, standard moral philosophical accounts are generally blind to this reality. They seek to justify the value or the moral significance of human beings in virtue of qualities they 'possess', qualities such as sentience, rationality or whatever. Such accounts do struggle to keep fully among us those human beings who lack or are deficient in the relevant quality and seem 'bound to issue in a problematic account of the moral standing of people with cognitive and other disabilities'.[102]

Even our grasp of the concept of love may be fragile. Cordner notes that 'modern [philosophical] habits of thinking have made it very difficult indeed even to express what is at issue' in his discussion of the meaning and significance of love as irreducible to its practical benefits.[103] His remark is borne out by the highly critical response of Christopher Hamilton to Gaita's appeal to the significance of the love of saints for moral philosophy. Hamilton complains that Gaita does not adequately characterise what justifies calling the nun's response 'love', since we 'are told nothing about what she actually *did* while visiting the patients in the psychiatric hospital or thereafter'.[104] Apparently for Hamilton, '*doing*' something does not include attending to or acknowledging another's very existence, 'seeing' their humanity:

> Did she remonstrate with the doctors in an attempt to get them to treat the patients better? Did she seek to get the institutional structures and organisation changed

---

[101] Cordner, 'Two Conceptions of Love in Philosophical Thought', p.320.

[102] Wynn, *Emotional Experience and Religious Understanding*, p.37. On this point, Wynn cites Peter Singer arguing for the moral equivalence of the 'imbecile' and the dog on the grounds that they share an equivalent rationality.

[103] Cordner, 'Two Conceptions of Love in Philosophical Thought', p.324.

[104] Christopher Hamilton, 'Raimond Gaita on Saints, Love and Human Preciousness', *Ethical Theory and Moral Practice*, 11 (2008): 181–195, p.183.

that the patients might be better cared for? ... [O]ne might think that, if she did nothing to ameliorate the situation of the patients, then this was no love at all. Or one might think it love, but not really worth a lot: it is not at all obviously wrong to think that the patients could well do without such love, and would be far better off being the beneficiaries of a bit more down-to-earth practical help.[105]

As Cordner rightly remarks, in certain circumstances, of course love requires practical expression. Yet to think, as Hamilton seems to, that for people whose lives were utterly devoid of acknowledgement of their *selves*, as distinct from their 'condition', that they 'could well do without such love' is astonishing. It suggests that we cannot take for granted that the possibility of the nun's love can be kept alive, either practically or conceptually, in a culture that does not know how to recognise or nourish it.

Gaita notes that the love shown by the nun for the psychiatric patients was shaped by a language of love, the love of God for his children, and by 'virtues of character, imagination and sensibility, given content and form by the disciplines of her vocation'.[106] Although it seems theoretically possible to extract this concept of love from the particular practices and disciplines that shape it, it is not clear exactly what other schools for moral formation might be capable of enabling this transfiguring love of saints. Indeed, Gaita says that he does not believe that the demeanour of the nun in the psychiatric hospital 'would have been possible for her were it not for the place which the language of parental love had in her prayers'.[107] Commenting on this, Wynn suggests that

> Gaita's view implies ... that while there may be no abstract conceptual
> requirement that saintly love be conditioned by the language of divine love,
> it may well be that, as a matter of contingent, historical fact, such love needs
> the language of religion, since that language offers our richest, most sustained
> exploration of the thought that we are all intelligibly the objects of love, in so far
> as we are all children of God, and beloved of God.[108]

If my suggestion about the centrality of the practice of dispossession is near the mark, then I suggest that it is not simply the language of parental love in prayer that conditions the possibility of the nun's love, but also practices such as worship (involving an *ek-stasis* of other-centredness), radical trust in relation to material security, surrender to the requirements of vocation, and so on. It is not that practices of this kind could not in principle be available in other contexts, but it is true that, as Rowan Williams has noted, the Christian church does exist

---

[105]   Hamilton, 'Raimond Gaita on Saints, Love and Human Preciousness', pp.183–184.

[106]   Gaita, *A Common Humanity*, p.20.

[107]   Gaita, *A Common Humanity*, p.22.

[108]   Wynn, *Emotional Experience and Religious Understanding*, p.43.

as an 'embodying structure' for an ethic of a particular kind.[109] For this kind of reason, Wynn suggests that 'a person who shares with Gaita a commonsensical range of moral commitments ought, at least, to be favourably disposed to religious traditions, and to hope that the language of those traditions, where it represents God's love for us as akin to that of a parent, continues to be vital'.[110]

I emphasise that at stake here is not simply a question of whether Christian language or belief or practice is the best place to form the kind of selves capable of the love of saints, or whether other secular schools for such formation might be possible. We are concerned here not simply with the possibility of the practice of love in particular instances, but with the continued intelligibility of a certain concept of goodness and the love with which it is interdependent. That is because unless we can see this kind of goodness enacted, the concept will become incomprehensible to us, unavailable to us. The world will not be visible in its light. The shape of moral possibility and impossibility will be different.

Gaita says: 'I want to show how the world appears to moral reflection about what to do and how to be when it is illuminated by the kind of goodness shown by people like … the nun and Mother Teresa … I say that it was not the superlative development of a natural or moral capacity that enabled Mother Teresa to respond as she did to the radically afflicted beggars in Calcutta'.[111] True, he continues, she was a compassionate person, but her compassion 'was informed by an understanding that it was elicited by people whose preciousness had not been even slightly diminished'.[112] For this reason, he says, his point is conceptual: 'It is about the concepts that must be available to us if we are to see things in a certain way, in this case, if we are to see people who are radically afflicted in a way that enables us to respond with a compassion that does not condescend'.[113]

I have followed Gaita and Murdoch in accepting that the good and the real are related, such that increasing virtue is the condition of deepening attention to reality. At a certain kind of limit, we have seen that encountering the reality of the full humanity of the afflicted is dependent upon that humanity being made visible by love whose purity is like that displayed by Mother Teresa or the nun in the psychiatric hospital. In this last part of the chapter, I have been considering the conditions of the possibility of that kind of love.

Although they are inextricably entwined, I have sought to distinguish the question of how a self might be formed so as to be open to receive the gift of such loving, from the question of the concepts that must be available to us, as Gaita puts it, if we are to see and respond to reality in this way. I have registered doubt about the extent to which the practice of this kind of love and the concept of

---

[109] Rowan Williams, 'Interiority and Epiphany: A Reading in New Testament Ethics', in *On Christian Theology*, pp.239–264, p.247.

[110] Wynn, *Emotional Experience and Religious Understanding*, p.43.

[111] Gaita, *Good and Evil*, p.xviii.

[112] Gaita, *Good and Evil*, p.xviii.

[113] Gaita, *Good and Evil*, p.xix.

goodness interdependent with it can continue to be vital when disconnected from the theological reality to which they are a testimony and response. What I hope to have done, therefore, is to have made room for a theological exploration of moral reality that is worth the attention of those who do not have existing theological commitments. It is to the beginnings of that exploration that we now turn.

Chapter 2
Resurrection and Transcendence

> What is most obvious is that this past complex event has left a trace or effect in our history which retires into its own uniqueness even as it is invoked. It occurs as a summons to wager oneself on the truth of what has been revealed, to be judged by it, to enter into its field of communication, to receive its witnesses, even without being able to 'signify' or ever represent it fully.[1]

When Gaita refers to God in whom he cannot believe, or Murdoch speaks of God who used to symbolise what is more perspicuously seen in the concept of the Good, neither attends in any depth to the meaning of this name, 'God'. Gaita does distinguish between the abstract God of the philosophers and God known by faith. He notes, following D.Z. Phillips, that the meaning of the language of religion, including the concept of God, must be learned from the place it has in the lives of those who believe rather than from *a priori* definitions in terms of omnipotence, omniscience, and so on. Nevertheless, his is not and is not intended to be a theological discussion of the Christian doctrine of God. As Gaita makes clear, he intends only to make conceptual space for an understanding of goodness in ethics that lies beyond what can be accounted for by ethical naturalism but that also does not rely on religious belief. Neither Gaita nor Murdoch has an interest in exploring or elaborating on that space in theological terms.

In the previous chapter, I argued that their reasons for refusing this theological elaboration do not establish that such an enterprise is impossible or illegitimate, and I suggested that there may be practical and conceptual costs to human life that follow from that refusal. In this chapter, I approach this question from, as it were, the other end. That is, whereas in the previous chapter I began from the side of philosophers arguing in non-theological terms for the significance of transcendence in ethics, in this chapter I begin from the side of theology exploring the shape of transcendence in the light of specifically theological revelation, the story of the life, death and resurrection of Jesus Christ. I am interested in the nature of the transcendent reality that is, in Murdoch's phrase, the 'proper background' to morals.

This approach may seem to beg all the relevant questions at the outset. Why begin theological elaboration of the space of transcendence from a Christian perspective, drawing on Christian doctrine and theological sources? What are those of non-Christian background or commitment to make of such a discussion? It may not be doubted that the space of transcendence *can* be elaborated in

---

[1]   Anthony J. Kelly, *The Resurrection Effect: Transforming Christian Life and Thought* (Maryknoll, NY: Orbis Books, 2008), p.124.

Christian terms, but what makes the choice to put it in those terms other than simply arbitrary? What does this kind of elaboration contribute to transcending the boundaries between a philosophical discussion that can make no serious sense of the language of theology, and prior dogmatic commitment to a religious, and specifically Christian, worldview?

Some remarks of Rowan Williams are helpful here. In reflecting on the relationship between theological and ethical discourse, and on the place of Christian commitment in contributing to general ethical discussion, he writes:

> The claims made by classical Christian theology for the universal pertinence
> of the proclamation of Jesus, the claims to a decisive authority in shaping the
> human world, can only be given flesh by trying to see if, in fact, the narrative
> of Jesus *can* offer resources for an ethic and an anthropology with some ability
> to liberate us from the manifestly self-destructive spirals of human interaction.[2]

This means that it is not a matter of establishing in advance that Christian theology, Christian conviction, is authorised to specify the space of ethical transcendence. It means that the authority of Christian proclamation will be granted insofar as it *can* actually offer resources for deepening and liberating our lives. So, Williams continues,

> a Christian theological statement has to be – at least – an invitation into a world
> of possible readings of the world in terms of the gospel, and possible responses
> to the given narrative of Jesus; not a provider of occult information, but ... a
> modification of sensibility.[3]

This does not mean that other readings of ethical transcendence might not also be possible, might not also offer 'readings of the world'. In seeking to explore the space of transcendence, the nature of transcendent 'reality', from a Christian theological perspective, I am not making *a priori* exclusivist claims. I am, however, suggesting this as a possible reading of the 'world' and then asking if and how such a reading offers a resource for 'an ethic and an anthropology with some ability to liberate us'. The question of *critical* engagement with the viability and truthfulness of this theological reading of the world will necessarily arise within the exploration itself as we ask about its power to illuminate reality. In the same way that Gaita's testimony to what was revealed by the love of the nun cannot be authenticated except in relation to what her love revealed and in relation to how her love deepened and shaped Gaita's moral imagination, so it is with the testimony of Christian theology to the event and the meaning of Jesus Christ for

---

[2]   Rowan Williams, 'Interiority and Epiphany: A Reading in New Testament Ethics', in *On Christian Theology* (Oxford: Blackwell Publishers, 2000), pp.239–264, pp.252–253.

[3]   Williams, 'Interiority and Epiphany', p.253.

human life. We begin necessarily in the midst of things. And, for reasons that I shall now elaborate, I begin from the resurrection.

Resurrection

I begin from the resurrection because without it there would be no Christian witness, no specifically Christian conception of God, no New Testament, no church. As Thorwald Lorenzen affirms in the introduction to his comprehensive study of theological approaches to the resurrection,

> The resurrection is not merely an object of faith, and it is not merely a credal statement to accept; it is the *origin* and *ground* of faith. Here the *nature* and *content* of faith, what Christian faith actually *is*, is decided.[4]

In a similar vein, James Alison notes:

> We have a faith at all because we receive a witness ... What the apostles witness to is the resurrection, the irruption of a happening into their lives and one that could be experienced in a variety of ways. It was not simply a fact that they could then tack on to the end of the creed, so that it would be a fuller account of what happened. It was what made it possible for there to be a creed at all. If there had been no resurrection, there would have been no New Testament, since the New Testament is the witness of the apostles to the resurrection, including their new-found ability to understand what led to it. Without it, there would have been no new story to tell.[5]

These contemporary statements echo the recognition in the earliest New Testament witness, that the resurrection is the *sine qua non* of the Christian gospel of salvation, the Christian account of God. So, as Paul wrote to the Corinthian church,

---

[4]   Thorwald Lorenzen, *Resurrection and Discipleship: Interpretive Models, Biblical Reflections, Theological Consequences* (Maryknoll, NY: Orbis Books, 1995), p.1.

[5]   James Alison, *Knowing Jesus* (Springfield, IL: Templegate Publishers, 1994), pp.5–6. The same point is made by almost every study of the resurrection. See, for example, Jürgen Moltmann, *Theology of Hope: On the Ground and the Implications of a Christian Eschatology* (Minneapolis, MN: Fortress Press, 1993), p.165; Jürgen Moltmann, *The Way of Jesus Christ: Christology in Messianic Dimensions* (London: SCM Press, 1990), p.213; C.F. Evans, *Resurrection and the New Testament* (London: SCM Press, 1970), pp.1–5; Pheme Perkins, *Resurrection: New Testament Witness and Contemporary Reflection* (London: Geoffrey Chapman, 1984), p.17; Peter Carnley, *The Structure of Resurrection Belief* (Oxford: Clarendon Press, 1987), p.6; Brian D. Robinette, *Grammars of Resurrection: A Christian Theology of Presence and Absence* (New York: Crossroad Publishing Company, 2009), p.63.

> If Christ has not been raised, your faith is futile and you are still in your sins.
> Then those also who have died in Christ have perished. If for this life only we
> have hoped in Christ, we are of all people most to be pitied. (1 Cor. 15.17–19)

Indeed, if Christ has not been raised we are 'even found to be misrepresenting God, because we testified of God that he raised Christ' (1 Cor. 15.15).

So much may be readily granted. But what is this 'happening' called resurrection? What does it mean? And why should it be believed? It is difficult to know how to begin engaging these questions for the purposes of this book. The relevant literature is vast, and could itself occupy many full-length studies. I am interested specifically in the question of the difference professing resurrection faith makes to moral imagination and moral life. Yet that presupposes some account of what this resurrection faith amounts to, and some reason for taking seriously how the world looks in its light. I suggest that a way into the terrain is via the category of testimony. I am going to begin with some conceptual remarks before turning to the New Testament witness to the resurrection.

Recall Gaita's discussion of being 'claimed in testimony' by the reality revealed by the love of the nun for the psychiatric patients, the reality of their full humanity. Gaita's account of this event involves the narration of certain facts, an eyewitness report of something that happened, which is at the same time his account of the meaning of that event. In other words, Gaita's testimony to his encounter with the nun is not simply a story about something that once happened to him (like the fact that he went to London for his holidays), but is an invitation to participate with him in a certain way of seeing it, a certain judgement about its meaning. This dialectic between narration and confession, fact and meaning is, in Paul Ricoeur's analysis, fundamental to the concept of testimony.[6] Testimony, he notes, 'is at the service of judgement … Testimony wants to justify, to prove the good basis of an assertion which, beyond the fact, claims to attain its meaning'.[7]

Two further significant features of testimony can be drawn from this example. The first concerns the relationship between the objectivity of the happening and the subjectivity of the experience. Gaita's testimony to the nun's love involves not simply a report concerning the fact of her visit but a testimony to a reality rendered visible by her love. But this 'reality' may not have been recognised by someone else. It is possible, for example, that one of the psychiatrists who saw the nun with the patients would not have seen what Gaita saw, would not have seen their full humanity in the light of her love. Does this mean that what Gaita thinks he saw was not 'really' there, because not perceptible to just anyone? Or does it mean that there are objective 'realities' perceptible only to a subjectivity capable of receiving them, those who have 'eyes to see' or 'ears to hear'? The category of testimony

[6] Paul Ricoeur, 'The Hermeneutics of Testimony', in Lewis Mudge (ed.), *Essays in Biblical Interpretation* (London: SPCK, 1981), pp.119–154, p.135.

[7] Ricoeur, 'Hermeneutics of Testimony', pp.123–124.

complicates a crude distinction between subjective and objective experience, which will be important as we turn to the resurrection narratives.[8]

Second and relatedly, there is the question of the credibility of testimony. What counts as evidence, as reason for believing the testimony of a witness? There are different modalities for determining truthfulness or reliability here. On the one hand, to the extent that testimony involves the narration of an event, certain historical facts may call it into question. If it is established that no nun had ever visited the psychiatric hospital, then Gaita's story ceases to be testimony and becomes instead an elaborately worked example. It may still, as an imaginable scenario, claim to illustrate a truth about meaning, but it is no longer testimony. On the other hand, to the extent that testimony involves the attestation of meaning, critical concepts other than factual correspondence are also required for assessing its credibility. If someone's testimony to a happening is sentimental, for example, or self-absorbed, or cynical, then these are critical concepts that are relevant to our assessment of the truthfulness of their speech. Moreover, testifying to something, seeking to be true to something, always involves a kind of moral risk for the witness. Gaita says that someone claimed in testimony to a particular experience of meaning 'must speak in authoritative and authentic response to what has moved him. Such speech is an act of trust that we have not been seduced by what we feel we must be true to'.[9] Basic to the act of testifying, then, is the self-implication of the witness:

What is a true witness, a faithful witness? Everyone understands that this is something other than an exact, even scrupulous narrator. It is not limited to testimony that... but he testifies for..., he renders testimony to.... By these expressions our language means that the witness seals his bond to the cause that he defends by a public profession of his conviction, by the zeal of a propagator, by a personal devotion which can extend even to the sacrifice of his life. The witness is capable of suffering and dying for what he believes.[10]

Part of what this means is that a judgement about the truthfulness of a testimony, of a witness, is connected to how that which is testified to shows itself in the life of the one testifying.[11] Gaita, for example, testifies to the nun's love and to what it

---

[8]   This issue is well discussed by Anthony Kelly, *Resurrection Effect*, chapter 7.

[9]   Raimond Gaita, *Good and Evil: An Absolute Conception*, second edition (London: Routledge, 2004), p.224.

[10]   Ricoeur, 'Hermeneutics of Testimony', p.129.

[11]   The question of what counts as evidence for the truthfulness of testimony is extensively discussed by C.A.J. Coady, *Testimony: A Philosophical Study* (Oxford: Clarendon Press, 1992). He notes that in assessing the reliability of 'astonishing reports' what is needed is not 'a criterion but a judgement' (p.198), although he tends to focus on judgement concerning the sufficiency of the grounds for belief rather than the way in which that which is attested shows itself in the life of the witness.

revealed, and his trust in that reality shows itself in his own life. It manifests itself through how he understands and responds to the humanity of the afflicted, and through his commitment to naming what is missing in accounts of moral reality that do not acknowledge this. He is not simply a witness *to* a particular happening and its meaning, but a witness *from* it.[12] Following Ricoeur, Williams puts it this way:

> testimony and *manifestation* belong together: in the 'testimony' of a life-commitment, that which is witnessed to declares or shows itself, becomes manifest as a comprehensive and unconditional source of meaning.[13]

If these remarks illuminate something of the character of testimony in general, how do they help us to engage with the apostolic testimony to the resurrection of Jesus from the dead? They enable us, I suggest, to respond more productively to a cluster of seeming problems or difficulties concerning faith in the resurrection and the meaning of this witness.

Let us begin with the most obvious question: did the resurrection 'really' happen, or is talk of resurrection just a way of saying that the 'meaning' of Jesus or the 'cause' of Jesus lives on?[14] In the resurrection, did something happen to the dead Jesus or not? If we begin with the New Testament texts, then they purport to speak of something happening to Jesus. In his letter to the Corinthian church, Paul writes: 'For I handed on to you as of first importance ... that Christ died for our sins ... and that he was raised on the third day in accordance with the scriptures, and that he appeared to Cephas, then to the twelve' (1 Cor. 15.3–8). The first preaching of the resurrection, as portrayed by Luke in the Acts of the Apostles, is announced to those who had known Jesus in the flesh. His crucifixion and resurrection are proclaimed equally as 'events', things that happened at a certain time and place to Jesus. Peter asks his hearers, 'You that are Israelites', to acknowledge that they knew this man Jesus of Nazareth, 'a man attested to you by God with deeds of power, wonders, and signs that God did through him among you, as you yourselves know' (Acts 2.22). This man whom 'you crucified and killed by the hands of those outside the law', is the same man whom 'God raised ... up, having freed him from death' (Acts 2.23–24). Of this raising up, 'all of us are witnesses' (Acts 2.32). The resurrection narratives in all four gospels speak of an utterly bewildering encounter with the 'fact' of something having happened to Jesus, either in the form of the absence of the body (the empty tomb) or in the form

---

[12]   See Alison, *Knowing Jesus*, p.7.

[13]   Rowan Williams, *Resurrection: Interpreting the Easter Gospel*, second edition (Cleveland, OH: The Pilgrim Press, 2002), p.56.

[14]   Summarising the state of scholarship on the resurrection is itself a large scholarly task. Among many possible references, an accessible summary is Gerald O'Collins, 'The Resurrection: The State of the Question', in Stephen T. Davis, Daniel Kendall SJ and Gerald O'Collins SJ (eds), *The Resurrection: An Interdisciplinary Symposium on the Resurrection of Jesus* (Oxford: Oxford University Press, 1997), pp.5–28.

of the appearance of the crucified and risen Jesus to one or more of his followers. And yet, it is not easy to know how to read this testimony, to understand what kind of assent it asks for.

The difficulties are numerous. For one thing, the dead do not rise and this claim was no easier for those in first-century Palestine to believe than it is for the 'modern' mind.[15] The narratives concerning the empty tomb and the appearances are not contemporaneous with the events, they are unable to be harmonised with each other, and they bear clear signs of theological commitment and redaction. It is impossible to get back fully behind these texts to discover what 'really' happened, and the texts themselves show little concern for forensic accuracy as we understand it: their interest is in the proclamation and elicitation of faith. These difficulties have prompted a spectrum of scholarly response, ranging from the apologetic attempt to prove the historicity of the empty tomb, to the abandonment of history in favour of existential or eschatological accounts of the reality of the resurrection, and various positions in between.[16]

Beginning with the understanding that the New Testament witness to the resurrection is indeed *witness*, testimony, a fruitful place to begin engaging these difficulties is by looking at the manifestation of this testimony in the lives of those who were first claimed by it. And here, it seems clear that being true to what they were claimed by had a profoundly transformative effect on the apostles, not only turning them, as James Alison engagingly remarks, from

> pusillanimous fisherfolk into international heroes and martyrs, but causing them to rethink the whole of their lives, their relationship with their homeland, their culture, its values, and radically altering their understanding of who God is.[17]

Now the fact that one is profoundly changed may attest to the impact of something, but it does not necessarily mean that that something is revelatory of truth or reality. As Ricoeur notes, the fact that a witness is willing to become a martyr does not by itself prove the truth or justice of a cause.[18] We can distinguish, at least in principle, between the faithfulness of a witness and the reality of that to which they testify. Thus, as Gaita says, just as one who is claimed in testimony must trust that they

---

[15]   As Williams notes, 'it is not a straightforward matter to say what the gospels understood by the resurrection of Jesus; but this seems to have something to do with the fact that the Christian communities of the last quarter of the first Christian century didn't find it all that straightforward either'. 'Between the Cherubim', in *On Christian Theology*, pp.183–196, p.187. See also Robinette, *Grammars of Resurrection*, p.34.

[16]   A recent discussion of some of these variants, which includes a summary of recent scholarship on the resurrection, is Gerald O'Collins, *Believing in the Resurrection: The Meaning and Promise of the Risen Jesus* (New York: Paulist Press, 2012).

[17]   Alison, *Knowing Jesus*, p.7.

[18]   Ricoeur, 'Hermeneutics of Testimony', p.129. Coady likewise notes that the willingness of martyrs to die for their beliefs may be evidence of their sincerity but is insufficient by itself to establish the truth of their testimony. *Testimony*, pp.52–53.

have not been seduced by that which claims them, so those who receive a testimony must determine that they worthily trust the witness. This is a question, ultimately, of judgement, interpretation, discernment. But surely this is precisely the question with which we began: on what basis may we judge the apostolic witness to the resurrection to be worthy of trust? How may we know what really happened?

At this point, I suggest, it is significant to see the *whole* of the New Testament as witnessing to the resurrection, and not simply the passages or narratives that speak of the event of Jesus rising on the third day. The resurrection, as we noted earlier, is not simply an event described or narrated alongside others within the New Testament writings: it is that from which the whole is generated.[19] It is part of this testimony, not simply that the event of resurrection occurred, but that because of that event everything is different. Because of that event, there is a new reality to inhabit: 'So if anyone is in Christ, there is a new creation: everything old has passed away; see, everything has become new!' (2 Cor. 5.17) The truth of the testimony concerning the resurrection, remembering that testimony encompasses both what happened (narration) and its meaning (confession), is necessarily interdependent with whether the reality testified to is capable of being inhabited in such a way that life lived in its light is indeed 'new', is experienced as more 'real', more deeply, truthfully and creatively engaged with its meaning.

This claim may seem to say that it does not matter whether the resurrection 'really' happened; what matters is only the capacity of resurrection faith to generate the possibility of living a certain kind of life. However, such an approach denies the self-designation of the New Testament as witness to a happening utterly unexpected, unforeseen, and bewildering in its newness. As Brian Robinette puts it,

> Even a superficial reading of the New Testament reveals that *because* 'Jesus is risen' there is faith – not the other way around. One is certainly entitled to disagree that an eschatological 'event' after Jesus' death took place, but only with exegetical violence can one conclude that the New Testament itself is not fundamentally interested in what happens to Jesus after Good Friday.[20]

Even though several of the narratives indicate that recognising the reality of the risen Jesus is connected in some way to the receptive capacity of the subject and may not be straightforwardly perceptible to a neutral bystander,[21] nevertheless

---

[19]   Lorenzen, *Resurrection and Discipleship*, p.2.

[20]   Robinette, *Grammars of Resurrection*, p.63.

[21]   The claim that the risen Christ could not have been seen by just anyone, a 'neutral' bystander, is disputed by Stephen T. Davis in '"Seeing" the Risen Jesus', in Davis, Kendall and O'Collins (eds), *The Resurrection*, pp.126–147, but I do not think his arguments are convincing given the significance of the theme of 'non-recognition' and epistemic transformation in the appearance narratives. Relevant here is my earlier point about the extent to which just anyone could have seen the reality by which Gaita is claimed in testimony. I return to these epistemological issues later in the chapter. See also Sarah

we must be willing to recognize that the *prima facie* testimony of the New Testament, no matter how pluriform its narratives and metaphors, is unified in its proclamation that something new and radical occurs after Jesus' death, and that Christian faith, while ever remaining in continuity with the pre-Easter Jesus, is also transformed and given new content and form by it.[22]

In short, I am suggesting that our first access to discerning whether the New Testament witness to the resurrection is worthy of trust is through discerning something of the new reality, the new lives, made visible and inhabitable because of it. This does not mean that the resurrection event is itself *reducible* to the transformation undergone by its witnesses, but that our access to it necessarily goes by way of its effects.[23] It is the purpose of the next section to trace some of those effects, so that we might be better placed to see the nature of the reality to which they attest.

Effects of Resurrection

When I was a child, my mother would sometimes come to my school – she would work in the tuck shop or come to a class event. Whenever my mother was at the school, I felt deeply safe and, as a result, free. I felt that, while she was there, I could not get into trouble with a teacher (not that I was a troublesome child); I grew less cautious and freer to express my views, my laughter; I felt less afraid of classmates – even the 'tough' kids – since they couldn't hurt me while Mum was there; I felt as though the anxieties and dramas of the playground were suddenly put in perspective, and didn't ultimately matter very much; I realised, in a way I hadn't noticed before, the extent of my unfreedom in a normal school day. And all this happened, not because of anything particular that she said or did when she came to school, but simply because she was there and I knew absolutely that she loved me and was for me. When she came she brought that deeper reality of my life into the context of my school life, and my day was altered. It is an

---

Coakley, 'The Resurrection and the "Spiritual Senses": On Wittgenstein, Epistemology and the Risen Christ', in *Powers and Submissions: Spirituality, Philosophy and Gender* (Malden, MA: Blackwell Publishing, 2002), pp.130–152.

[22] Robinette, *Grammars of Resurrection*, p.63.

[23] The 'effects' of resurrection include not simply the kinds of lives and understanding now made possible for the apostolic witnesses themselves, but the textual 'traces' of that event in the resurrection stories. Robinette helpfully puts it this way: 'What is it about the resurrection that might make the historical, textual, and conceptual ambiguities found in the New Testament an unavoidable outcome? Might it be that the ambiguities of the resurrection narratives are uniquely disclosive as textual traces of an event whose eschatological character necessarily exceeds and overwhelms the capacity of representation, thereby reflecting something of the dynamism and historical ambiguity of the resurrection itself?' *Grammars of Resurrection*, pp.33–34. See also Williams, 'Between the Cherubim'.

incomplete analogy but, as well as showing how fortunate I am in my mother, this story illuminates for me something of the dynamics of the disciples' experience of the resurrection that I now explore in more depth.[24]

Feeling safe was not the immediate experience of the disciples faced with the risen Jesus. The gospel accounts all insist upon their fear, amazement, startling and incomprehension. Mark's gospel ends, in the oldest manuscripts, with the testimony of the women silenced by their fear (Mark 16.8), and nowhere is Jesus' first appearance welcomed as the familiar and safe presence that my mother's was for me at school. In fact, so unfamiliar was he that he was mostly unrecognised at first, and so fearful were the disciples that Jesus has to preface his speech to them with 'Peace' and 'Do not be afraid' (Luke 24.36; Matt. 28.10; John 20.19).

James Alison has sketched the strands of the fear that marked the first encounters with the resurrected Jesus. There was the sheer shock of encountering something utterly beyond any anticipated experience, 'quite outside the possibility of human vocabulary'.[25] There was consciousness of their shame, guilt and complicity in the betrayal and abandonment of Jesus to his death.[26] Most significantly perhaps of all, there was a vertiginous sense of nothing being certain any more: 'now there was no security, no rules, nothing normal could be trusted in. And worse, terror because everything difficult and frightening which Jesus had taught had to begin to come about: he went before them, as he had told them'.[27] As Alison continues, 'there is nothing pretty about Christian hope. Whatever Christian hope is, it begins in terror and utter disorientation in the face of the collapse of all that is familiar and well known'.[28]

Nor was safety a conspicuous outcome of the disciples' witness to this happening. From the stoning of Stephen in Jerusalem to the Pauline communities enduring faithfully in the midst of persecution, the witnesses to the resurrection suffered and were killed for the story they had to tell. And yet, despite these beginnings in fear and insecurity, the lives of the apostles come to rest in the 'sure and certain hope of the resurrection', and to be empowered by the conviction of absolute safety.[29] If God has raised Jesus from the dead, then there is no need

---

[24]   My account here is substantially indebted to what I have learned from James Alison.

[25]   Alison, *Knowing Jesus*, p.14.

[26]   Alison, *Knowing Jesus*, p.16.

[27]   James Alison, *Raising Abel: The Recovery of the Eschatological Imagination* (New York: Crossroad Publishing Company, 1996), p.161.

[28]   Alison, *Raising Abel*, p.161.

[29]   In his 'Lecture on Ethics', Wittgenstein referred to 'the experience of feeling *absolutely* safe' as an experience that helped him to fix his mind on what he meant by 'absolute or ethical value'. 'I mean the state of mind in which one is inclined to say, "I am safe, nothing can injure me whatever happens"'. Wittgenstein noted that, at one level, such an expression is nonsense; yet it expressed for him the way in which religious and ethical speech seeks '*to go beyond* the world and that is to say beyond significant language'. From a theological perspective, it is tempting to say that such an experience is a depth experience of the human condition whose source and meaning is revealed more explicitly in the

to fear either death or the authorities that wield it. If God is for them, then who can be against them? So, as Paul writes in his letter to the Romans, 'It is God who justifies. Who is to condemn? It is Christ Jesus, who died, yes, who was raised, who is at the right hand of God, who indeed intercedes for us. Who will separate us from the love of Christ? Will hardship, or distress, or persecution, or famine, or nakedness, or peril, or sword? ... No, in all these things we are more than conquerors through him who loved us' (Rom. 8.33–37). This sense of ultimate safety empowers the radical risk taking, the boldness of speech, of the early community (Acts 4.8–12, Acts 7).

The fact of individuals or a community feeling absolutely safe in the face of death or persecution, however, need imply no more than some kind of delusion. Suicide bombers and cult leaders may also express a sense of ultimate impregnability that frees them for radical and risky action in the world. What signals that the 'sure' hope of the resurrection is other than this? What entitles us to believe that it takes us closer to, rather than away from, the truth about reality? Here I suggest we need to look more closely at what turns the disciples' fear to rejoicing and so at the *content* of their new security and freedom.

Let me begin again with analogy. When my mother came to school, she was outside its world – she was not caught up in its fears and ways, not subject to its authority. By being from beyond and yet for me, she loosened for me the constrictions it imposed. She showed me that it was not the whole of reality, that I had access to a world safer and more accepting than it. She freed me from my judgement of myself as inadequate in the school's world, as not being cool or tough or pretty enough, such that I was empowered actually to *be* differently. How did I know that this was a truthful experience, an experience that enabled me to live more closely connected to how things 'really' were? I knew it just because in the light shed by my mother's visit on the world of the school and on me within it, I saw that I was smaller, less 'myself' at school than at home; I knew that what loomed so large at school did not loom large everywhere, and so on. And something like this happened to the disciples through their encounter with the risen Jesus. In its light they see more deeply into the reality of the world they inhabit, they see the limits of that reality, and they are freed to live in response to and empowered by a radically different reality.[30]

Three features of the resurrection experience are particularly important in this regard. First is the significance of the return to the disciples of the Jesus they had

---

resurrection encounters, but that suggestion would need fuller elaboration and exploration than I can undertake here. See *Philosophical Review*, 74/1 (1965): 3–12, pp.8, 11.

[30]   Charles Taylor has spoken of practical reasoning as a kind of reasoning in transitions. In the light of B, I now see that A was limited in certain ways: I now have access to a 'better account' of the way things are. 'We show one of these comparative claims to be well founded when we can show that the *move* from A to B constitutes a gain epistemically'. *Sources of the Self: The Making of Modern Identity* (Cambridge, MA: Harvard University Press, 1989), p.72.

known in the flesh, who lived a certain way and died a certain death, the Jesus from the particular provincial town of Nazareth who taught in the temple and was known to the authorities, 'this Jesus', says Peter, has been raised up by God and 'of that all of us are witnesses' (Acts 2.32). The early testimony to the resurrection is not primarily concerned with belief about a form of life after death, but is focused around the particular life that is raised. The meaning of the resurrection is necessarily connected, in the experience of its first witnesses, with the manner of Jesus' life because it is 'this' Jesus and no other who has been exalted by God.

It is therefore the life of Jesus that gives a concrete shape to the reality in whose light the world is now seen differently. 'By raising Jesus Christ from the dead', Lorenzen writes, 'God revealed, confirmed, verified, and enacted the mission of the life and death of Jesus. The resurrection is God's concrete and unconditional "Yes" to Jesus' life and death. At the same time, the ministry of Jesus also gives content to the resurrection'.[31] In other words, the new perspective on the world received by the disciples because of the resurrection is connected to what the vindication of 'this' Jesus shows about the nature of God and of God's way and will for the world. Williams writes,

> Jesus proclaims the indefeasible and indiscriminate and indestructible regard of God for all, regardless of merit and achievement; yet he falls foul of the religious and political authorities and is executed. But to proclaim that he has been raised from death is to say that both the proclamation and the practice of Jesus cannot be brought to an end by an authority, even one that has the power of life and death. What Jesus does is, in theological language, owned and vindicated by God as *God's* proclamation and practice; as such, it is not ultimately vulnerable to history, in the sense that its continuance is never at the mercy of human will or the institutions of the world.[32]

The resurrection shows that Jesus and all that he taught and lived, his ministry of healing and forgiving, his radical inclusiveness and love for the alienated, unlovely and 'legally unsatisfactory', has not been cancelled by the violence done to him. Because of that, its witnesses begin to see that there is a reality, an infinitely larger and more abundant reality, beyond the violent, envious, excluding and fear-driven world that cast him out. In the light of this larger reality manifested in Jesus' resurrection, they begin to understand just how completely they have been constricted by and caught up in the dynamics of that smaller, violent and fearful world, and they glimpse the possibility of sourcing their lives from a different place.

Central to this possibility, however, and the second important feature of the experience of resurrection, is the *manner* of Jesus' return. As Jesus yielded to the authorities and death, the disciples had despaired at his seeming failure, mostly

---

[31]   Lorenzen, *Resurrection and Discipleship*, p.242.
[32]   Williams, 'Interiority and Epiphany', p.251.

betraying, denying and abandoning him at the time of his most desperate need and vulnerability. In the gospel accounts of the disciples gathering after the crucifixion, we catch echoes of shame, disillusionment, terror, grief and hopelessness. To these friends and disciples, Jesus returns as forgiveness. For Alison, the 'resurrection is forgiveness: not a decree of forgiveness, but the presence of gratuity as a person'. Indeed, he suggests,

> The simple fact of Jesus' appearance to his disciples, as soon as they had recovered their consternation at the presence of what was quite outside their experience, was the presence of forgiveness. Their sorrow, and guilt, and confusion, could be loosed within them, because the focus of their sorrow and guilt and confusion had come back from right outside it, and was not affected by it. There was no element in the presence of the risen Jesus of any reciprocating by Jesus of what had been done to him. If there had been his presence would not have been outside our human tit-for-tat, it would not have been gratuitous, and it would not have been forgiving.[33]

This manner of Jesus' return is significant because it not only shows that there is a reality that cannot be cancelled by the violence of the world, but that this reality is inexhaustibly inviting and hospitable. The disciples are given yet another chance to understand what Jesus has been about and the nature of the life into which he has been inviting them for years. 'Oh, how foolish you are, and how slow of heart to believe all that the prophets have declared!' (Luke 24.25), says the risen Jesus to the two on the road to Emmaus, who are still failing to recognise the meaning of his life and death. He explains it afresh from the Scriptures, shares fellowship with them once more, and finally 'their eyes were opened' (Luke 24.31).

If the resurrection were merely the vindication of Jesus, it is conceivable that it could have led the disciples to despair of themselves, their being trapped inside the system that crucified him, their oppression by it and complicity with it. But that is not how the resurrection occurs for them. Because Jesus returns to them in peace, they see the full truth of themselves and their situation in the context of being already loved and forgiven. So, at the very same time as they are enabled to see clearly who they really are and what they have been a part of, they are set free of its power and invited into a reality that has nothing to do with that.[34]

Robinette has spoken of God's vindication of Jesus and his return as forgiveness as 'reversal' and 'double-reversal'.[35] There is judgement of a particular human way of being – judgement in the sense of God's vindication of Jesus' life and teaching, and God's 'no' or refusal of the judgement enacted against him. But this judgement is of a different order than the kind of judgement Jesus suffered. It is not simply a 'no', a reversal or negation, but is a judgement that offers hospitality

[33] Alison, *Knowing Jesus*, p.16.
[34] See Alison, *Knowing Jesus*, p.16.
[35] Robinette, *Grammars of Resurrection*, pp.184ff.

and freedom from the whole realm of tit-for-tat, win or lose, victim or victimiser. As Williams remarks, it is a 'judgement of judgement'[36] such that 'when God receives and approves the condemned Jesus and returns him to his judges through the preaching of the Church, he transcends the world of oppressor–oppressed relations to create a new humanity, capable of other kinds of relation – between human beings, and between humanity and the Father'.[37]

How do we know that this was the experience of the disciples? Not because, as in my school story, we have first-person reportage. Rather, we have the preaching of the resurrection – the effects of the resurrection enacted in proclamation. Perhaps because of the familiarity of this tale we often fail to attend to its strangeness and power. For this is preaching by the followers of a condemned and executed criminal in the same city, indeed before the very court, that had recently convicted their leader. This is preaching undertaken by 'uneducated and ordinary men' (Acts 4.13) with no illusions about the power and the willingness of this court to dispose of its opponents. And it is to this court that the apostles Peter and John proclaim not only God's reversal of their judgement, but God's offer of forgiveness, God's invitation into a new structure of social relations. 'This Jesus is "the stone that was rejected by you, the builders; it has become the cornerstone"' (Acts 4.11).[38] The proclamation is that there is no will to exclude in God, that God's invitation is for all, including those who have been involved in the rejection and execution of God's anointed. The wonder and freedom of that new understanding, its gift quality, is evident by the fact that, even after they are arrested, the apostles are prepared to risk becoming victims of the court that crucified Jesus to make available that new world to their would-be persecutors. As Alison argues, the proclamation of the resurrection is not itself enacted violently, but is prepared to become a victim of violence in the service of unmasking it.[39]

The third feature of the resurrection vital to the transformation of the disciples' perception of reality and its possibilities is a profound experience of their lives being newly opened to and directly empowered by divine life. Jesus' resurrection is closely related to the giving of the Holy Spirit. In Luke's account, the physical appearances of the resurrected Jesus come to an end after forty days, Jesus ascends into heaven, and shortly afterwards the Holy Spirit comes upon the apostles. Peter's first bold proclamation of the resurrection is presented as arising directly from this moment, 'in the midst of a Pentecostal gathering in which members of the primitive Christian community have become saturated with the presence of the Spirit ... that enables them now to say and do as Jesus instructed them'.[40] The risen Jesus is now understood to be with God, 'exalted at the right hand of God' (Acts 2.33), and pouring out God's Spirit on humanity.

---

[36]   Williams, *Resurrection*, chapter 1.
[37]   Williams, *Resurrection*, p.9.
[38]   See Williams, *Resurrection*, pp.2–3.
[39]   Alison, *Knowing Jesus*, p.45.
[40]   Robinette, *Grammars of Resurrection*, p.194.

John's gospel presents this differently, with Jesus breathing the Holy Spirit into the apostles on the first evening of the resurrection (John 20.22). In both cases, however, as Alison emphasises, the 'Holy Spirit is the Spirit of the risen Lord, the Spirit that was in Christ. The Spirit constantly makes present the crucified and risen Lord, thus perpetually reproducing those changes of relationship which the risen Lord had started to produce as a result of the resurrection'.[41]

Robinette notes that this feature of the resurrection is expressed in the language of fulfillment and fruition, the proclamation that 'eternal life [is] breaking in upon and transforming the present age'.[42] The transformation in question is not to a more 'supernatural' or 'ethereal' way of being, but quite specifically empowers those who receive the Spirit to live in Jesus' own way.[43] So the signs of this transformation of human life and possibility include boldness of speech, enduring persecution without anxiety, hospitality to enemies, sharing goods and possessions in common, healing the sick, and distributing to those in need. Robinette affirms:

> However much the resurrection of the dead remains an outstanding reality that we anticipate with eager longing, it is also real and effective through the ongoing work of the Holy Spirit. Here we may speak of *theosis*, or 'divinization', by which I mean the progressive transformation of the whole human person who, now liberated from the cycle of those social mechanisms that perpetuate sin and violence in the human community, is freed for genuinely human flourishing, for realizing more fully the original vocation of humanity.[44]

These, then, are the three features of resurrection experience that flesh out the disciples' testimony that, in its light, they see more deeply into the nature and limits of untransformed human reality, and are freed to live in response to and empowered by a radically new reality. The resurrection, they are adamant, is something that happens to Jesus, but it both reveals and makes available a new life, a new creation. This new life is characterised by freedom, even in the face of fear and persecution, forgiveness, and trust in the inexhaustible hospitality, the grace of God. It begins to be lived out in the earliest Christian communities in the form of proclaiming the 'good news' of God's acceptance and forgiveness, invitation into a life of discipleship and transformation, provision and care for those in need, and a ministry of healing and social inclusion. Jesus' resurrection enacts, in Robinette's words, 'justice for victims, forgiveness for victimizers, and participation for all ("divinization") in the trinitarian life of God'.[45] Through the Spirit poured out by the risen Jesus, this is the pattern that characterises the early Christian community and makes it a community of resurrection.

---

[41] Alison, *Knowing Jesus*, p.26.
[42] Robinette, *Grammars of Resurrection*, p.194.
[43] Alison, *Knowing Jesus*, pp.28–29.
[44] Robinette, *Grammars of Resurrection*, p.194.
[45] Robinette, *Grammars of Resurrection*, p.181.

Witnessing Resurrection

I have been suggesting that our first access to evaluating whether the New Testament witness to the resurrection is worthy of trust is through discerning something of the reality made visible and the new lives made possible because of it. The previous section focused on the effects of the resurrection on its early witnesses, recognising that an even fuller sense of the meaning of the resurrection emerged over time, as it was reflected upon and lived from. This fuller understanding deeply affects the Christian community's understanding of God and humanity, and so, among other things, is the source of all Christian doctrinal development[46] and the radical reimagining of ethical concepts such as righteousness, law, purity and judgement.

Part of the testimony to the event of resurrection, however, is that becoming a 'witness' to it is not necessarily a straightforward matter. A number of the appearance narratives suggest that recognising Jesus after he was raised required some kind of shift in perception. All testimony, we noted earlier, implicates the witness in the sense that the witness must trust that they have not been 'seduced by what [they] feel [they] must be true to',[47] but the resurrection seems to implicate its witnesses even more radically. Clarifying the strange epistemological character of becoming a witness to the resurrection is a second access to engaging with the credibility of the apostolic testimony, and is the task of this section.

Commentators have routinely noted that the New Testament texts imply, in various ways, that 'seeing' the risen Jesus, becoming a witness to the resurrection, was not like seeing and becoming a witness to a car accident. Sarah Coakley points out the significance in this regard of the narratives that 'chart a *change* of epistemological response' or that 'indicate the possibility of simultaneous and different responses to the same event'.[48] For example, there is the interaction between Mary Magdalene and the 'gardener' in John, 'where Mary has to "turn" several times before she recognizes Jesus' (John 20.11–13); the story of the walk to Emmaus where Jesus is recognised only in the breaking of the bread (Luke 24.13–35); the possibility of simultaneous recognition and doubting in Matthew (Matt. 28.17); and the disciples' only gradual recognition of Jesus by the lakeside in Galilee after the miraculous catch of fish (John 21.1–14).[49] Not all these features, surely, Coakley inquires, 'can be explained away as merely redactional or apologetic embroidery? And if not, what do they tell us about the epistemological conditions under which the risen Christ *comes to be* apprehended?'[50]

A variety of responses has been given to this question. Coakley draws on the 'spiritual senses' tradition to suggest that the capacity to 'see' Jesus risen is related

---

[46]   See James Alison, *The Joy of Being Wrong: Original Sin through Easter Eyes* (New York: Crossroad Publishing Company, 1998), p.115.

[47]   Gaita, *Good and Evil*, p.224.

[48]   Coakley, 'Resurrection and the "Spiritual Senses"', p.135.

[49]   Coakley, 'Resurrection and the "Spiritual Senses"', p.135.

[50]   Coakley, 'Resurrection and the "Spiritual Senses"', p.135.

to maturity of spiritual perception. This maturing is necessarily a process that begins with an initial 'turning' around, practice at seeing the world differently, and deepening love or communion.[51] Although, as she notes, the epistemic transformations described in the New Testament narratives seem to have been relatively swift, this account reflects the dynamics of the shifts of perception narrated in the gospels and helps to make sense of the possibility of people *coming* to know or 'see' the risen Christ after the era of the apostolic appearances.[52]

Without drawing specifically on the notion of spiritual senses, others also note the internal relationship between recognising the risen Christ and being transformed by the encounter. Lorenzen does not consider faith to be a *pre-condition* of encountering the risen Jesus,[53] but he points out that all who participated in these appearances emerged as believers. Thus, he claims, 'faith must be considered to be a necessary ingredient for the proper understanding and appropriation of the resurrection of Jesus Christ. Therefore, there were no neutral, unaffected, and in that sense objective witnesses of the resurrection appearances'.[54] Alison emphasises that the witnesses to the resurrection are necessarily witnesses from it, such that 'the gap between subjective and objective has disappeared. What happened "out there" – Jesus' appearances to the apostles, and what happened "in here" – the transformation that this produced, are part of the same phenomenon: the presence of the risen Lord'.[55] Kelly too comments on the way in which the polarities of 'objective' and 'subjective' are undone in the resurrection encounter:

> The objectivity of the event enhances the subjectivity of those who witness it and of those who will profit from such testimony. Conversely, the transformed subjectivity of those who have experienced the self-disclosure of the risen One, and who now know themselves caught up in his risen life, makes them key witnesses to the world-transcending objectivity of what has taken place.[56]

I want to explore three features of the 'transformed subjectivity' of those who recognise and become witnesses to the risen Christ. They can be characterised as distinct but related dimensions of a radical process of decentring of self and a coming-to-be centred in a new way in Jesus' own relationship with God such that, as Paul expresses it, 'it is no longer I who live, but it is Christ who lives in me' (Gal. 2.20).

We have already seen that the risen Jesus appears to the disciples as the presence of forgiveness. This forgiving, gracious presence loosens the shame, guilt

---

[51] Coakley, 'Resurrection and the "Spiritual Senses"', pp.136–141.

[52] Coakley, 'Resurrection and the "Spiritual Senses"', pp.140–141.

[53] Lorenzen adduces the appearances to Paul and James in support of this claim. *Resurrection and Discipleship*, p.145.

[54] Lorenzen, *Resurrection and Discipleship*, p.145.

[55] Alison, *Knowing Jesus*, p.7.

[56] Kelly, *Resurrection Effect*, p.125.

and desolation that has enveloped them since the crucifixion, and sets them free to proclaim the availability of radical forgiveness for all. Being forgiven, however, is a denser and often more painful process than we might superficially imagine. It is, as Williams has said, 'no bland legitimation of all we are and do',[57] but involves a costly re-membering of our past, its diminutions and evasions. If we attend to this process in a little more depth, we begin to see why recognising the presence of the risen Christ is necessarily connected to the transformation of the self.

In the final resurrection appearance narrated in John's gospel, for example, we find that recognition of 'the Lord' is interdependent for Peter with being recalled painfully to the full truth of his betrayal and desertion of Jesus, and thereby to the full truth of himself. As Williams has pointed out, in this episode the disciples are depicted as having returned to their old lives, fishing again in Galilee, as if their life with Jesus had never been.[58] Only gradually do they recognise the risen Jesus standing on the shore, as he directs them to where they will find fish, pointing them again towards abundance and life (John 21.6). They share breakfast with him over a 'charcoal fire' like the fire (*anthrakia*) over which Peter had denied Jesus three times in the High Priest's courtyard. And after breakfast, recapitulating Peter's threefold denial of him, Jesus asks Peter three times if he loves him. Williams notes that in this exchange Jesus addresses Peter as 'Simon, son of John' – the name he had when he was first called to discipleship. 'Simon has to recognize himself as betrayer: that is part of the past that makes him who he is. If he is to be called again, if he can again become a true apostle, the "Peter" that he is in the purpose of Jesus rather than the Simon who runs back into the cosy obscurity of "ordinary" life, his failure must be assimilated, lived through again and brought to good and not to destructive issue'.[59]

It is easy to confuse the nature of the relationship between acknowledgement of failure, repentance and forgiveness here. It is not that the painful acknowledgement of his betrayal is a precondition of forgiveness in the sense that Jesus requires a little grovelling before being willing to show mercy. It is rather that, unless Peter can be present to the full truth of himself and what he has done, then he cannot be given back to himself and called into renewed relationship. Without this acknowledgement and naming, a part of himself would have to be resisted, avoided, covered over perhaps by fear and self-loathing. Forgiveness is freely offered to Peter, but it costs him something to receive the gift. To be present to the One who returns as forgiveness necessarily involves seeing and relating to oneself in a new way.

This process of repentance and forgiveness as giving back and liberating the 'old' self is shown in a different way in the story of Mary's coming to recognise

---

[57]   Williams, *Resurrection*, p.45.

[58]   Williams, *Resurrection*, pp.27–28. I am indebted to Williams's discussion of the whole theme of forgiveness and re-membering, as well as to his interpretation of the appearance narratives in John.

[59]   Williams, *Resurrection*, pp.28–29.

Jesus in the garden outside the empty tomb. Mary's past with Jesus is not, like Peter's, one of desertion and betrayal, but simply of need, loss and desolation. Jesus had given her identity and acceptance, the gift of a self, and with his death not only he but the self he had known and called into life was lost.[60] In the gospel narrative, Mary turns back looking for Jesus three times – she returns to the tomb she had found empty, she turns to speak to the 'gardener', and she turns again on hearing Jesus call her name. In this final turning, she recognises Jesus as she herself is recognised and remembered.[61] Writes Williams,

> Jesus is 'lost' by our betrayal, or simply 'lost' as we are carried away from him in the violent turmoil of the human world; whether by sin or by suffering (to use the conventional categories), our value and our self-love is lost with him. But conversion, the turning of *metanoia*, the repentance of which the New Testament speaks, is the refusal to accept that lostness is the final human truth.[62]

Recognising the risen Jesus, then, is connected in the resurrection narratives to being restored fully to the truth of oneself, and restored to life and hope.[63] It is, affirms Williams, 'the learning of one's own self as gift, allowing it to be returned – whatever the initial pain or shame – by the risen Christ, hearing one's true name from his lips'.[64] No wonder encountering the risen Christ is transformative.[65]

The self that is thus returned, however, is not held, is not mine in the same way as before. The past is not cancelled out, but able to be embraced and reconciled in the context of the freely offered forgiveness and love of Jesus. The knowledge of need, lostness, weakness and fallibility are able to be borne in the light of this love, but there can no longer be illusions about the possibility of self-making and self-justification. The self is received as gift rather than possessed and defended against accusation or hostile fortune. The Peter who is forgiven his betrayal knows his vulnerability and his weakness. He will no longer brashly promise that, in his own strength, he will never betray his Lord (John 13.37). The Mary who is given back herself as loved and known, knows that her life and hope do not belong to her but are sourced in the endless life of Jesus: 'because I live, you also will live' (John 14.19).[66] Their selves are now constituted essentially by their relationship

---

[60]   Williams, *Resurrection*, p.39.
[61]   Williams, *Resurrection*, p.38.
[62]   Williams, *Resurrection*, p.40.
[63]   This is true of the Emmaus story too, where the disciples on the road are given back their own experience of their life with Jesus but in a way that reveals its full meaning and truth (Luke 24.32).
[64]   Williams, *Resurrection*, p.38.
[65]   Paul's 'late' and unique encounter with the risen Jesus has exactly this dynamic. Being present to Jesus is interdependent with being made present to who he is and what he has done in persecuting others, and then being called into a new identity, given a new name: '"Saul, Saul, why do you persecute me?"' (Acts 9.4)
[66]   Williams, *Resurrection*, p.41.

to, their being loved by, the risen Jesus – and this has two striking implications. The first is to do with relationship to the future and the second with relationship to other people.

All those who encounter (are encountered by) Jesus after he is raised from the dead are sent. They are given a task, a commission to tell the others, to go to Galilee and from there to the ends of the earth (Mark 16.7; Matt. 28.19; John 20.37).[67] Not only are the disciples sent into new futures, but they are called in a sense from the future. The risen Jesus promises to be with the disciples, but he is always ahead of them, inviting them to meet him in Galilee, ascending to the Father. Just as the empty tomb means that the human history of Jesus can never be sealed off or finalised, so the ascension of Jesus to the right hand of the Father means that relationship with the risen Christ is never possessed as something fixed and absolute.[68] 'Do not hold onto me', 'do not cling', says Jesus to Mary (John 20.17). He is to be known not in memory but encountered afresh through the Spirit, still alive as one who forgives and calls his disciples to share in the creative and recreative work of God in the world. This means that the disciples are asked to live into an open horizon, and to receive their identity through their responsiveness to this call. So, as the Letter to the Colossians says, 'you have died, and your life is hidden with Christ in God. When Christ who is your life is revealed, then you also will be revealed with him in glory' (Col. 3.3–4). Or, as 1 John expresses it, 'Beloved, we are God's children now; what we will be has not yet been revealed. What we know is this: when he is revealed, we will be like him, for we will see him as he is' (1 John 3.2).

Those who are in the process of receiving their identity from the future through their relationship to the risen Jesus are also in the process of being brought into a particular kind of relationship with one another. As they come to share in Jesus' relationship with the one he called 'Father', 'Abba', so they understand themselves as belonging to one another in new ways.[69] They become 'brothers and sisters' since they share the one Father, and they become witnesses to the possibilities for human being and becoming made available through relationship with Jesus. In a sense, they become what Jesus looks like when his life is embodied in concrete human relationships and so, in Paul's language, they become the 'body' of Christ. And yet, Williams emphasises, the community of disciples, the church, can never be simply identified with Christ – Christ remains 'other' to the church: 'Jesus grants us a solid identity, yet refuses us the power to "seal" or finalize it, and obliges us to realize that this identity only exists in an endless responsiveness to new encounters with him in the world of unredeemed relationships'.[70]

The transformed subjectivity of those who become witnesses to the resurrection, then, involves a decentring of the self in at least these three dimensions. The

---

67   Williams, *Resurrection*, p.41; Alison, *Knowing Jesus*, p.17.
68   Cf. Williams, *Resurrection*, p.76.
69   Williams, *Resurrection*, p.64.
70   Williams, *Resurrection*, p.76.

disciples who encounter the risen Jesus know themselves in a new way. They are able to receive fully the whole of themselves, the gift of themselves, because of being loved and accepted by him, but this 'gift' is not something they possess self-sufficiently, independently of their relationship with him. This gift of self always involves the call to give themselves away, responsive to the one who is ahead of them, so that their being over time extends into the life of God. And it invites them to belong to one another in new ways but, again, not such that this belonging becomes another fixed identity, a closed source of meaning. The community is what it is only insofar as it remains answerable and responsive to the one who calls it into existence, judges and recreates it.[71]

In turn, the fact that encounter with the risen Jesus transforms subjectivity along these lines helps to reveal something of the nature of the resurrection event itself. Jesus is encountered as a human being alive on the other side of death and capable of giving life in a new way. Something happens *in* history (on the third day) that the disciples understand as at the same time the judgement of history and the revelation of creation's true end. This is what it means to say that the resurrection is an eschatological event. Robinette writes,

> It is 'historical' insofar as it irrupts within our history and produces a history of effects. It is 'historical' insofar as it reveals (and proleptically accomplishes) the ultimate future of salvation history ... On the other hand, the resurrection is 'more-than-historical' insofar as it cannot be plotted within time as just one temporal link in an indefinite succession. It stands as God's definitive act of salvation *for* history; thus it comes to us from *beyond* history.[72]

The stories of recognition and non-recognition, of presence and absence, can be understood as themselves a kind of testimony to this paradox.[73] Jesus is still alive in the human world, still engaged concretely with the transformation and reconciliation of individuals, communities and creation itself, but he is never owned or controlled by those to whom he gives himself. His absence as much as his presence is a gift, since in the space opened up by his withdrawal there is room and time for the transformation and fulfilment of all things.[74] There is room for the participation of human beings in God's work of reconciliation. This is the time of the church, which, through its relationship to Jesus in the Spirit and bodied forth in community, sacrament and praxis, is the place where the risen Jesus may now be 'seen'.[75]

---

[71] Cf. Williams, *Resurrection*, p.76.

[72] Robinette, *Grammars of Resurrection*, p.41. See also pp.64–66.

[73] So Robinette argues that, rather than the ambiguities of this testimony becoming a 'problem' for resurrection faith, they are revelatory of the kind of (eschatological) presence that the risen Christ is. *Grammars of Resurrection*, p.66.

[74] See Robinette, *Grammars of Resurrection*, p.25.

[75] Robinette, *Grammars of Resurrection*, p.28.

There is clearly a kind of circularity in this testimony. Recognising Jesus as risen is interdependent with the transformation of perception brought about through encounter with him. So, says Lorenzen, 'We can only "know" that Jesus Christ is risen from the dead, when in our life the gospel has created new life. We can only know the power of the resurrection if we have accepted the call and cost of discipleship and have become engaged in the passion of God to make human life whole'.[76] As he points out, however, there are other realities that can likewise only be known through participation – love is one of them.[77] Robinette also notes the circularity in saying that resurrection itself provides the ground from which the truth of the resurrection can be seen and affirmed, but denies that this means abandoning oneself to irrationality.[78] It means, rather, that the epistemology appropriate to encountering this phenomenon is necessarily transformed by the phenomenon in question. Other critical approaches, historical and literary, may have contributions to make, but they 'are never formally constitutive of resurrection faith and knowledge … [F]aith is never something to be apologetically secured. It remains a self-involving risk'.[79]

Where, however, does that leave those who do not find themselves 'involved' in this way, as witnesses from the resurrection? In this chapter, I have been fleshing out something of the effects of the resurrection in the lives of those who testified to it, and something of the process of becoming a witness. On this account, it belongs to the nature of the event itself that there could be no neutral testimony as to its truth. If we believe the testimony, that is, in part, because we find ourselves on the inside of the reality it is and to which it points, knowing its truth as we live from it and experience the difference that it makes.[80] This is not simply a matter of a drastic 'leap' of faith and nor is it a matter of having one's own private resurrection appearance. Becoming a witness of resurrection can be lived into or 'learned' through participation in the life of the community which grows from this event. Robinette suggests that it involves 'becoming immersed in a habitus – a world, a cultural–historical setting, a community of shared beliefs and practices'.[81] It is like 'learning a language'. Like learning a language, however, this is not

---

[76] Lorenzen, *Resurrection and Discipleship*, p.146. In a similar vein, Moltmann avers that '[b]elieving in Christ's resurrection … does not mean affirming a fact. It means being possessed by the life-giving Spirit and participating in the powers of the age to come'. *Way of Jesus Christ*, p.218.

[77] Lorenzen, *Resurrection and Discipleship*, p.146.

[78] Robinette, *Grammars of Resurrection*, p.55.

[79] Robinette, *Grammars of Resurrection*, p.56.

[80] Cf. Wittgenstein's remark: 'It is *love* that believes the Resurrection … What combats doubt is, as it were, *redemption* … So this can come about only if you no longer rest your weight on the earth but suspend yourself from heaven. Then *everything* will be different and it will be "no wonder" if you can do things that you cannot do now'. From *Culture and Value*, 33e quoted by Coakley, 'Resurrection and the "Spiritual Senses"', p.142.

[81] Robinette, *Grammars of Resurrection*, pp.26–27. See also Alison, *Knowing Jesus*, pp.103–106. A fuller discussion of this point would focus on the ways in which Jesus has

merely a self-referential process. It is true that there is no place wholly outside the journey of being transformed by the event of resurrection from which it is possible finally to evaluate its truth. Nevertheless, it is possible to invite those on the 'outside' to begin to explore how the world looks in the light of resurrection through participation in the practice of resurrection faith.

As I said at the beginning of this chapter, the claims to the truthfulness and universal significance of Christian theological statements can only be made out by seeing if in fact the narrative of Jesus *can* offer resources for an ethic and anthropology that is liberating. It is the aim of the following chapters to offer a reading of possibilities for moral imagination and the moral life that become available in the light of the resurrection.[82] For this reason, it will be helpful to conclude this chapter with some preliminary reflections on the shape of ethical transcendence made manifest by the resurrection. How is the transcendent reality given form and content by the resurrection of Jesus related to the reality of Goodness to which Murdoch and Gaita testify and which, in their view, is the necessary background to moral life?

Resurrection and Transcendence

According to the apostolic testimony, the nature of transcendent reality experienced in the light of resurrection is inexhaustibly forgiving and hospitable. It is alive in a way that is not shaded by death; loving in a way not shaded by violence. It is self-dispossessing, liberating and reconciling, and offers human beings the possibility of participating in the dynamic and the project of this divine life. It thereby reveals that becoming like and animated by this life is our access to becoming fully who we are. Like the mysterious, indefinable and 'non-representable blankness' of the Good, this reality always exceeds us and remains to some extent unknown. Otherwise, as Murdoch rightly insists, we have strayed into idolatry. Nevertheless, because of the narrative of the life, death and resurrection of Jesus, there is not quite such inarticulacy about the form and content of this transcendence as there is about the 'non-dogmatic mysticism' or the 'ethical other-worldliness' to which Murdoch and Gaita appeal. The transcendent reality revealed and testified to by the resurrection can be learned, explored and participated in through the language and practices of the community that has arisen from being transformed by its encounter with it.

At this stage, I want to highlight three features in particular of the reality made visible and humanly accessible by the resurrection, noting more explicitly

---

given himself to be known in the sacraments of the church, particularly baptism and the Eucharist. See Williams, *Resurrection*, pp.51–52ff.

[82]   Cf. Robinette, 'the task undertaken here is one of *showing*, of extending an invitation to the reader to explore a world of meaning, thinking, speaking and living'. *Grammars of Resurrection*, p.29.

differences from the philosophical account of ethical transcendence. Each suggests the significance of the Christian conception of transcendence as personal. We saw in the previous chapter that for Murdoch there is a significant difference between the Idea of the Good and the personal God of religion and that this difference speaks in favour of her account. The concept of the Good, she believes, is much less at risk of degenerating into anthropomorphism and idolatry than the concept of a personal God. This may be true, but, as I suggested, there is also a cost involved in refusing theological articulation of the space of transcendence. We are now in a position to indicate more fully what is at stake here in terms both of our understanding of the Good and of the formation of the moral self.

The New Testament speaks, in the light of the resurrection, of God's 'will' to save and transform. The language of divine 'will' and 'desire' is notoriously difficult and vulnerable to projection and abuse. Nevertheless, it is central to the Christian account of reality that God's goodness and love is defined by God's action to reconcile and redeem, to bring creation to fulfilment. This truth is manifest in the light of the resurrection because it comes to be understood that God will go *this far* in order to liberate humanity from the endless cycle of violence and death, and to redeem and transform the betrayals, deceptions, ignorance and futility of human life. That is, on the Christian account, God not only actively desires the good of creation but God is willing to suffer a violent and shameful death at human hands to make this possible. Or, as the writer of John's gospel puts it, 'God so loved the world that he gave his only Son, so that everyone who believes in him may not perish but may have eternal life' (John 3.16). The resurrection is of the *crucified* Jesus, and this is not incidental to what it reveals about the nature of God.

If, however, the goodness of God is actively reconciling, then this is a significantly different conception from Murdoch's Good. For one thing, God cares about us. The Idea of the Good remains unaffected by our striving to reach it, a distant reality in whose light we see aright; in Jesus, by contrast, God enters our world and dies to liberate us, inviting us to share with him in the abundance of the divine life. For another thing, the goodness of the reconciling God is not simply a judgement of our imperfection, but seeks our wholeness and our good. This is goodness that is generative and that makes goodness possible.[83] In the language of Martin Luther, it is a righteousness that makes us righteous.[84]

I have already characterised the encounter with the resurrected Jesus in terms of forgiveness and acceptance that restores and makes whole. This encounter

---

[83]   Here notice again the significance of Christopher Cordner's point that, whereas on the Platonic conception of love as expressing lack in the one loving, the Good cannot love, in the Christian conception God loves out of fullness. 'Two Conceptions of Love in Philosophical Thought', *Sophia*, 50 (2011): 315–329, p.318.

[84]   Luther describes this as 'passive' righteousness, as opposed to the 'active' righteousness that can only condemn our failure. See Rowan Williams, *The Wound of Knowledge: Christian Spirituality from the New Testament to Saint John of the Cross*, second edition (Cambridge, MA: Cowley Publications, 1991), p.156.

issues not in the excision of those parts of the self that are failed and 'wrong' but transforms and redeems them, making of them a gift to ourselves and others. So, Peter's betrayal of Jesus becomes the occasion for his being called afresh, capable precisely because of his now redeemed failure to 'tend the sheep'. Julian of Norwich speaks in this sense of our sins become our glory.[85] Goodness here is connected to a wholeness that is offered and received through a process of repentance and forgiveness, rather than a perfection that has never been broken. The active goodness of reconciling love thus has a very different flavour from the Goodness connected to the Idea of Perfection in whose light we are never quite enough, and which reveals the truth about us but is not *for* us.

The Christian conception of transcendent reality as personal is significant also for the formation of the moral self. Murdoch and Gaita speak of 'unselfing' as necessary for deepened perception of the Good, and as a condition of the love that is capable of revealing the full reality of another human being. Yet how, on their account, is such unselfing, such radical restructuring of human identity and desire, accomplished? Murdoch speaks of the importance of loving the Good, contemplating it and being changed by its energy. She speaks of coming to know the distance between even good acts and the idea of perfection that beckons us further into the infinite depth of reality and virtue.

The problem, however, with this account is that it remains too optimistic and too intellectual to lead to the radical restructuring of the self that is needed. What is missing is a relationship between the Good and the self robust enough to call and sustain someone in the place of death and shame in which she loses all pretensions to possess or justify her own existence.[86] The *idea* of the Good points us in the direction of perfection; Jesus calls us by name. Would contemplating the idea of the Good, for example, have allowed Peter to own himself as betrayer and to receive back the gift of the whole of himself as forgiven?

The significance of this point is well made by Williams, who claims that the proclamation of resurrection is not simply a 'paradigm' of the process of salvation or transformation but an 'indispensable *agent*' of it. This is 'because it witnesses to the one personal agent in whose presence we may have full courage to "own" ourselves as sinners and full hope for a humanity whose identity is grounded in recognition and affirmation by nothing less than God. It is a story which makes possible the comprehensive act of *trust* without which growth is impossible'.[87] Discipleship of Jesus means being loved into wholeness, given an identity in God that cannot be lost and so becoming free to give ourselves away as Jesus did. The objection that the Christian account of transcendent reality merely reflects a

---

[85] Julian of Norwich, *Revelations of Divine Love*, trans. Clifton Wolters (Harmondsworth: Penguin, 1966), chapter 39, pp.120–121.

[86] This process is well discussed by James Alison in a number of places, including the essay 'Discipleship and the Shape of Belonging', in *Broken Hearts & New Creations: Intimations of a Great Reversal* (London: Darton, Longman and Todd, 2010), pp.54–72.

[87] Williams, *Resurrection*, p.43.

preference for anthropomorphism rather than a supposedly more austere vision must therefore face the question of how in practice the vision of the Good effects the transformation of the human self and enables the love of saints to which Murdoch and Gaita appeal as evidence for the Good's reality.

The personal nature of God and hence the possibility of relationship with God points to one final feature of the Christian conception of transcendent reality. It is that this reality is alive. God is a living God. Paradoxically, this suggests that, rather than the Christian concept of a personal God being peculiarly at risk of degenerating into idolatry, it is the abstract Goodness of the philosophers that begins to seem at least as likely to be a projection of human values and ideals, an idea we have rather than a living reality by whom we are grasped.[88] The God of Abraham, Isaac and Jacob, the God of Jesus Christ, is a God who addresses humanity. This God is often enough experienced as radically Other to us, *not* who we expect, capable of doing a new thing and calling people into surprising and unanticipated ventures. Think of Abraham setting out from Ur, Sarah laughing incredulously at the promise that she would bear a son, Moses and Jeremiah protesting their unfitness to speak on God's behalf, Mary asked to be the mother of God, and Jesus driven into the desert. The doctrine of revelation expresses this *resistance* of God, this independence of God from merely human definition. We know God at all, not because we have an Idea of Goodness, but because God makes God's self known.

Moral responsiveness is thus connected to what I earlier described as the possibility of participating in the dynamic and project of divine life. It is not primarily about making 'justifiable' moral choices, or managing competing claims and interests, or measuring up to our ideals, but is in the service of life's renewal and healing and energised by God's active presence. To 'share Christ's risen life', in the shorthand of the New Testament, is to share in a life 'where God is the only ultimate horizon – not death or nothingness'.[89] This new horizon profoundly affects moral life and thought, transforming moral agency and imagination. To explore its nature and the conditions of our participation in it is the task of the next chapter.

---

[88]   I am indebted to Scott Cowdell for suggesting this line of thought to me.
[89]   Williams, *Wound of Knowledge*, p.22.

Chapter 3
Resurrection, Imagination and Ethics

So if you have been raised with Christ, seek the things that are above, where Christ is, seated at the right hand of God. Set your minds on things that are above, not on things that are on earth, for you have died, and your life is hidden with Christ in God. When Christ who is your life is revealed, then you also will be revealed with him in glory. (Col. 3.1–4)

Say over a period of time, I have slipped into a habit of anxiety. I haven't really noticed it happening and I am not conscious of dramatic bouts of panic or dread. It is just that everything is coloured by vague unease and discontent. This affects my enjoyment of my job, my friendships, my sense of myself, and even the way I think. The strange thing is that it is not until I begin to come out of this period of anxiety, that I notice how much it has been affecting me. Or, more happily, consider how the world appears and is experienced by someone in love. Tasks and people that previously were the occasion of frustration now seem easier, lighter. Life is coloured by a deep and pervasive contentment.[1]

These examples show how, psychologically, a background state can impinge on consciousness and constitute a filter for experience without our necessarily being aware that it is doing so. The same thing is true at the level of our conceptual awareness, our perception and cognition of what we take to be 'reality'. Wittgenstein drew attention to the significance of underlying pictures and forms of life for our relationship to and understanding of the world. These background pictures or contexts may be virtually invisible, and yet generate what seem to be problems for thought and set the terms in which they are debated. When the background is brought to the fore, often the 'problem' takes on a different aspect or disappears altogether. Writing critically of what is taken for granted in many contemporary philosophical accounts of morality, for example, Raimond Gaita has said:

> Just as we do not notice what sets the stage for certain performances (standing in front of an object, pointing to it and uttering a sound, for example) to count as naming an object, so we do not notice what sets the stage for our taking a negotiated rule or principle, or a disposition of character, to be the kind we call 'moral' – for it to have the *kind* of significance in our lives to justify our calling it that.[2]

---

[1] See James Alison, *Knowing Jesus* (Springfield, IL: Templegate Publishers, 1994), pp.40–41.

[2] Raimond Gaita, 'Common Understanding and Individual Voices', in Jane Adamson, Richard Freadman and David Parker (eds), *Renegotiating Ethics in Literature, Philosophy, and Theory* (Cambridge: Cambridge University Press, 1998), pp.269–288, pp.272–273.

In this chapter, I argue that the resurrection of Jesus transforms moral life and thought at this level. That is, the resurrection and the form of life to which it gives rise affects not simply the *content* of particular moral norms or values (forgive as you have been forgiven; love your enemies), but the *horizon* against which moral life assumes its shape, force and meaning. This underlying structure, the taken-for-granted background to moral life and thought, is what I am calling our 'moral imagination'.[3]

I emphasise the double layer of reflection involved in this argument. Already in the New Testament, it was clearly understood that the change in possibilities for human being brought about by Jesus' life, death and resurrection had profound significance for moral life. The boundary of death, thought to be fixed, is now believed to be penultimate. The being of God and so, among other things, the character of God's love and judgement are now understood with reference to the person, practice and resurrection of Jesus. Paul exults that God in Jesus has overcome the power of sin and death (Rom. 6.8–11), and so the possibilities of human life, freedom and relationship are made new. *Therefore*, he writes, live out the implications of this reality, and in accordance with it (Rom. 6.12).

This structure of so-called 'indicative' and 'imperative' in Paul's teaching is the customary logic of his ethics.[4] What God has done for us determines what believers must do. If in Christ, we have 'died to the elemental spirits of the universe, why do you live as if you still belonged to the world?' (Col. 2.20); indeed, 'if you have been raised with Christ' you must therefore '[p]ut to death ... whatever in you is earthly' (Col. 3.5).[5] Likewise, 1 Peter exhorts those who have 'been born anew ... through the living and enduring word of God' to 'rid yourselves, therefore, of all malice, and all guile, insincerity, envy, and all slander' (1.23, 2.1). This relationship between resurrection and moral life expresses what might be called

---

[3] Philip Kenneson claims, 'Human persons are always the recipients of an imaginative world within which they are called to live and through which they are encouraged to understand themselves and their place within that world. This imaginative whole is produced and reproduced by means of various human social structures, institutions, and practices, all of which shape and animate human lives in ways that presuppose and reinforce a particular understanding of how things hang together. Thus, every time that people engage in particular practices, interact with and have their lives shaped by certain institutions, come to believe certain things and hold certain convictions, and in all of this have certain desires instilled or fulfilled, these people are having their imaginations profoundly shaped with regard to what the "whole" of human life is about'. 'Worship, Imagination, and Formation', in Stanley Hauerwas and Samuel Wells (eds), *The Blackwell Companion to Christian Ethics* (Malden, MA: Blackwell Publishing, 2004), pp.53–67, p.56.

[4] Brian S. Rosner (ed.), *Understanding Paul's Ethics: Twentieth Century Approaches* (Grand Rapids, MI: Eerdmans, 1995), p.17.

[5] See the discussion of Christology and ethics in Colossians in John Webster, '"Where Christ Is": Christology and Ethics', in F. LeRon Shults and Brent Waters (eds), *Christology and Ethics* (Grand Rapids, MI: Eerdmans, 2010), pp.32–55. See also 1 Cor. 5.7; Gal. 5.1; Gal. 5.25; Eph. 4.1ff; Rom. 12.

first-order teaching concerning the behaviour and understandings that accord with and follow from the new reality in Christ.

These first-order questions are not, however, my focus at this stage. Rather, I seek to explore the difference made by the resurrection to our imaginative sense of moral life as a whole: the difference it makes to the content and significance of moral concepts; the practice of moral thinking and judgement; the formation of the moral self, and so on. These second-order issues affect and are affected by first-order moral reflection, but are also distinct.[6] Although the work of a number of contemporary theologians contains significant insight into these questions, it is commonly remarked that this remains a neglected topic in Christian ethics.[7]

---

[6]   Just as, in doctrinal development, it took time for the fuller implications of the resurrection for the Christian conception of God to be noticed and worked through, the same is true for its implications for our conception of morality. Speaking of doctrine, Rowan Williams expresses the point succinctly: 'Christian faith has its beginnings in an experience of profound contradictoriness, an experience that so questioned the religious categories of its time that the resulting organization of religious language was a centuries-long task'. *The Wound of Knowledge: Christian Spirituality from the New Testament to Saint John of the Cross*, second edition (Cambridge, MA: Cowley Publications, 1991), p.11.

[7]   For example, Rowan Williams has explored New Testament ethics in the light of resurrection in 'Interiority and Epiphany: A Reading in New Testament Ethics', in *On Christian Theology* (Oxford: Blackwell Publishers, 2000), pp.239–264, and 'Resurrection and Peace: More on New Testament Ethics', in *On Christian Theology*, pp.265–275. James Alison has touched on the significance of resurrection for moral theology in numerous places, including *The Joy of Being Wrong: Original Sin through Easter Eyes* (New York: Crossroad Publishing Company, 1998), *Raising Abel: The Recovery of the Eschatological Imagination* (New York: Crossroad Publishing Company, 1996), and 'The Place of Shame and the Giving of the Spirit', in *Undergoing God: Dispatches from the Scene of a Break-in* (London: Darton, Longman and Todd, 2006), pp.199–219. See also John Milbank, 'Can Morality Be Christian?', in *The Word Made Strange: Theology, Language, Culture* (Oxford: Blackwell Publishers, 1997), pp.219–232, and *Being Reconciled: Ontology and Pardon* (London: Routledge, 2003). Although resurrection may feature implicitly in much Christian ethical reflection, there has been little direct attention paid to its moral theological or ethical significance. Brian Johnstone has claimed that a review of scholarly texts in Christian ethics and moral theology 'indicates that authors have given the theme of the resurrection only a marginal importance' and, over a decade later, Anthony Kelly and Gerald O'Collins have echoed that claim. See Johnstone, 'Transformation Ethics: The Moral Implications of the Resurrection', in Stephen Davis, Daniel Kendall SJ and Gerald Collins SJ (eds), *The Resurrection: An Interdisciplinary Symposium on the Resurrection of Jesus* (Oxford: Oxford University Press, 1997), pp.339–360, p.340; Anthony Kelly, *The Resurrection Effect: Transforming Christian Life and Thought* (Maryknoll, NY: Orbis Books, 2008), p.159; Gerald O'Collins, *Believing in the Resurrection: The Meaning and Promise of the Risen Jesus* (New York: Paulist Press, 2012), pp.166ff. The only book-length treatment of the topic is Oliver O'Donovan, *Resurrection and Moral Order: An Outline for Evangelical Ethics*, second edition (Leicester: Apollos, 1994).

Goodness beyond Good and Evil

'The knowledge of good and evil appears to be the goal of all ethical reflection. The first task of Christian ethics is to supersede that knowledge'.[8] Dietrich Bonhoeffer's startling claim offers a key by which the transformation of ethics by Jesus' life, death and resurrection, can be explored. I begin by considering the relationship between God and human moral systems.

For Bonhoeffer, the very possibility of knowing good and evil is already a falling away from human origin in God. This is because when human beings are wholly in God, they know 'nothing but God alone'. Anything else is known only 'in the unity of their knowledge of God'.[9] Thus to know something apart from God, opposed to God, already presupposes a disunion and estrangement. Bonhoeffer draws on the story of the 'fall' in Genesis 3 to illuminate this claim.[10] What interests Bonhoeffer in the story is its portrayal of the relationship between the human project of self-possession or self-origination, and knowledge of good and evil. The serpent tempts Eve to grasp onto equality with God, encouraging her to eat of the 'tree of the knowledge of good and evil' and so to become 'like God, knowing good and evil' (Gen. 3.5). Eve succumbs and, eating of the fruit, she and Adam come to self-consciousness: they know themselves to be other than God, naked, and immediately seek to hide themselves (Gen. 3.7). Instead of seeing only God, they see themselves separate from God and shame appears.[11] Attaining to the knowledge of good and evil is thus, in the story, interdependent with falling away from an original communion with God and, indeed, with each other. The 'knowledge' that is thereby gained is fundamentally distorted, because it is knowledge apart from God, knowledge whose possession cuts them off from the source of life (Gen. 3.22, 24).[12]

This story could be interpreted as merely a mythological account of 'God' as despotic and jealous, serving sociologically as an instrument of social or religious control. What should make us consider that it has anything to teach us about true knowledge of the Good?[13] Bonhoeffer's basic insight is that the Goodness of God is beyond the dualism of good and evil. Any conception of 'good' that can be opposed to 'evil' is itself already outside of God, which means that it cannot be truly Good. It is a simulacrum whose origin and judge is not God but human beings seeking to possess themselves independently of their relationship to God. And,

---

    [8]   Dietrich Bonhoeffer, *Ethics*, Dietrich Bonhoeffer Works, Volume 6, ed. Clifford J. Green, trans. Reinhard Krauss, Charles C. West and Douglas W. Stott (Minneapolis, MN: Fortress Press, 2009), p.299.

    [9]   Bonhoeffer, *Ethics*, p.300.

    [10]   Bonhoeffer, *Ethics*, pp.300–305.

    [11]   Bonhoeffer, *Ethics*, p.303.

    [12]   Bonhoeffer, *Ethics*, p.302.

    [13]   In this section, I shall use a capital 'G' to refer to non-dualistic goodness, the goodness of God, to distinguish it from the 'good' that is defined with reference to 'evil'.

says Bonhoeffer, it is this Good beyond good and evil that becomes accessible again because of the reconciliation wrought by Jesus Christ.[14]

I shall return to Bonhoeffer's argument, but let me first develop the claim that the true Good is beyond the dualism of good and evil, drawing on a suggestive discussion by James Alison. Alison has noticed a seeming anomaly in Paul's logic in the Letter to the Galatians, which bears directly on this question. Paul is urging the Gentile believers in Galatia to resist pressure from certain Jewish Christian teachers to put themselves under the authority of the law of Moses. In particular, he is urging them not to presume that their standing with God, their righteousness, has anything to do with practices such as circumcision and dietary observance (Gal. 2.11–14). He reminds them that they did not receive the Spirit by doing the works of the law, but by believing in Christ crucified (Gal. 3.2–5) and argues that, just as it was Abraham's faith in God's promise that was 'reckoned to him as righteousness' rather than any adherence to law, so also God blesses the Gentiles through their faith in Jesus (Gal. 3.6, 8).[15] So, in a preliminary summary of this argument at Galatians 3.10, Paul writes:[16]

> For all who rely on the works of the law are under a curse; for it is written, 'Cursed is everyone who does not observe and obey all the things written in the book of the law'.

Alison points out that Paul's scriptural quotation ('for it is written') seems to undermine his argument.[17] It claims that anyone who does not observe and obey all that is written in the book of the law is cursed, but Paul himself has just claimed the opposite: 'all who rely on the works of the law are under a curse'.[18] If we read Paul as seeking to provide a proof text for his argument, then his logic seemingly does not make sense.

One way to interpret this apparent incoherence is in terms of there being a suppressed premise: all who rely on the works of the law are under a curse because no one is able actually to keep the law, which means that the law condemns their failure and so curses them (cf. Rom. 7.19). In his commentary on Galatians, Philip Esler suggests that this is the 'most plausible view' of Paul's meaning, and is the

---

[14] Bonhoeffer, *Ethics*, p.311.

[15] I elaborate later in this chapter on the Christian proclamation of the relationship between Christ's death and resurrection, and the reconciliation of humanity with God and creation.

[16] Alison, 'The Place of Shame and the Giving of the Spirit', p.199.

[17] Alison, 'The Place of Shame and the Giving of the Spirit', p.200. The passage is Deut. 27.26: 'Cursed be anyone who does not uphold the words of this law by observing them'.

[18] Alison, 'The Place of Shame and the Giving of the Spirit', p.200.

Deuteronomic meaning of the curse.[19] Alison, however, suggests there is another way of understanding what Paul is doing:

> Paul is quoting the text, not as we would usually imagine it, as a proof text, a way of saying 'you see, the text agrees with me'. It doesn't agree with him. Rather he is quoting it as internal evidence of an anthropological structure. He quotes the verse so as to show that *because it curses those who don't obey the Law* the text of the Law itself shows that it is part of a system of goodness which divides between good and bad, and thus that even those who uphold it, who are apparently blessed by it, are in fact dwelling in the sphere of the curse. In other words he is quoting the words in a way that stands back from them and says: 'Look at what this sentence gives away about the sort of system of which it is an integral part'.[20]

On this reading, the curse of the law is not the justified consequence of a culpable failure to keep it. Rather, the 'sphere of the curse' is internal to the law itself. Insofar as it operates in this way, the law (whether it is kept or not) cannot make us righteous before God (Gal. 3.11). In support of this reading, Alison points to Paul's claim that, by being put to death on a cross, Jesus is accursed according to the law and yet it is through faith in him and the gift of the Spirit that new life in God is received. Paul writes: 'Christ redeemed us from the curse of the law by becoming a curse for us – for it is written, "Cursed is everyone who hangs on a tree"' (Gal. 3.13). Alison rejects the view that 'God had set things up so that someone needed to be cursed, then God got Jesus to stand in for being cursed, and now that that has been done, the curse has been lifted'.[21] Rather, he argues, what Jesus does by undergoing the curse of the law is to disconnect righteousness according to the law from righteousness in relation to God.[22] What he does is to

---

[19] Esler thinks that Paul's argument implies that this failure to keep the law was an 'in practice' rather than 'in principle' failure, since although difficult, Paul does not really suggest that keeping the law is impossible (Gal. 5.3). Philip F. Esler, *Galatians* (London: Routledge, 1998), p.187.

[20] Alison, 'The Place of Shame and the Giving of the Spirit', pp.200–201.

[21] Alison, 'The Place of Shame and the Giving of the Spirit', p.203.

[22] Significantly, arriving by a different route, Esler interprets the essential import of Paul's argument in just this way. He suggests that Paul is arguing from his experience of Christ and his knowledge that because of their 'faith in Christ gentile communities had actually experienced life and blessings in the Spirit (2.19–3.9)'. This must mean that life did not come from the law, and that the law has become more of a blockage than a source of blessing. Esler, *Galatians*, pp.187–188. There is also, however, a significant difference between Alison's and Esler's approaches. Esler interprets Paul's argument within a 'social identity framework', arguing that Paul is seeking to protect his mixed congregations of Israelites and gentiles against being persuaded by the circumcision party to conform to the group identity norms of the Israelites. This means that part of his strategy is to remind them that they received life and blessing from outside the law (by faith and the Spirit)

subvert reliance on the law and its curse, reliance on 'a system of goodness which divides between good and bad'.[23]

What is wrong with a 'system of goodness which divides between good and bad'? Alison argues that, at its core, it fatally contradicts itself. That is because, in a system that divides between good and bad, righteous and unrighteous, 'goodness' is defined by its relationship to 'badness' and is thus dependent on it. That is, '[i]f I rely, for my goodness, on holding onto, and obeying, everything in the system, then that means my goodness is "over against" someone else's badness, and thus, being dependent on it, is part of it'.[24] Not only is goodness in such a system tacitly dependent on the continued existence of the badness against which it is defined, but even that which 'goodness' requires is unable to be fulfilled. The commandment that sums up the law, to love my neighbour as myself, cannot be fulfilled because 'the Law as a system of goodness will prevent me from recognizing the neighbour who is *as myself* and who needs loving'.[25] This is because often enough my neighbour will show up as 'cursed', beyond the pale and not remotely as 'myself'. 'In other words', Alison concludes, 'the lived anthropological effect of the system

---

and part of it is to stereotype or denigrate those of the 'other' group (suggesting that those who rely on the law are 'cursed', because they have failed to keep the law). Whereas, then, Alison attributes to Paul an argument concerning the anthropological effects upon *any* group seeking to establish its 'righteousness' according to the law, Esler attributes to him an attempt to stigmatise the Israelite party as wrongly reliant on the Sinaitic covenant in order to persuade the gentile Christians to resist their blandishments (p.191). Clearly, there is an oppositional thrust in Paul's argument, but I am uneasy at the suggestion that he is simply trying to assert his own 'in-group' identity against the Israelite 'outgroup' (Esler uses these phrases, for example, pp. 184, 203), since this seems inconsistent with Paul's own sense that through faith in Christ Jesus comes the possibility of *all* being one in Christ, 'no longer Jew or Greek, slave or free' and so on (Gal. 3.28–29). That is, along with the abolition of the law comes the abolition of 'inside' and 'outside'.

[23]   Paul's argument is that the essential mode of the relationship between God and humankind is promise and trust, established by God's blessing of Abraham through whom all people are to be blessed (Gal. 3.8). Although the law was added 'because of transgression', it was only a temporary device, ordained 'through angels by a mediator' and not directly from God. It has validity as a 'disciplinarian' until the coming of Christ, who restores the possibility of unmediated relationship to God through faith in the promise: 'But now that faith has come, we are no longer subject to a disciplinarian, for in Christ Jesus you are all children of God through faith' (Gal. 3.25-26). As noted above, the direct result of this is that there is no means in Christ of defining oneself over against another: 'There is no longer Jew or Greek, there is no longer slave or free, there is no longer male and female; for all of you are one in Christ Jesus' (Gal. 3.28). See also Rom. 7.4: 'In the same way, my friends, you have died to the law through the body of Christ, so that you may belong to another, to him who has been raised from the dead in order that we may bear fruit for God'.

[24]   Alison, 'The Place of Shame and the Giving of the Spirit', p.201. See on this point also Williams, 'Resurrection and Peace', p.267.

[25]   Alison, 'The Place of Shame and the Giving of the Spirit', p.201

of goodness is, in practice, that of nullifying the goodness towards which the commandment points'.[26]

Bonhoeffer emphasises precisely this difference between a conception of goodness that is necessarily dependent on its relation to the bad, and Goodness that is of a different order. On his account, the knowledge of good and evil is connected with disunion from God, and what becomes apparent in the New Testament is the possibility of 'rediscovered unity' or reconciliation.[27] The difference this makes to ethics begins to be manifest in the encounter of Jesus with the Pharisees. Bonhoeffer insists that we mistake the seriousness of this encounter if we caricature the Pharisees as hypocritical, holding others to moral standards they do not keep themselves.[28] In fact, in doing good and avoiding evil, they 'judge themselves as sternly as their neighbours' and their whole lives are organised with reference to obeying the law in all its complexity and demand.[29] Yet, the more they seek to be and do the good, the more they are enmeshed in the dynamic that Alison identifies.

On the one hand, they require the existence of the bad against whom they secure their own goodness, living in a state of perpetually envious comparison and judgement. The parable of the Pharisee and the tax collector at prayer, which Jesus told 'to some who trusted in themselves that they were righteous and regarded others with contempt' (Luke 18.9), names the self-defeating nature of this goodness. Yet, the Pharisees seem impervious to the teaching, persisting in their dividing of the world into good and bad, able to engage with Jesus only by reference to his relationship with the law. A *reductio ad absurdum* of this way of defining goodness is attained in John 9, where the import of the healing of the blind man is entirely eclipsed for them by Jesus' breaking the Sabbath.[30] On the other hand, as John 9 also illustrates, it is this very obsession with goodness defined dualistically that condemns the Pharisees to failure. They *cannot* fulfil the law they seek to obey because their conception of goodness necessarily involves defining themselves over against their neighbour. As their casting out of the blind man and the parable of the Good Samaritan decisively show, those who are 'good' in this way cannot love their neighbours as themselves (Luke 10.25).[31]

---

[26]   Alison, 'The Place of Shame and the Giving of the Spirit', p.201.

[27]   Bonhoeffer, *Ethics*, p.309.

[28]   Bonhoeffer, *Ethics*, p.309.

[29]   Bonhoeffer, *Ethics*, p.310.

[30]   See too Luke 11.38 – 'The Pharisee was amazed to see that he did not first wash before dinner' – as well as the stories concerning healing on the Sabbath.

[31]   Note also the inability of Simon the Pharisee to 'see' as neighbour the 'sinful' woman in his house, who washed Jesus' feet with her tears. The Pharisee 'said to himself, "If this man [Jesus] were a prophet, he would have known who and what kind of woman this is who is touching him – that she is a sinner". Jesus spoke up and said to him: "Simon, I have something to say to you" … "Do you see this woman?"' (Luke 7.39–40, 44)

There are two seemingly natural readings of Jesus' dispute with the Pharisees that fail to appreciate the extent of its challenge to a dualistic understanding of good and evil, and hence to their moral imagination. One follows from not taking seriously the moral world of the Pharisees. Their concerns with ritual purity and Sabbath observance are not ours, and we all know who is 'right' in the parable of the Good Samaritan. It is easy to think that Jesus' dispute with the Pharisees concerns not so much their being zealous, as their being zealous over the wrong things. They are focused on petty legalism rather than what really matters to God, as Jesus points out when he criticises them for tithing 'mint, dill and cumin' and yet failing to observe the weightier requirements of justice and mercy (Matt. 23.23; Luke 11.42).[32] There is something true in this reading, but we need to beware the danger of merely inserting different moral content into an otherwise unchanged dualistic system.

Jesus criticises not only the *object* of the Pharisees' moral concern, but also the very structure of their desire to be good. When the Pharisees test him on the law, he refuses the terms in which the questions are posed. Their framing of what is at stake presupposes the conception of goodness and of God that he is seeking to undo. So, as Bonhoeffer notes, the Pharisees and Jesus talk past one another and, although Jesus in some sense evades their questions, this is not a debating strategy as much as evidence of the fact that they 'speak on completely different planes'.[33]

In other words, it is not just that Jesus treats sinners 'well' or has compassion for prostitutes with hearts of gold and therefore models how we are to treat those who are morally suspect. Much more radically, he subverts the whole division of the world into good and bad, righteous and unrighteous. He refuses to allow himself to be designated as good: 'Why do you call me good? No one is good but God alone' (Mark 10.18). He understands God to be unconcerned with our division of each other into such categories, for God 'makes his sun rise on the evil and on the good, and sends rain on the righteous and on the unrighteous' (Matt. 5.45), and gives the labourer who has worked least in the fields the same wage as the one who has worked longest (Matt. 20.1–16).[34] Jesus is not simply proposing a new principle of moral life, a new norm of judgement within an alternative system of goodness. He is making available a far deeper way of *being* Good.

A second reading of the dispute with the Pharisees interprets Jesus as relaxing the rigid and stultifying letter of the law to make visible its true spirit. 'The sabbath was made for humankind, and not humankind for the sabbath' (Mark 2.27) might

---

[32]   See similarly the teaching on the defilement that comes from the heart rather than from eating with unwashed hands (Matt.15.19–20).

[33]   Bonhoeffer, *Ethics*, p.311.

[34]   This logic of God's generosity being in no way related to desert is exemplified too in the parable of the Prodigal Son (Luke 15.11-32), and the many teachings on the last being first.

be cited in support of this reading.[35] Again, there is something true in the view that Jesus understands the law as being concerned with human maturity rather than arbitrary demand, but we need to beware the assumption that Jesus was concerned primarily to inject some licence into the Pharisees' overly scrupulous observance. Bonhoeffer notes that the Pharisees knew full well that there could be exceptions or mitigations of the requirements of the law. 'Special circumstances and crises receive special consideration. The seriousness of the knowledge of good and evil does not rule out leniency and mercy. Rather, such lenience is an expression of that seriousness'.[36] Law may be more or less rigidly observed and may even be overturned entirely, while the basic structure of moral imagination remains untouched. This is the insight that emerges from Paul's wrestling with the 'twin temptations of antinomianism and moralism' that turn out to be 'simply two sides of one and the same temptation, which he called "the flesh"'.[37]

As we have seen, those who are righteous according to the law can all too easily be seduced into thinking that it is their righteousness, their 'goodness', that secures their standing and identity before God and their value as human beings. Paul is painfully aware from his own experience that such self-possessed goodness may become a justification for the rejection of those designated 'unrighteous' (Phil. 3.6). He also recognises that it blocks those who are certain of their goodness from true understanding of themselves and their own sinfulness, and so from trustful and humble relationship with the real source of life (Rom. 2.1; Gal. 2.16).[38]

It may seem as though the antidote to the moral and spiritual danger of such self-justification and self-righteousness is to refuse to prescribe norms of goodness at all, to live without law. Without norms there are no bases for envious comparison and assessment, so fewer opportunities for classifying each other as successful or unsuccessful performers in moral and religious life. In the idiom of contemporary liberalism, each must live according to her 'own' values and interests, and refrain from imposing her values on others.[39] The problem is, however, that the mere

---

[35]   Conversely, Jesus' insistence that 'not one letter, not one stroke of a letter, will pass from the law until all is accomplished' (Matt. 5.18) might give such a reading pause.

[36]   Bonhoeffer, *Ethics*, p.310.

[37]   O'Donovan, *Resurrection and Moral Order*, p.12. O'Donovan draws attention particularly to Paul's discussion of law and lawlessness in Romans and Galatians.

[38]   As Alison writes, 'systems of goodness are especially dangerous ... to the "good" guys as well, since the "good guys" are unlikely to perceive that, far from worshipping God, becoming dependent on God and being given their identity by God, who is not over against anything at all, they are in fact being given identity by that violent "over against" by which they build themselves up. In other words, they are the ones most prone to become violent nihilists, thinking themselves servants of God'. 'The Place of Shame and the Giving of the Spirit', p.202. Jesus says similarly to the Pharisees at the end of John 9, 'If you were blind, you would not have sin. But now that you say, "We see", your sin remains' (John 9.41).

[39]   Williams has fruitfully discussed the limits of Western political liberalism and contractual moral theory and their relationship to 'lawlessness' in both 'Resurrection and Peace' and 'Interiority and Epiphany'.

refusal of law does not transform the dynamic that underlies this human tendency towards envy, competition and threatenedness, and it is this tendency that is inimical to the possibility of true fellowship, true Goodness.

Rowan Williams has argued that the writer of the Letter to the Ephesians identifies just this underlying dynamic, saying that *both* those who seek to secure their identity by their relationship to law *and* those who have no sense of being accountable to a reality beyond the self, who live 'following the desires of flesh and senses' (Eph. 2.3), 'are locked in a demonic symbiosis of hostility'.[40] That is, as Williams paraphrases, 'The life that defines itself confidently in its ordered doing, *and* the life that steps aside from the painful question of meanings and continuities together form a pathology of the human world'.[41]

For the law abiding, the problem is the delusion that, by following the rules, doing the 'right' thing, we control our meaning and our righteousness: 'what *we* do establishes us in the world'.[42] For those outside law-structured patterns of common life, however, the self's meaning and identity is also constructed by what the self does, this time in seeking to fulfil its own desires or aspirations. Whereas the identity of the law abiding is defined over against the 'badness' of others, the identity of the libertarian is defended in the face of all that might limit or thwart its fulfilment. So, suggests Williams, although its oppositional presuppositions might be more muted, nevertheless it 'works with no less intensive a model of competition for limited space than the order and success model'.[43] It is thus equally inimical to the possibility of true fellowship, true neighbourliness, because it evades the task of negotiating a common good, a shared future, leaving humanity 'trapped in a stage of consciousness where the other is always liable to be apprehended as a threat or a rival'.[44] So, as Williams observes,

> The 'freedom' of the life of passion, the organization of life around gratification, is intrinsically incapable of producing a properly social sense at all (witness the erosion of community sense in the wake of advanced capitalism), yet can foster a picture of human living together that is rigid and oppressive in its very resistance to the possibility of a shared future for which it is necessary to reflect, plan or sacrifice.[45]

---

[40] Williams, 'Resurrection and Peace', p.266. The writer proclaims that this is the hostility that has been overcome, made into peace, by the 'blood of Christ': 'For he is our peace; in his flesh he has made both groups into one and has broken down the dividing wall, that is, the hostility between us' (Eph. 2.14).

[41] Williams, 'Resurrection and Peace', pp.266, 268. Williams notes that while at one level Ephesians identifies these opposing possibilities with reference to the Jewish and Gentile communities, the writer implies that they are internal to all 'human self-interpretation and social construction', just as Paul in Romans also sees 'law and lawlessness at work in a single self'.

[42] Williams, 'Resurrection and Peace', p.266.

[43] Williams, 'Resurrection and Peace', p.267.

[44] Williams, 'Interiority and Epiphany', p.243.

[45] Williams, 'Resurrection and Peace', p.268.

This means that, despite their seeming opposition, law and lawlessness issue from and reflect a common imaginative horizon. Each involves accepting separateness and competition as built into human life and so fail to make possible, conceptually and practically, a universal community of genuine neighbour love and 'a common future'.[46] The source of this dynamic, suggests Williams, is the insistence that 'ultimately ... human identity is for humans to *control* – either in the overt form of the construction of successful human performances, or, more subtly, in the enacting of the desires of a given and unconstrained selfhood'.[47] Oliver O'Donovan summarises the point as follows: 'Every way of life not lived by the Spirit of God is lived by "the flesh", by man taking responsibility for himself whether in libertarian or legalistic ways, without the good news that God has taken responsibility for him'.[48]

Goodness as Grace

What, then, is the deeper order of Goodness to which, according to the New Testament witness, Jesus gives us access? To begin to explore it, I need to say a little more about the relationship between moral life and the self.

I have so far used a number of different expressions connecting certain ways of being in the world with what I am arguing is a problematic conception of goodness and moral responsiveness. I have referred to the human desire for self-possession and self-origination, self-justification and self-righteousness; I have spoken of those who seek to secure their own identity and meaning, quoting Williams on the distorting effects of the human desire to control identity and O'Donovan on unredeemed 'man's' tendency to take 'responsibility for himself'. Implicit in these descriptions is the sense that it is possible for human beings to 'be' differently, and that this other way of being makes possible another form of Goodness.

We saw in the previous chapter that the appearance of the risen Jesus to the disciples was interdependent with a transformation of their subjectivity. It involved their being able to own their failure and lostness as they were encountered by Jesus and received his forgiveness and commissioning; it involved their coming to belong to one another in new ways and to entrust themselves to a call that came, as it were, from the future. Their identities are no longer fixed, possessions of the self, but they are enacted and lived into in responsiveness to God's call. '[F]or you have died, and your life is hidden with Christ in God. When Christ who is your life is revealed, then you also will be revealed with him in glory' (Col. 3.3–4).

This experience of *being* forgiven, restored to themselves and empowered to live by the Spirit out of the resources of the divine life, gives rise to the New Testament proclamation of newness of life, being born from above (John 3.3). In

---

46   Williams, 'Resurrection and Peace', p.268.
47   Williams, 'Resurrection and Peace', pp.268–269.
48   O'Donovan, *Resurrection and Moral Order*, p.12.

its light, the disciples realise the true nature and extent of their former condition, their state of 'self-exclusion from the Creator and consequent disharmony with each other and with the universe'.[49] In Christian theology, this realisation comes to be understood as pertaining, not simply to the state of the disciples, but to humanity as a whole. It is described by the doctrine of original sin,[50] which, as Sebastian Moore emphasises, points not primarily to the sins people commit but to 'a cut-offness from God that was somehow woven into the human condition and had been so since the beginning of human time'.[51] It is with reference to the recognition of this essential alienation and the possibility of its healing that I seek now to explore how the event of the resurrection opens up new possibilities for human being that are interdependent with the possibility of participating in God's Goodness, Goodness beyond good and evil.

There are two points to emphasise at the outset. The first is that the doctrine of original sin is not simply a theological interpretation of phenomenological reflection about 'the human condition'. Too often, Alison writes,

> the doctrine of original sin is treated as a starting point relatively independent of revelation, as though it were simple human common sense that there is something terribly wrong with the human race. This 'something terribly wrong' then becomes a foundational reality, from which we can understand salvation.[52]

Theological understanding of what requires healing in the human condition, however, is discovered through the experience of that healing itself, and not by some *a priori* account of what fully human flourishing would look like. Thus, for example, it is in the experience of finding ourselves in communion in a deeper way with other people and with the energy of divine life, that we realise the extent to which we have previously been isolated or defended or whatever. Without this experience of healing, peace and belonging, our previous condition just defines the limits of reality and its possibilities.

Second, once we begin to glimpse the essential alienation of unredeemed human being, we must (says Moore) wonder how it got to be this way.[53] This wondering is not simply the idle desire for explanation but is connected to the need for radical engagement with our condition as part of our journey towards healing.[54] Alison

---

[49] Sebastian Moore, *Let This Mind Be in You: The Quest for Identity through Oedipus to Christ* (London: Darton, Longman and Todd, 1985), p.87.

[50] James Alison notes that the doctrine of original sin is a derivative doctrine, arising out of the 'new perception on God and on humankind brought about by the events and interpretations that constitute the apostolic witness'. *Joy of Being Wrong*, p.64.

[51] Moore, *Let This Mind Be in You*, p.87.

[52] Alison, *Joy of Being Wrong*, p.64.

[53] Moore, *Let This Mind Be in You*, p.87.

[54] So Moore criticises fundamentalist insistence on the literal truth of the Adam and Eve story precisely because it blocks a sufficiently deep engagement with the meaning, or

speaks of the need for accounts that mediate between what the resurrection reveals about the possibilities of receiving new life from 'above' and the human patterns of thought and being in which we are actually enmeshed.[55] This is not because revelation needs to be translated uncritically into terms acceptable to modern anthropology or psychology but because, without reference to such anthropological understandings, it is difficult to know how we move from acceptance of the *doctrine* of our alienated being to 'the practical discovery of the way out of ... entrapment'.[56] It is likewise with reference to such mediating accounts, I suggest, that we are able to explore at greater depth the significance for moral life of the revelation of our alienation and the possibility of our transformation.

In what follows, then, I offer an account of human identity formation that fleshes out the claim that we are in some sense 'cut off' from God, ourselves and each other in ways that distort moral imagination. This is a necessary precursor to characterising the Goodness that Jesus enacts, a deeper order of Goodness that becomes humanly accessible through the resurrection.

For the purposes of our discussion, it will serve to identify what I believe are three significant and relatively uncontroversial theses concerning the emergence and formation of human self-consciousness or identity. First, the human self is essentially relational. We come to be selves at all through our relationship with others, by learning language and desire, by being 'seen' by another.[57] Second, the self experiences itself *as* itself 'over against' what it is not. Often enough, this is an experience of lack or threatenedness.[58] Third, distortions in perception and response arise when this 'over against' identity is solidified and grasped at, issuing in defensive responses of various kinds.[59]

James Alison sketches an account of the process of human identity formation that includes these elements, drawing upon the theory of desire based on imitation, or *mimesis*, developed by René Girard and deployed in developmental psychology

---

the symbolic resource of the story. The literal reading confines its attention to sin as definite, deliberate decision, whereas the doctrine of original sin expresses the view that prior to any deliberate choice there is that in us which resists life. *Let This Mind Be in You*, pp.90–91.

[55] He notes that this process of seeking understanding was necessary even for the disciples since although Jesus 'is shown to have perceived and spoken and acted from out of a particular perspective on human beings', the disciples themselves had to discover this perspective and come to inhabit it 'in an authentic human labor, or struggle, to understand and to perceive'. *Joy of Being Wrong*, p.24.

[56] Alison, *Joy of Being Wrong*, p.24.

[57] For example, Williams, 'Interiority and Epiphany', p.240; Alison, *Joy of Being Wrong*, p.28.

[58] See, for example, Moore, *Let This Mind Be in You*, pp.71ff; F. LeRon Shults, *Reforming Theological Anthropology: After the Philosophical Turn to Relationality* (Grand Rapids, MI: William B. Eerdmans Publishing Company, 2003), pp.90ff.

[59] See discussion in Alison, *Joy of Being Wrong*, p.33; Shults, *Reforming Theological Anthropology*, p.91.

by J.-M. Oughourlian.[60] Although, as I have already indicated, my argument requires some account of the essential alienation of unredeemed humanity from God, ourselves and each other, it does not depend on the final adequacy of either Girard's theory or Alison's development of it. I believe, however, that this account offers an important and illuminating model for conceptualising the formation of human self-consciousness and so for specifying anthropologically how the resurrection of Jesus may be understood as a source of transformation of human subjectivity.

Alison begins with the observation that human infants are drawn or moved towards an adult. Following Girard, Oughourlian calls this draw '*mimesis*', arguing that it is what enables the infant to be socialised and learn language, to become a human being. In this way, the 'other' is both anterior to and the condition of the possibility of any given self. Initially, the infant's imitation of the adult involves no sense of a separate 'me': the imitation is of the 'form, or appearance of the model'.[61] Later, however, the infant is drawn to things, toys or rattles, to which its adult model points. The adult demonstrates how to play with the designated object, and it 'is this movement towards an object that is exterior to the model which we call desire'. This desire 'pulls us away from the model and begins to make us autonomous'.[62] What finally constitutes the 'me', however, is a third sort of imitation that depends on the preceding stages. This is where the infant, imitating what a model has, wants to *be* the model, to assert 'the incipient self over against the model, in order to take the model's place, or be him or her'.[63] Alison insists that this does not mean that we are all 'would-be murderers'.[64] Nevertheless, it seems, there is an implicit and necessary dynamic of being 'over against' another in the constitution of the self.[65]

Sebastian Moore has elaborated how this dynamic plays out in adult life:

> I naturally think that my desire is mine, is of me, that I am its subject and I know what I want. But so to think is not to see that desire is *making me*. Desire is awakened in me by the sight of another desiring. This model-aroused desire

---

[60] Alison, *Joy of Being Wrong*, p.27. For a good summary of the development and location of Girard's theory, see Scott Cowdell, *Abiding Faith: Christianity Beyond Certainty, Anxiety and Violence* (Eugene, OR: Cascade Books, 2009), pp.78ff. This account of human beings becoming selves by imitating the desires of others is apparently supported by scientific research on mirror neurons in the brain. See Alison's discussion in 'Love Your Enemy: Within a Divided Self', in *Broken Hearts & New Creations: Intimations of a Great Reversal* (London: Darton, Longman and Todd, 2010), pp.160–175.

[61] Alison, *Joy of Being Wrong*, p.29.

[62] Alison, *Joy of Being Wrong*, p.29.

[63] Alison, *Joy of Being Wrong*, p.30.

[64] In this he says that Girard's analysis of the Oedipus complex undercuts the 'necessarily murderous element of infantile rivalry postulated by Freud'. *Joy of Being Wrong*, p.30.

[65] Moore offers another account of this development in *Let This Mind Be in You*, pp.69ff. For our purposes, the significant point is that the coming into separate consciousness of the infant is here also experienced as a conflictual process and connected with lack.

feels the other as rival, and it is this over-against-the-otherness that makes me feel *me*. Me is me against.[66]

Moore says he experienced this mechanism in himself when he was passed over by a superior and found in himself a 'jostling, rivalry-shaped feeling' clothed in moral outrage. It is this *feeling* that constitutes the sense of a separate, autonomous self who was there first and who is doing the desiring, standing up for its rights and so on. That, however, is an illusion. The 'real order of events' is that the self I oppose to the other, the self as the 'cause into which we pour our energy', is the 'creation of desire'.[67] So 'me is me against' and me is also, in some sense, illusory. What we take to be our solid, separate self is constituted, if this account is true, by our imitation of the desires of others and our 'forgetting' of this very fact. The 'forgetting' is necessary, but becomes problematic and self-deceptive when it turns from simple 'unknowing' into active denial of the prior other-dependence of the self, and so into the need to expel the other who is our rival.[68] The formation of a separated identity or 'ego' is a necessary stage in the development of human consciousness, but distortions in perception of both self and other arise when my self becomes something 'I' generate or possess, something 'I' need to build up or defend.

In summary, then, human beings start out as radically dependent on others, not simply for our bodily needs but also for becoming selves, for our very identities. Alison notes that the better we are parented, the more we receive a sense of our own 'being' without having to grasp at it. Nevertheless, our need for being is never fully met.[69] This means that the very process by which we develop our identity may lead also to our seeking to build or shore up our identity or our group's identity over against others. 'As if by magic we know, as small children, how to strengthen our group: by finding someone weak to cast out, someone against whom we can all be'.[70] Although it is possible for us simply to recognise where we have come from, to allow ourselves and others to be given and receive our selves peaceably, our condition more often than not is the self-deceived condition of refusing to acknowledge our existential dependence and so needing either to defend and uphold our ego's 'persona' or to wrest more 'being' from others.[71] The

---

[66]   In his Foreword to Alison's, *Joy of Being Wrong*, p.viii.

[67]   Foreword to Alison's, *Joy of Being Wrong*, p.viii.

[68]   Alison, *Joy of Being Wrong*, p.32.

[69]   He writes, 'there is what might (with great care) be called an ontological need, a radical need to *be*, a need which draws us to others and to imitate them in order to acquire a sense of being, something felt as a lack'. *Joy of Being Wrong*, p.33.

[70]   Alison, *Joy of Being Wrong*, p.33. See also, *Undergoing God*, p.5.

[71]   In *Let This Mind Be in You*, Moore discusses the formation of the self and self-consciousness in terms of the early crisis of separation from the mother, but suggests a similar existential condition: 'our fundamental uncertainty touches not our *character* ("Am I a good person?"), as to which others could reassure us, but our very *existence*, which is beyond the reach of others, who in any case suffer the same radical uncertainty', p.72. To

healing of the self and human community, on this kind of account, is connected to being able to let go of the illusion of the possibility and necessity of self-making, learning to accept vulnerability and dependence without fear of annihilation.

This, then, is one way of articulating the experience of salvation undergone by the disciples in the company of Jesus. Jesus himself models freedom from any project of self-making, trusting himself entirely to God as the source of his life and meaning, revealing thereby the unconditional hospitality and generosity of the 'Father' who is in no form of competition or rivalry with us. Through his own practice of hospitality, his stories of the profligate compassion of God, and his resurrection from the dead, Jesus enacts God's endlessly giving life in the human world, inviting his disciples to 'follow me' in that same trusting dependence.[72] In relationship with such a 'gratuitous' other, the self can relax into the process of its own becoming without defensiveness or grasping, letting go the illusion of its essential separateness and autonomy, its need to establish itself in the face of threat. Indeed, as the mystical tradition expresses it, as the self comes to know and embrace its own nothingness (no-thingness) it can finally authentically become itself, receive fullness of being.[73] Williams notes that theology 'has formalized the teaching of Jesus on the "non-competitive difference" of God and God's indiscriminate welcome in terms of justifying grace; we are reckoned to have a right to be, by God's free determination'.[74] F. LeRon Shults expresses the transformation of the believer's identity similarly:

---

say that the self is in some sense 'illusory', originally and necessarily other-dependent, does not negate the reality of inwardness or the possibility of struggling to attain personal integrity or authenticity. It does, however, alter our image of that process. As Williams has noted, rather than the 'true' self being conceived as a pre-existing substance, prior to any relationship with others and needing to be unearthed from deep within, our self is born of desiring and in language, and with more or less need to build or defend itself over against others. Williams, 'Interiority and Epiphany', pp.240–241.

[72] For example, John's gospel portrays Jesus as praying for his disciples immediately before his betrayal: 'The glory that you have given me I have given them, so that they may be one, as we are one. I in them and you in me, that they may become completely one, so that the world may know that you have sent me and have loved them even as you have loved me' (John 17.22–23).

[73] St John of the Cross writes, 'That you may possess all things, seek to possess nothing. That you may be everything, seek to be nothing'. *Ascent of Mount Carmel*, Book I, cited by Ruth Burrows, *Ascent to Love: The Spiritual Teaching of St John of the Cross* (London: Darton, Longman and Todd, 1987), p.46. Burrows comments: 'We can never come to our true fulfilment, our authentic being, unless we undergo an undoing, a noughting … We must allow God to bring us to the fulfilment he has made for us … We must be brought to dispossession, emptiness, formlessness. A dreadful prospect? Does not this spell death to a human being? Paradoxically, no, it is the other side of the plenitude of life. It is to enter into him who is all, to be filled by the all'. *Ascent to Love*, pp.46–47.

[74] Williams, 'Interiority and Epiphany', p.250.

> In the normal (i.e., sinful) process of identity formation, the ego strives to hold its world together around itself. But for the kind of relational unity in which we are "one spirit with the Lord", the ego ... must be inverted so that the self as human spirit can rest transparently in the Infinite Power that established it ... it now accepts its identity and destiny as a gift of grace. This was intuited by Martin Luther when he insisted that believers exist *extra se in Christo* (outside themselves in Christ).[75]

What are the ramifications of this discussion for moral life? I began this section seeking to elucidate the claim that attempts to control, possess or establish our identities for ourselves are connected to a problematic conception of goodness, and block access to the deeper order of Goodness revealed by Jesus. I suggest now that this is because such attempts involve a kind of self-deception, a dynamic of being 'over against' another. They are expressions of threatenedness or lack. Insofar as being good or seeking one's good are means by which one seeks to secure identity, moral life partakes of this same dynamic. It is dualistic and contains the threat of violence.[76] Indeed, Williams suggests that both the moralist and the person impatient of external limits 'work in different but recognizably related modes of acquisitiveness'.[77] They 'have not learned to lose what they believe to be crucial to their identity', each resisting 'a belonging that cannot be dictated or constructed by the human self', and unable to receive as gift the lives and the identities they seek so desperately to own.[78]

The proclamation of the New Testament is that the felt need to grasp at identity and the systems of goodness that are interdependent with it are overcome by the crucifixion and resurrection of Jesus, which makes available an order of Goodness that is not defined over against anything else and that is not afraid. This Goodness does not belong to us and is not under our control. It is only gift, grace.

Participation in Goodness

So how does this work? I have spoken of the transformation of subjectivity arising from the disciples' encounter with the risen Jesus, but here I seek to elaborate how it is that Jesus' death and resurrection makes possible our coming

---

[75]   Shults, *Reforming Theological Anthropology*, p.91.

[76]   This is a theme to which I shall return. It has been extensively explored by Alison and Girard, as they connect the creation of victims or scapegoats as a necessary correlate of attempts to shore up the felt deficit in our 'selves'.

[77]   Williams, 'Resurrection and Peace', p.269.

[78]   Williams, 'Resurrection and Peace', p.269. Bonhoeffer says that, in grasping at equality with God, human beings grasp at and misappropriate their own origin. 'What God gave them, human beings now wanted to be on their own. But God's *gift* is intrinsically *God's* gift. The origin constitutes the gift. Changing the origin changes the gift'. *Ethics*, p.301.

to share in this new reality and so makes available participation in God's Goodness.[79] Alison, Bonhoeffer and Williams each emphasise different aspects of this event in discussing its significance for ethics. Together they illuminate the richness of its challenge and resource for moral imagination, and I draw on their discussions in turn.

Alison emphasises Jesus' free giving of himself to become the victim of a system of goodness. Instead of working to stay on the right side of the religious authorities, the enforcers of the system, Jesus goes into the space of being cursed by them. In doing so, he unmasks the mechanism through which the identity and goodness of the group is secured over against its designated 'other'. This revelation pertains not simply to the actions of this particular system of goodness in this particular case, but to all systems of goodness that maintain themselves by creating victims.[80]

This account emphasises both the freedom and the innocence of Jesus. Many people become victims of systems that shore up a sense of identity and goodness at the expense of those cast out. So, as Alison says, the 'class fairy' may be the victim by means of which the school class secures itself; the racially other may be the victim by means of which the political grouping secures itself. What makes Jesus' victimisation redemptive is that he occupies the space of shame voluntarily and without in any way being run by it. In ordinary human life, we seek desperately not to be designated the 'cursed one', the class fairy: 'any of us would do anything we could to avoid such a fate, including making damn sure that it's someone else who occupies that space in our group, and if that fails, then we are pushed kicking and screaming into that place and are destroyed by it'.[81] It is in this context, Alison suggests, that we read Galatians 3.13, where Paul writes, 'Christ redeemed us from the curse of the law by becoming a curse for us – for it is written, "Cursed is everyone who hangs on a tree"'.

Paul's insight, claims Alison, is that, by going voluntarily into that place, 'knowing full well that it constituted the psychological space which the Law, backed by crowd psychology, designated as "cursed by God"',[82] Jesus breaks the hold of the curse over us:

---

[79]   These questions take us to questions of atonement and redemption, which vast field for theological reflection I only touch on here.

[80]   In support of the claim that this is the New Testament's understanding, Alison points to Paul's insistence that the story of Jesus and the giving of the Spirit enables believers to do likewise, being baptised into Christ's death so as to be 'set free from being run by any system of goodness and badness over against others, any system of belonging which blesses by cursing'. 'The Place of Shame and the Giving of the Spirit', pp.207–208.

[81]   Alison, 'The Place of Shame and the Giving of the Spirit', p.205.

[82]   Alison, 'The Place of Shame and the Giving of the Spirit', p.205. Alison cites other places in Scripture where Jesus is said to occupy that same place, standing 'as a Lamb slain' or 'going outside the camp as did the scapegoat from the Levitical rite' (Rev. 5.6; Heb. 13.13).

> It is as if by his living in the midst of the curse and refusing to regard it as a curse, or be run by it as a curse, or react to it as a cursed-one does, the trap door of the trap got permanently stuck just, just, open, so that it could never close again. And with that, the curse lost its power, and the system of goodness became powerless, or moot.[83]

It is as though, Alison continues,

> the class fairy could be glimpsed, unperturbed, glad to have occupied, and to be occupying, the space of shame, and happy to be doing so. He does this because he knows that the class will fatally choose a fairy, because that is the only way they know to keep themselves together, to keep good 'good' and bad 'bad', which is the only way they have ever structured their bonding, their jockeying for prestige and their playing. But if someone could occupy the place of shame, the place of the curse, without being in reaction to it in any way, then the moment some in the class begin to glimpse him or her doing this, they can see that the place of shame, the place of the curse, is survivable, its toxicity quietly evanescent. From the moment they perceive this, then their system of goodness starts to fall apart ....[84]

It is important to clarify the sense in which victims of systems of goodness are innocent. From the point of view of such a system, the actual guilt or innocence of its designated victim in relation to any particular offence is largely irrelevant. What matters is that the group agrees on the necessity of the expulsion or 'cursing' of the victim for the sake of the identity and goodness of the whole (cf. John 11.50). Often it may be that this victim is innocent both in the sense that her expulsion is arbitrary and in the sense that she has committed no offence – the class fairy, the Jew, the old woman called a witch. It may be, however, that a victim of a system is guilty of a particular offence while still 'innocent' *qua* victim of the system. For example, someone may be guilty of paedophilic behaviour, and yet also be the victim of a mob that shores up its own sense of goodness and identity by lynching this designated other. In another context, the offence deemed to legitimate the lynching might be blasphemy or being unpatriotic or being caught in adultery (John 8.3–11).

When Jesus undoes the power of the system of goodness, he does not make it impossible to make judgements about or respond to particular behaviours. He does, however, radically subvert our construction of our own goodness and identity by means of casting others into the place of shame and death. This is the sense in which, regardless of their guilt or innocence of particular offences, at one level all victims of systems of goodness are innocent. That is, whatever the supposed justification for their victimisation, insofar as the system requires victims for its

---

83   Alison, 'The Place of Shame and the Giving of the Spirit', p.205.
84   Alison, 'The Place of Shame and the Giving of the Spirit', p.205.

own maintenance, it is the need of the system rather than the behaviour of its victim that drives the expulsion. This means that the 'justification' is no real justification at all. This is the sense in which Jesus is innocent, and reveals the innocence of all victims of systems that define their goodness over against the wicked other.

So on Alison's analysis, what the crucifixion and resurrection of Jesus save us from is the necessity of either being or creating victims.[85] It becomes possible to be the one cast out or shamed, and to know that this has nothing to do with God. It is merely a mechanism of human identity formation, which cannot separate its victims from the true source of life and Goodness. And it becomes possible to imagine the formation of human identity and human community without victims, realising that all are beloved of God and that identity and community do not need to be secured 'over against' anyone. Ethics in such a community is then decisively disconnected from a conception of goodness defined and maintained over against badness.

I have emphasised that the construction of identity by means of goodness defined against badness is inimical to true neighbour love and leads at worst to victimisation of others. We have also seen, however, that this dynamic is internal to the self as well as external. If I experience myself as lacking somehow in 'being', needing to build up my identity, then my sense of my own need and insufficiency occurs as a threat, something that must be either denied or covered over. This is the source of the drive to make myself good that distorts moral imagination and responsiveness.[86] To be liberated from this drive involves my daring to acknowledge 'inner contradiction, failure, the breakdown of performance and the emptiness of gratification',[87] to see myself and be 'seen' in all my lack such that I no longer have to deny or cover it over with a goodness I possess for myself. For Bonhoeffer, this is the liberation made possible not so much by Jesus' innocence, but by his transgression (2 Cor. 5.21). At issue here is the nature of Jesus' solidarity with humanity.

---

[85]   Alison remarks elsewhere that what goodness looks like after Christ is 'boring intermediary forms of process and protection, and insisting on rules of evidence'. The due process of the law is what replaces the lynch mob. 'Sacrifice, Law and the Catholic Faith: Is Secularity Really the Enemy?' in *Broken Hearts & New Creations*, pp.73–91, p.85.

[86]   Andrew Shanks has recognised the distortion of moral responsiveness arising from the need to see ourselves and be seen as 'just' or 'innocent' in his exploration of the work of Gillian Rose. He describes the distinction between the desire to be innocent and the desire to be just as being at the core of Rose's discussion of law. He writes, 'Some people's idea of morality simply stems from their wanting to be just, to do justice to others. Other people are driven, instead, by a desire to be recognized as innocent. Most of us, most of the time, are a mixture of both. Our morality stems from both sorts of motive, so intertwined that we are all too easily oblivious of the difference. But is not the desire to be innocent, properly understood, the great distraction, turning us away from the authentic desire to be just? If we want to be just, we must first of all give up wanting to be innocent. In terms of Christian theology, this is surely the true meaning of "original sin"'. Andrew Shanks, *Against Innocence: Gillian Rose's Reception and Gift of Faith* (London: SCM Press, 2008), p.30.

[87]   Williams, 'Resurrection and Peace', p.269.

If I have failed, it is one thing if someone is kind to me, refrains from judging me, invites me to try again. It is another thing entirely if someone shares with me her own story of failure and walks with me. This is the difference between charity and solidarity. I may be grateful for the first response, but I am empowered, liberated and able to integrate and transform my failure in a wholly different way through the second.[88] Likewise, it is one thing if God declares from on high that we are forgiven our sins, loved despite them, and exhorted into fuller life. It is another thing entirely if God enters fully into human life, knows the power and suffering of sin, and liberates us from alongside us.

Bonhoeffer emphasises again and again that, in Jesus, God takes the latter course. It is not just that God takes on the 'cause of human beings', but takes on 'humanity bodily'.[89] The humanity that God loves and becomes is not 'an ideal human, but human beings as they are; not an ideal world, but the real world'.[90] And since real human beings are alienated from God and each other, that is the humanity that Jesus takes on. So God does not just love us as we are, but (daringly) God becomes who we are.

> In an incomprehensible reversal of all righteous and pious thought, God declares himself as guilty towards the world, and thereby extinguishes the guilt of the world. God treads the way of humble reconciliation and thereby sets the world free. God wills to be guilty of our guilt; God takes on the punishment and suffering that guilt has brought on us. God takes responsibility for godlessness, love for hate, the holy one for the sinner. Now there is no more godlessness, hate, or sin that God has not taken upon himself, suffered, and atoned. Now there is no longer any reality, any world, that is not reconciled with God and at peace.[91]

---

[88] I am thinking of the way in which 12-step programmes, such as Alcoholics Anonymous, lead people to freedom through this kind of solidarity. Simone Weil emphasises the difference between pity or kindness that, however well meant, condescends and so in some sense destroys its recipient, and a response of the 'supernatural virtue of justice': 'He who treats as equals those who are far below him in strength really makes them a gift of the quality of human beings, of which fate had deprived them. As far as it is possible for a creature, he reproduces the original generosity of the Creator with regard to them'. 'Forms of the Implicit Love of God', in *Waiting on God*, trans. Emma Craufurd (London: Fontana Books, 1959), pp.94–166, p.101.

[89] Bonhoeffer, *Ethics*, p.84.

[90] Bonhoeffer, *Ethics*, p.84. In similar terms, Douglas John Hall gives an account of this compassionate (suffering-with) movement of God in Luther's theology of the cross. 'To feel compassion … is to overcome the subject/object division; it is to suffer *with* the other. Not just to have a certain fellow feeling for him or her, and certainly not only to look with pity upon another – a pity that in its actualization accentuates one's *distance* from the other. Rather, it means to be thrust into a solidarity of spirit with the other – to experience, in one's own person, the highest possible degree of identity with the other'. *The Cross in Our Context: Jesus and the Suffering World* (Minneapolis, MN: Fortress Press, 2003), p.22.

[91] Bonhoeffer, *Ethics*, p.83.

This is how Bonhoeffer understands the mystery of reconciliation effected in the person of Jesus. Somehow in him, the abyss of God's love embraces the abyss of evil such that there is now no reality 'that is not reconciled with God'.[92]

Bonhoeffer's discussion of how this is so and what it means for ethics is not systematic. What I find significant is the suggestion that Jesus does not simply occupy the place of shame while being in reality innocent, but that he takes on *being* a transgressor. This is Christologically complicated. On the one hand, Jesus is understood to be sinless, the one truly innocent human being and so the only one capable of forgiving human sin without in any way being complicit in it. On the other hand, if Jesus truly shares our human condition, then he is not just understanding and forgiving of our weakness, but bears it with us and knows what it is to bear it.

Bonhoeffer writes, 'Only as judged by God, can human beings live before God; only the crucified human being is at peace with God'.[93] Through the lens of a certain understanding of atonement, Bonhoeffer can be interpreted as saying that sin is taken away only by punishment and that Jesus takes on our sins in order to bear our punishment. The debt is paid, and peace is restored.[94] A problem with this reading, in my view, is that it conflates the concepts of punishment and judgement. Although Bonhoeffer's argument does not directly deal with this issue, I want to offer a reading of his insistence on judgement as connected not to the need for punishment but vulnerability.

We resist judgement. Even if we are not avoiding acknowledging particular crimes, we resist owning fully our pettiness and fear, our lack of love and freedom. Such acknowledgement confronts us directly with the sense of lack and insufficiency we are trying to make good, and the impossibility of our succeeding. We are like Adam and Eve, hiding ourselves and frightened. As long as we pretend we are not as we are and as long as we seek to justify ourselves, there will be separation from God, ourselves, and others. Reconciliation comes when we allow the truth to be told, which is judgement. Bonhoeffer says, 'God judges people because, out of sheer love, God wants them to be able to stand before God. It is a judgement of grace that God in Christ brings on human beings'.[95] Judgement is grace because we are confronted with ourselves in such a way that we may 'own' ourselves and suffer being loved not for our perfection but in our imperfection.

What might it mean to say that Jesus takes God's judgement of us upon himself or that in Jesus we are 'seen' as we really are, and how might this make a difference? If Jesus is the innocent victim of alienated humanity, in what sense is he also a 'transgressor'? Alison suggests that he is a transgressor only in the sense that he is deemed a transgressor, because he goes willingly into the place of shame,

---

[92] Bonhoeffer, *Ethics*, p.83.

[93] Bonhoeffer, *Ethics*, p.88.

[94] Bonhoeffer says, 'Only by executing God's judgement on God can peace grow between God and the world, between human and human'. *Ethics*, p.88.

[95] Bonhoeffer, *Ethics*, p.90.

the place of the cursed one. It is his innocence that reveals the mendaciousness of the system that crucifies him. Bonhoeffer is saying, I suggest, something in addition to that. He insists that Jesus shares fully in being human. His love is such that he wills to be guilty as we are guilty, so that he is able to undergo God's judgement of humanity on our behalf and as our brother. This is not a judgement that punishes, but a judgement that heals and liberates. Nevertheless, undergoing it is necessarily and excruciatingly humiliating and painful since it involves the death of the self that seeks to possess itself.

Holding this paradox requires that we distinguish between two notions of sin or transgression, which in human experience are inseparable.[96] On the one hand, there are the particular wrongs we do to others and ourselves, identifiable failures of love, generosity, courage and compassion. On the other hand, there is our experience of lack and creaturely vulnerability that tempt us to seek security and power, and from which all our 'sins', including those that masquerade as our righteousness, proceed. Jesus is like us in that he shares our basic human experience, but unlike us in that he refuses to allow it to separate him from trustful dependence on God in search of a self-made security. The gospel narratives of the temptations in the desert and the agony in the Garden of Gethsemane point to the liveness of Jesus' choice in this regard. As the Lenten Eucharistic preface expresses it, 'He was tempted in every way as we are, yet he did not sin'.

We tend to hear this overcoming of temptation by Jesus as a triumph of moral will, something we are exhorted to emulate. This reading, however, misses the real source of Jesus' sinlessness, which lies not primarily in will but in absolute openness to God's life. This absolute openness, expressed in obedience, is understood theologically as the work of the Spirit.[97] Whereas we resist judgement, resist the vulnerability of being fully seen and known, Jesus (in the power of the Spirit) does not. He does not grasp at moral success or any other strategy for self-protection or self-justification. He entrusts himself entirely to God.[98] And because ultimately he is given identity and life on the other side of what promises

---

[96]   Sebastian Moore's discussion of the twofold meaning of 'sin' as predicated *of* the human condition and a defect observed *within* the human condition is significant here. *The Crucified is No Stranger* (London: Darton, Longman & Todd, 1977), p.32.

[97]   Colin Gunton writes of the Trinitarian dimension of the atonement: '[Jesus] goes, as man, where we cannot go, under the judgement, and so comes perfected into the presence of God. But it is grace because he does so as God and as our representative, so that he enables us to go there after him. That is what is meant by the ancient teaching that Christ is our mediator. He brings us to the Father as one of us, but does so as one who, because he is God incarnate, is able to do so'. And later: 'Jesus was free in the midst of the pressures towards enslavement to the demonic because his life was maintained in freedom by the action of the liberating Spirit. So it is in general: the Spirit is God enabling the world to be itself, to realize its eschatological perfection'. *The Actuality of Atonement: A Study of Metaphor, Rationality and the Christian Tradition* (London: T&T Clark, 1998), pp.166, 167.

[98]   'His concern is neither success nor failure but willing acceptance of the judgement of God'. Bonhoeffer, *Ethics*, p.90. Jesus' silence at his trial dramatises this undergoing.

annihilation, through and in him we have access to a life that does not need to secure or make itself good.

> Ecce homo – behold the human being, accepted by God, judged by God, awakened by God to a new life – see the Risen One! God's Yes to this human being has found its goal through judgment and death ... In Jesus Christ, the one who became human was crucified and is risen; humanity has become new.[99]

How is Jesus surrendering to his crucifixion as 'transgressor' redemptive? I was tempted to articulate its logic in terms of the necessary crucifixion of the 'sinful' part of our selves. This is the self that wants to make itself whole, justify itself, and that ends up crucifying others. But that view makes crucifixion a weapon that God uses to kill something in us. What is wrong with that formulation is that it attributes violence to God when that is a weapon that belongs to us alone,[100] and that it solves the 'problem' of alienation by excision rather than reconciliation. I propose, then, that what is redemptive about Jesus' going to death and judgement as transgressor (entrusting himself radically naked and undefended to God), is that the alienated humanity in which he shares is restored by God's life and love. In being seen in truth and suffered for what it is, it is made whole utterly gratuitously, by gift.[101] The alienation of humanity from God is, in him, reconciled. What is redemptive is not that the crucifixion kills the 'sinful self', but that the 'sinful self' offered to God in truth and trust is made whole. Jesus crucified and risen *is* restored humanity.

How does this make a difference to us? How is the restoration of humanity in Jesus shareable by us? According to the New Testament, it is as we offer our alienated selves to God in repentance, sorrow and vulnerability that we receive as gift the same restoration and wholeness. That self-offering is, often enough, an intensely painful process, involving the cracking open of a settled identity or persona, coming to the end of our resources for self-making in experiences of broken heartedness and failure. It is made possible by the Holy Spirit breathed on the disciples by the resurrected Christ, and results in receiving the gift of the same Spirit. It is ultimately in and through Christ's death that we come to share in Christ's risen life (2 Cor. 5.14–15; Gal. 2.19–20). This means that a new possibility has opened up for human life, which is both already given and awaiting realisation by persons and communities. So, again there is paradox. Under the shadow of Nazism, Bonhoeffer could claim, in the passage previously quoted, 'there is no

---

[99]   Bonhoeffer, *Ethics*, p.91.

[100]   I have already endorsed Alison's argument that it is the fearful, self-justifying part of us that crucifies Jesus; Moore proposes that it is this same part of ourselves (roughly designated 'ego') that crucifies our 'true selves' – which is the true sense in which we are both crucifiers and crucified. *The Crucified Is No Stranger*, p.11.

[101]   Recall the discussion in the previous chapter of the risen Jesus 'seeing' the self-alienated Peter in Galilee such that he is restored to himself.

longer any reality, any world, that is not reconciled with God and at peace', while recognising that the realisation of this reality occurs in fullness only as surrender to cross and resurrection is undergone in particular lives.[102]

I do not think that Alison and Bonhoeffer are essentially at odds here. Alison emphasises the Johannine portrayal of Christ, peacefully and freely handing himself over to the space of death and godforsakenness without being run by it, assured of his unbroken oneness and unity with the Father.[103] In doing so, he reveals the violent futility of our systems of goodness and invites us into a new way of relating to ourselves, each other and God. Bonhoeffer emphasises the portrayal by the synoptic gospels of Christ suffering the depths of human alienation from God, so that precisely that alienation may be overcome in God's love and life. Perhaps Alison's account remains more exemplarist (we follow Jesus into the space of shame with confidence because we have seen him there and know ourselves forgiven for our complicity in the system), whereas Bonhoeffer focuses on the reconciliation effected through judgement of human alienation in the person of Jesus. On both accounts, however, Jesus enacts a radical freedom from humanly constructed systems of goodness and their correlative projects of attempted self-justification. Through the resurrection and the giving of the Holy Spirit, life in this freedom becomes newly possible for human beings. It is Williams who draws out most fully how this new life is transmitted to the disciples and becomes, through them, the church's proclamation and a new horizon for ethics.

Williams notes that the crucifixion leads not only Jesus into the place of shame and failure, but his disciples also. As Jesus fails, he writes, the 'incipient "new Israel" of the Twelve is scattered'.[104] They have been led by Jesus outside the religious and moral belonging they have known; 'they have become marginal in the world of public law-keeping'.[105] Yet their 'longings for power' and positions of influence in the new age have also been disappointed. There has been no fire from heaven to vindicate Jesus, no new authority for them, no restoration of Israel. The 'embryonic new identities they had begun to learn in the company of Jesus' are exposed as weak and confused 'as they find they cannot survive his failure and dereliction'.[106] The disciples are thus left stripped of the possibility of self-making by either means. So, says Williams,

> Any identity, any reality they now have will have to be entirely gift, new creation;
> not generated from their effort or reflection or even their conscious desire ...
> Jesus has taken his friends beyond the normal bounds of law and lawlessness,
> and they have found that beyond those bounds they cannot survive in their own

---

[102] Bonhoeffer, *Ethics*, pp.94ff.

[103] See also Alison, 'Discipleship and the Shape of Belonging', in *Broken Hearts & New Creations*, pp.54–72, p.68. See, for example, John 14–17.

[104] Williams, 'Resurrection and Peace', p.270.

[105] Williams, 'Resurrection and Peace', p.270.

[106] Williams, 'Resurrection and Peace', p.270.

resource; the loss that threatens is too sharp and humiliating to be borne. So life beyond law and lawlessness must be the life of God's gift, the assurance that failure and loss do not mean final destruction or emptiness. Meaning, promise, the future, the possibility of continuing to live in freedom and in the resource to love – all these are 'held' in the being of God, which is communicated to us as mercy, absolution.[107]

Williams emphasises that to interpret Jesus' failure in this way depends upon 'a transformation of self-perception' that is itself a gift. It is to speak from the perspective of resurrection, where new life and new identity are given not only to Jesus but to those who had followed and then abandoned him. 'Resurrection, the new life from a moral and material nothing', judges both the attempt to safeguard goodness and identity through a system of goodness and the 'sentimental assumption' that we can generate and sustain our lives for ourselves 'independently of relation to a "giving" reality'.[108] The self that is given life on the other side of this death does not possess its goodness for itself, but learns to trust and participate in a Goodness that transcends it.

How is it that the crucifixion and resurrection of Jesus makes available an order of Goodness that is not defined over against anything else and which is not afraid? The responses to that question I have been considering in the work of Alison, Bonhoeffer and Williams do not exhaust theological wondering.[109] Like all authentic doctrinal reflection, they are not so much explanations as testimony from a transforming encounter that seeks to create access to that same encounter for others.[110] The apostle Paul, writing to the Corinthians, expressed it this way:

> God chose what is foolish in the world to shame the wise; God chose what is weak in the world to shame the strong; God chose what is low and despised in the world, things that are not, to reduce to nothing things that are, so that no one might boast in the presence of God. He is the source of your life in Christ Jesus, who became for us wisdom from God, and righteousness and sanctification and redemption. (1 Cor. 1.27–30)

---

[107] Williams, 'Resurrection and Peace', p.270.

[108] Williams, 'Resurrection and Peace', p.271.

[109] No discussion of the atonement and reconciliation effected by the cross and resurrection of Christ can provide a 'final account' of this event. In his fine discussion of the dominant metaphors deployed by theologians to explore its meaning, Gunton writes: 'The metaphors with which we are concerned in this book have the importance that they do because they help to articulate a central feature of the human condition. It is for that reason that they are finally unfathomable and present to the theologian ever new possibilities for insight and development'. *Actuality of Atonement*, p.105.

[110] Cf. Williams, 'Beginning with the Incarnation', in *On Christian Theology*, pp.79–92, pp.82–83.

The proclamation of the New Testament is that God in Jesus brings to nothing any attempt to make, own, possess or control identity just because it is those attempts that perpetuate alienation from God, our neighbours and ourselves. When conceptions of goodness and the moral systems based on them partake of this alienation, they are necessarily distorting and potentially violent. The only true Goodness is the Goodness of God, which we receive as gift and in which we learn to participate to the extent that we are in the process of surrendering our possession of ourselves and our righteousness.

What this means is that reconciliation with God and neighbour are not new moral norms imposed within the old horizon, as if to be good what I need to be is reconciling, loving and so on. Rather, they constitute a new horizon, a new habitation, a new imaginative framework. We are formed by this new framework such that all moral responsiveness flows through that transformed perspective. We do not see resurrection, but we see from it. This has implications for normative moral judgement, moral epistemology, and the formation of the moral self.

Chapter 4
Living beyond Death and Judgement

'Very truly, I tell you, anyone who hears my word and believes him who sent me has eternal life, and does not come under judgement, but has passed from death to life.' (John 5.24)

Salvation is bound up with judgement, which therefore forbids any Christian talk of reconciliation from collapsing into a sentimentality that ignores moral right and wrong.[1]

I have argued that God's Goodness is distinct from much of what goes by the name of morality, the systems of goodness that construct themselves over against a necessary badness and that are bound up with projects of self-justification and self-righteousness. God's Goodness is, by contrast, grace. It is not in rivalry with anything and it does not belong to us. We receive it as a gift, and are enabled to participate in it as the anthropological condition of alienation is overcome by Jesus' crucifixion and resurrection. God's Goodness transcends and judges the world (in its light we see things as they really are), but it is a reconciling reality. It is working to recreate the world, and to bring all things into wholeness and communion. God's Goodness is simply God's being, God's life. The apostle John calls it love; Bonhoeffer reminds us that it is none other than Jesus Christ.

But what, practically speaking, does this reality of God's Goodness mean for moral life? In Christ all things might be reconciled but we need still to distinguish between justice and injustice, to make moral choices and judgements. On what basis do we discern and act? What are the moral norms proper to resurrection life, and how do we enact them without recreating goodness as a 'system'? What does moral reasoning look like when it no longer intermingles our concern for justice with our desire for self-justification? And how is a moral self formed who lives according to the Spirit rather than the moralistic flesh? These questions will be our focus in the next three chapters. Before we turn to them, however, I need briefly to situate this discussion in relation to broader currents in moral philosophy.

Ethical Foundations

Philosophical theories of morality dominant since the Enlightenment have sought to provide foundations for ethics capable of justifying our moral responses and

---

[1]   Colin Gunton, *The Actuality of the Atonement: A Study of Metaphor, Rationality and the Christian Tradition* (London: T&T Clark, 1998), p.108.

offering guidance in situations of moral difficulty. What has mattered is that these foundations be capable of rational justification since, so the argument goes, to ground them in the authority of tradition or belief alienates human freedom and renders us arbitrarily subject to superstition and prejudice. The Enlightenment believed 'with some justification', notes Colin Gunton, 'that its mission was to free humanity from the shackles of a dead past in order to make possible the free development of rationality and science'. In the sphere of moral life, 'it taught that salvation was to be found in the autonomous moral activity of the individual, discovering and doing for himself what was right, responsible to nothing but the dictates of reason and conscience'.[2]

In practice, two major theories of morality developed from this approach, each of which assumes a conception of the nature and purpose of morality, and derives from this conception a normative framework defining criteria for moral judgement.[3] Consequentialist moral theories have understood the purpose of moral life as to bring about the best overall state of affairs.[4] Justification of a moral choice, what makes one course of action morally preferable to another, is in terms of what conduces to the best possible state of affairs all things considered. Contemporary Kantian and contractual moral theories assume a world peopled by autonomous rational agents, each pursuing their own interests and values, their own conceptions of the good. The purpose of moral life is to ensure the freedom of all while respecting the equal rights of each to choose their own lives. A justifying moral reason is one that can be accepted by all rational agents as universal. The need for serious moral reflection arises mainly in those difficult cases where rights conflict in a particular situation.

In this philosophical climate, Christian ethics struggled for legitimacy. Based on a conception of the nature of reality that is ultimately a matter of faith,[5]

---

[2]   Colin Gunton, *Enlightenment & Alienation: An Essay towards a Trinitarian Theology* (Basingstoke: Marshall Morgan & Scott, 1985), p.71.

[3]   The notion that moral theories unavoidably assume a 'metaphysics', a background conception of the nature of reality, was highlighted by Iris Murdoch in the 1950s, as she sought to expose the spurious claim to 'neutrality' in certain linguistic approaches to moral philosophy. See 'Vision and Choice in Morality', *Proceedings of the Aristotelian Society*, supp. vol. 30 (1956): 32–58; Murdoch's argument is well discussed in Cora Diamond, '"We Are Perpetually Moralists": Iris Murdoch, Fact, and Value', in Maria Antonaccio and William Schweiker (eds), *Iris Murdoch and the Search for Human Goodness* (Chicago, IL: University of Chicago Press, 1996), pp.79–109.

[4]   What counts as the 'best state of affairs' has been understood in a range of ways, from Jeremy Bentham's utilitarian calculation of maximal happiness to contemporary conceptions of preference satisfaction. Joseph Fletcher's 'situation ethics' sought to Christianise the utilitarian calculus, describing the 'best state of affairs' in terms of what is 'most loving' in any situation. See Joseph Fletcher, *Situation Ethics: The New Morality* (London: SCM Press, 1966).

[5]   Bonhoeffer writes: 'The source of a Christian ethic is not the reality of one's own self, not the reality of the world, nor is it the reality of norms and values. It is the reality of

theological reflection on morality has been assumed to lack universal relevance and the authority that rational justification alone can confer.[6] In recent years, however, the cogency of the modern theoretical approaches to morality has been questioned. Feminist critics have disputed the assumption that rationality and autonomy are morally the most significant features of human beings, as well as drawing attention to gender blindness in conceptions of what counts as 'rational' thought. Aristotelian and virtue ethicists have drawn attention to the limits of instrumental reason in accounting for moral understanding. They have reminded us that moral perception is connected to the development of character or sensibility, such that moral thought must always involve more than the application of theoretical rules or principles to a neutrally described 'reality'.[7] The epistemological significance of virtue and narrative is emphasised, and questions raised about the very project of theory construction in the moral domain.[8] Finally, a number of philosophers including Iris Murdoch and Raimond Gaita dispute naturalistic accounts of the overall purpose of morality, asking whether it can be defined by ends exclusively internal to human life such as the furtherance of happiness or communal well-being or freedom, or is answerable also to a reality that transcends us.[9]

These recent shifts make the philosophical climate more conducive to serious engagement with an approach to moral life and thought centred in the Christian story. Nevertheless, I wonder if there remains difficulty in grasping quite what a radical challenge this story constitutes to philosophical approaches to morality. It is not simply that Christian ethics proposes an alternative foundational principle (love rather than rational freedom, for example, as the criterion for moral judgement), or an alternative account of the virtuous self. It is rather that

God that is revealed in Jesus Christ. This is the demand, before all others, that must honestly be made of anyone who wishes to be concerned with the problem of a Christian ethic. It places us before the ultimate and decisive question: With what reality will we reckon in our life?' Dietrich Bonhoeffer, *Ethics*, Dietrich Bonhoeffer Works, Volume 6, ed. Clifford J. Green, trans. Reinhard Krauss, Charles C. West and Douglas W. Stott (Minneapolis, MN: Fortress Press, 2009), p.34. It might, of course, be charged against modern theories of morality that their conceptions of reality are equally a matter of 'faith', in the sense that their world-pictures can no more be 'proved' than a religious one.

[6]   See, for example, Stanley Hauerwas, 'How "Christian Ethics" Came to Be', in John Berkman and Michael Cartwright (eds), *The Hauerwas Reader* (Durham, NC: Duke University Press, 2001), pp.37–50.

[7]   Martha Nussbaum has been a significant voice in this conversation, emphasising the significance of Aristotelian virtue and practical wisdom (*phronesis*), and practices of moral discernment and attention exemplified in literature. See, for example, *Love's Knowledge: Essays on Philosophy and Literature* (New York: Oxford University Press, 1990).

[8]   On the question of theory in ethics see, for example, Bernard Williams, *Ethics and the Limits of Philosophy* (Cambridge, MA: Harvard University Press, 1985).

[9]   'Naturalistic accounts' of the purpose of morality include not only contemporary Kantian and consequentialist theories, but also Aristotelian conceptions that define its *telos* in terms of human flourishing.

it claims that the ground and end of moral life is a living reality, the divine life revealed and made humanly shareable by Christ. Bonhoeffer describes the subject matter of 'a Christian ethic' as '*God's reality revealed in Christ becoming real ... among God's creatures*'.[10] This personal and living reality constitutes the field within which moral life occurs, and is the empowering dynamic of authentic moral responsiveness and agency. Drawing on the Letter to the Colossians, John Webster exegetes the matter in these terms:

> Jesus Christ 'is before all things, and in him all things hold together' (Col. 1.17). Jesus Christ is the absolutely existent one and, by virtue of that absolute existence, the one in whom creaturely reality in its entirety coheres. Together, this *autos* [he] and its correlative *en auto* [in him] are the foundation of creaturely existence, as well as of its intelligible unity and its movement toward perfection. And so to invoke the name of Jesus Christ in a moral context is to indicate the one by whom *ta panta* [all things] are moved, the one in whom action has its ground and telos. Creaturely moral action is action in the economy of grace, the ordered disposition of reality in which in Jesus Christ God's goodness is limitlessly potent.[11]

It is, I shall argue, the livingness and the self-dispossessing dynamic of this reality that prevents moral life sourced here from becoming merely another system of goodness, a fixed measure according to which we can assess our moral performance, though this has many times been obscured in the practice of Christian moral life.

Moral Life in Christ

I have already spoken of the reality revealed and inaugurated by the risen Christ as a reality of reconciling love, which transforms the subjectivity of those who encounter it. I have sketched some of the implications of this conception of reality for moral life, and want now to fill out that sketch a little further. I begin with its implications for the temporal horizon by which moral life and imagination are shaped.

In Chapter 2, I noted that the resurrection is an eschatological event: it is an event within history that is at the same time, in Brian Robinette's words, 'God's definitive act of salvation *for* history', coming to us 'from *beyond* history'.[12] For this reason, it profoundly affects the human experience of time. The Jewish imagination conceived of time as moving towards judgement and so as linear,

---

[10]   Bonhoeffer, *Ethics*, p.49. Emphasis in original.
[11]   John Webster, '"Where Christ Is": Christology and Ethics', in F. LeRon Shults and Brent Waters (eds), *Christology and Ethics* (Grand Rapids, MI: William B. Eerdmans Publishing Company, 2010), pp.32–55, p.34.
[12]   Brian D. Robinette, *Grammars of Resurrection: A Christian Theology of Presence and Absence* (New York: Crossroad Publishing Company, 2009), p.41.

historical.[13] This conception of time was bounded in two dimensions. It was bound in duration: time will come to an end. And it was bound by judgement, which was experienced often enough as uncertainty and fear. Although in this tradition the criteria for judgement have been set out in advance through the law, it is always difficult to be sure that one has fulfilled them adequately: the question of the law-abiding rich man to Jesus, 'Good Teacher, what must I do to inherit eternal life?' (Mark 10.17), seems evidence of that. With the resurrection of Jesus, it becomes conceivable to live (at least in part) on the other side of both these boundaries. Once again, James Alison will be our guide in exploring this terrain.

Let us consider first the conception of 'the end'. Time is for us, notes Alison, an 'ambiguous reality'.[14] In time, life is born and grows and develops, but it also grinds down, decomposes and dies. Human life runs towards death, towards its end, which means we experience time in some sense as an enemy. Time is 'running out'; time needs to be grasped or seized. With the resurrection of Jesus from the dead, what comes into view is the possibility of time beyond death, time without end. This possibility, Alison suggests, is most fully visible in the apostolic witness of John's gospel, which speaks frequently of 'eternal life' or 'life without end'.[15]

From the point of view of moral imagination, the significant thing about 'eternal life' is not that it promises life after death as a reward for good behaviour, but that it transforms the experience of life before death. By going to his death 'as if death were not', by inaugurating the belief that we could live now as if death were not, Jesus 'also enables us to live as if there were no end'. And what this means is quite extraordinary. It introduces

> the possibility of a [human] story which is only one of growth, of coming into existence, of development, and which is in no way shaded by its contrary. And this, logically enough, tends to relativize the time which we all know and live normally, the ambiguous time where we grow and decay. It means that two different qualities of time co-exist: the time of that which is coming into existence, which has no end, and the time which is subject to human violence, a time by means of which we seek our security, fortifying ourselves, grasping our existence in a struggle against the universal tendency to pass away.[16]

---

[13]   James Alison suggests that this conception came about during the time of the prophets and was interdependent with 'the birth of the understanding of human responsibility and of the possibility of choosing between this or that course of action in a particular historical circumstance'. *Raising Abel: The Recovery of the Eschatological Imagination* (New York: Crossroad Publishing Company, 1996), p.125.

[14]   Alison, *Raising Abel*, p.110.

[15]   Alison, *Raising Abel*, p.110.

[16]   Alison, *Raising Abel*, pp.110–111. In the next chapter, I consider in depth the relationship between mortality and moral meaning. I refer particularly to Raimond Gaita's argument that our finitude is in part what conditions the seriousness of morality and our sense of the preciousness of human life, as well as Iris Murdoch's claim that only in accepting our 'finitude' can we be truly Good.

As for the conception of judgement to which human life is answerable, I have already argued that it is transformed by the resurrection in two ways. First, God's judgement is of a different order from the judgement that violently casts out and curses. When the resurrected Jesus returns to his disciples, he comes as forgiveness, reconciling them to themselves and others, sending them into the world to invite all people into radical belonging to God and radical community among creatures. God's judgement is in the service of reconciliation and truth, not punishment.[17] And second, it is a judgement that has already happened in the world. On a view of time running towards judgement, judgement hangs over human life as a threat, its general criteria known but its application in any particular case uncertain. We can never be quite sure of having 'made it', of being found worthy of the reward of eternal life.[18] By contrast, the proclamation of the New Testament is that, in the crucifixion and resurrection of Jesus, judgement has already happened and happened as the free offer of acceptance.

As we saw in the previous chapter, this reality and our means of access to it may be understood in different ways. Sometimes the emphasis falls on the notion that Jesus, in some sense, *bears* God's judgement of the world; sometimes the emphasis falls on the insight that Jesus *reveals* the true nature of the system that judges and expels him, and alienates us from God and ourselves, so enabling humanity to live free from its thrall. Either way, the apostolic witness understands that for those who are 'in Christ Jesus' there is no more judgement to be undergone; there is no separation from life in God. Putting together these shifts in the understanding of time and judgement, leads to John's proclamation (5.24): 'Very truly, I tell you, anyone who hears my word and believes him who sent me has eternal life, and does not come under judgement, but has passed from death to life'. Anyone who allows their identity to be given by the crucified and risen Christ is learning to live on the other side of death and judgement, death and fear.

Of course, our experience of time and our human way of being remain shot through with what the writer of John's gospel might call 'unbelief' (John 20.31) or what Paul calls 'death' (Rom. 6.23). The new reality is imperfectly realised in and by us; the new identity is imperfectly received. Christ is the 'first fruits' of a new humanity, a new creation, but this way of being is only learned through a

---

[17]   Thus, Alison argues, Jesus subverts the violent apocalyptic imagination (sometimes using its language) and makes possible an eschatological imagination that involves a new understanding of God and God's judgement, now shorn of all violence. *Raising Abel*, pp.124ff.

[18]   This, notes Rowan Williams, was the source of the young Luther's agonised fear of damnation. Luther saw that God 'demanded conformity to his righteousness and condemned failure to conform. He demanded whole-heartedness; but how could the endlessly self-regarding, self-observing, self-dividing human soul produce such simplicity? Nothing in human action and motivation could be clear; by what right can a person ever satisfy himself or herself that an action is "good"?' *The Wound of Knowledge: Christian Spirituality from the New Testament to Saint John of the Cross*, second edition (Cambridge, MA: Cowley Publications, 1991), p.155.

long and costly process of discipleship and transformation. Thus, our inhabiting of this eschatological reality is characterised by the dynamic of 'now' and 'not yet'. Beginning from the resurrection, it becomes possible to live letting go our fear, our grasping at our lives and our righteousness, but 'this process of letting go is violent, because we don't let go easily, or at once'.[19]

Moral life occurs against this eschatological horizon, shaped by this possibility of life beyond death and judgement now present and active, but not yet fully realised.[20] This is how I understand Bonhoeffer's reference to the 'subject matter of Christian ethics being God's reality revealed in Christ *becoming real* among God's creatures'.[21] Until we are fully 'in Christ', Christ remains in some sense our 'judge', the criterion according to which our refusals of love, solidarity and forgiveness are measured.[22] Yet, at the same time, it is because of the presence of Christ's reconciling love that we are increasingly empowered to be conformed to him, not condemned for our failure but redeemed into eternal life.

What does this mean concretely in the human world? The reality of these two qualities of time, one running towards death and one liberated from fear of the end, is perhaps nowhere more clearly visible than in situations where solidarity with others puts us at risk of becoming victims of the world's violence. A portrayal of life responsive to this eschatological reality and its agonising human cost is offered by the 2010 film *Of Gods and Men*,[23] which tells the story of the Trappist monks of the Atlas Monastery in Algeria, killed in 1996 by radical Islamists.

As they and the Muslim villagers alongside whom they live come under increasing threat of violence from Islamic fundamentalists, the monks must decide whether to remain in Algeria or to go back to France. The authorities urge them to flee for their lives, and a number of the monks wish to do so. What is the point of staying only to die? What good will it do? Do they not also have a right to live? Others in the monastery believe they are called to remain with the villagers, with those who have no chance of escape. They wish to remain in solidarity with them, even if they can do nothing to avert the coming destruction. The monks enter a period of community discernment and together agree to stay. At one point during

---

[19]   Alison, *Raising Abel*, p.135.

[20]   Webster, analysing the ethical exhortation in the Letter to the Colossians, writes that the believer's moral history occurs in the gap between resurrection and exaltation, thus giving rise to the assurance of 'having been raised' and the imperative to 'seek'. The need to 'seek' is connected to our imperfect conformity to the reality of Christ; it is to 'be directed in one's moral history by the reality which grounds that history and toward which that history moves, namely "Christ is"'. '"Where Christ Is"', p.51.

[21]   Bonhoeffer, *Ethics*, p.49. My emphasis.

[22]   So, for example, the parable of the sheep and the goats in Matthew 25 shows how Jesus constitutes the criterion for judgement even when neither the 'good' nor the 'bad' is conscious that Jesus is present in their treatment of their neighbour in need. See Alison, *Raising Abel*, p.158.

[23]   Directed by Xavier Beauvois. Its original French language title is *Des Hommes et des Dieux*.

this painfully difficult process their abbot, Christian de Chergé, reminds one of the brothers that he has *already* given his life: it was given when he decided to follow Christ and to leave everything for his sake.

Here we have the construction of what Alison calls a 'counter-story' in the midst of the world's violent story, and a concrete illustration of the two qualities of time.[24] There is the time that is going out of existence, which would need to be defended or seized against destruction. And there is a choice to live from faith in a time and a reality that is without end. This is not a separate, heavenly time, which will be given to the monks as a 'reward' for being good. It is time that already partakes of eternity, the life without end that is God. In the film, the monks' living from this reality is movingly depicted in their final meal together, which, though shot through with the profound sorrow of human existence, becomes a foretaste of the heavenly banquet. They have come to share in the belief that Jesus inaugurated when 'he went to his death as if death were not, with his imagination absolutely fixed on the God who has nothing to do with death',[25] and this enables them to give themselves to being the presence of the possibility of reconciling love in the face of persecution and fear.

In his final Testament, the abbot de Chergé writes that if he should be killed he will, 'if God wills', at last be able to immerse his gaze in that of the Father and 'to contemplate with Him His children of Islam as He sees them … filled with the Gift of the Spirit whose secret joy will always be to establish communion and to refashion the likeness, playing with the differences'.[26] Like Jesus, the monks become judges of the violence that casts out and murders, but the shape this judgement takes is an invitation to forgiveness and friendship. Addressing in advance the unknown 'friend' who will take his life, de Chergé includes him among those to whom he gives thanks:

> And you too, my last minute friend, who will not know what you are doing, Yes, for you too I say this 'thank you' and this '*a-dieu*' – to commend you to this God in whose face I see yours. And may we find each other, happy 'good thieves' in Paradise, if it please God, the Father of us both.[27]

---

[24]   Alison himself speaks of Oskar Schindler in this context, and we might equally think of the witness of others such as Archbishop Oscar Romero in El Salvador and Sister Dorothy Stang in Brazil.

[25]   Alison, *Raising Abel*, p.110.

[26]   Dom Christian expresses his dismay that his death may justify a contempt for Algerians and a caricature of Islam, whereas for him 'Algeria and Islam is something different. It is a body and a soul', worthy of profound respect. His Testament was composed by Dom Christian de Chergé OCSO in Algiers, 1 December 1993, and produced in Tibhirine, 1 January 1994. It was opened on Pentecost Sunday, 1996, shortly after he and others of his Trappist community were murdered in Algeria. *Monastic Interreligious Dialogue Bulletin*, 55 (May 1996).

[27]   de Chergé, Testament.

As an illustration of moral life in Christ, however, this story may seem problematic. It appears uncritically to laud the kinds of self-denial and self-sacrifice that, in other contexts, have come to be seen as morally damaging or, at the least, ambiguous.[28] Furthermore, it occurs in a situation of oppression and victimisation that resonates in a fairly straightforward way with Christ's commitment to radical fellowship with the outcast and vulnerable. What about other situations of moral difficulty and choice? What about questions to do with medical ethics, warfare or sexuality, or situations where it is not clear what being in solidarity with the most vulnerable looks like? How does conceiving of ethics as responsive to an eschatological reality of living and reconciling love shape moral thought and being in 'ordinary' life, or provide guidance for moral discernment and choice in other contexts?

I suggest that there are three critical marks of moral life sourced in the eschatological reality of the risen Christ, the reconciling Goodness of God in our world. My claim is that moral life from resurrection is necessarily revelatory, vulnerable and compassionate. These marks can be seen in the story of the monks of Atlas, but are present also in less dramatic and more ambiguous moral circumstances. Although they provide nothing like a set of rules by which to measure moral outcomes, nor a fixed procedure for moral decision making, they are normative for moral life in the light of the resurrection. Exploring how this is so is the necessary background to engaging with the questions I have just raised.

Revelatory

Thomas Merton tells a famous story of the moment he realised his communion with the whole human race:

> In Louisville, at the corner of Fourth and Walnut, in the center of the shopping district, I was suddenly overwhelmed with the realization that I loved all those people, that they were mine and I theirs, that we could not be alien to one another even though we were total strangers. It was like waking from a dream of separateness, of spurious self-isolation in a special world, the world of renunciation and supposed holiness ... This sense of liberation from an illusory difference was such a relief and such a joy to me that I almost laughed out loud. And I suppose my happiness could have taken form in the words: 'Thank God, thank God that I *am* like other men, that I am only a man among others.'[29]

---

[28]   See, for example, Sarah Coakley's discussion of feminist criticism of Christian exhortations to self-emptying (*kenosis*) in '*Kenosis* and Subversion: On the Repression of "Vulnerability" in Christian Feminist Writing', in *Powers and Submissions: Spirituality, Philosophy and Gender* (Malden, MA: Blackwell Publishing, 2002), pp.3–39.

[29]   Thomas Merton, *Conjectures of a Guilty Bystander* (Tunbridge Wells: Burns & Oates, 1995), pp.156–157.

It was, Merton continues, 'as if I suddenly saw the secret beauty of their hearts ... the person that each one is in God's eyes. If only they could all see themselves as they really *are*. If only we could see each other that way all the time'.[30]

Merton's testimony resonates with Gaita's account, discussed in Chapter 1, of the reality made visible in the light of the nun's love for the psychiatric patients. Both stories express the extent to which the full humanity of other people and the sharedness of our lives may be, and usually is, hidden from us. They suggest that the reality to which moral thought and action is seeking to respond is visible at depth only to and in the light of love of a particular kind. The first mark of moral life sourced in the risen Christ is its power to reveal this reality, to deepen perception of what is before us.[31]

I emphasise that this revelatory capacity applies not only to seeing the full humanity of individuals, but also to perception of what is morally at stake in our lives. It is only as we see people, as Merton expresses it, 'as they really *are*' that we truly understand what it might mean to harm them or condescend to them, or even what particular moral questions amount to. Let me illustrate this claim with reference to another nun, Sister Helen Prejean, as portrayed in the 1995 film *Dead Man Walking*.[32] The film tells the true story of Matthew Poncelet, a murderer and rapist condemned to death in the US state of Louisiana, and of Sister Helen's accompanying him through the weeks and days leading up to his execution. On the film's account at least, this was no straightforward journey for her. She struggled with her own revulsion for this man and his crimes, as well as with her ostracism from systems of goodness that condemned her for committing to remain in solidarity with him. Yet, what grew from this struggle was a love that had the power of revelation in at least three dimensions.

First, her love rendered visible the humanity of someone in whom it had become obscured. Where the nun in Gaita's story revealed the humanity of those whose affliction had taken from them all that gives sense to our lives, here it was on account of his evildoing that it was difficult to recognise Matthew Poncelet as fully our fellow human being.[33] This recognition is a far deeper matter than believing that even someone who has committed terrible crimes has rights that must be respected by the legal system and that inform the way he may be treated. As with the psychiatrists in Gaita's story, it is perfectly possible to protect the rights, and even to believe sincerely in the 'inalienable dignity' of another, and yet fail to know their humanity as 'like ours' in any serious way.[34]

---

[30] Merton, *Conjectures of a Guilty Bystander*, p.158.

[31] I am not here claiming that *only* life sourced in Christ can be present to or make manifest this reality, simply that this revelatory power is a proper mark of Christian moral life.

[32] Directed by Tim Robbins.

[33] See Raimond Gaita, *Good and Evil: An Absolute Conception*, second edition (London: Routledge, 2004), p.xxiv.

[34] Indeed, the film shows the radical disjunction between the protocols designed to protect the prisoner's 'rights' and the capacity of those who carry them out to be present

But what does this mean? What *does* love make visible such that our responsiveness to such people is potentially transformed? I think it is to do with becoming present to the depth of a person, the unrepeatable particularity, mystery and wondrousness of a life. In the case of Poncelet, through Sister Helen's eyes we begin to see his childhood and its vulnerabilities and hurts, his need to belong, his inarticulate love for his mother and brothers mixed with an indiscriminate rage at their poverty, their social deprivation and impotence. We see tragedy in the pathetic bravado and pointless waste that has led him to death row.

Philosopher Cora Diamond has referred to a scene in Tolstoy's *War and Peace* that illustrates a similar shift in registering the particularity of another, and its profound significance for moral response.[35] In the story, Pierre is brought as a prisoner before General Davout. When Davout first looks up from his papers, he sees Pierre standing before him 'only as the present prisoner, the present circumstance to be dealt with'. Then, 'something in Pierre's voice makes him look at him intently', and in that moment, in Tolstoy's words, 'an immense number of things passed dimly through both their minds'. Diamond says that Tolstoy does not say *what* things, but, she thinks, 'they may be such things as scenes of childhood, of courtship, of the death of a parent or sibling ... they may be hopes and dreams, perhaps in Davout's case those inspired, many years earlier, by the Revolution'. In that second look 'human relations between the two men are established; and it is that look which saves Pierre's life'.[36]

Love is this profound 'seeing' of another that leads us to recognise and acknowledge the sharedness of our lives and yet, at the very same time, reveals the mysterious otherness of others, the impossibility of assimilating them to ourselves and our plans, treating them merely as the 'present circumstance to be dealt with'. In the light of Sister Helen's love, we cease seeing Poncelet merely as an instance of a class (prisoner, evildoer) and we begin to see him 'whole' – a murderer and rapist, yes, and unfathomably mysterious to us, but also our fellow, a sharer in our common humanity. This is the basis of any serious moral response to him.

The second dimension in which Sister Helen's love had the power of revelation was in relation to Poncelet's own moral understanding. I have said that, when the risen Jesus returned to his disciples as forgiveness, this was no 'bland legitimation' of all they had been and done.[37] For Peter, for example, to receive the love that saw

---

to his humanity. There is an 'inhuman' coldness in the bureaucratic procedures, forms and systems that surround the mechanism of judicial execution that blocks any sense of shared humanity between the guards, doctors and prison staff, and their prisoner.

[35] Cora Diamond, 'Losing Your Concepts', *Ethics*, 98 (1988): 255–277. See my discussion of this in 'Beyond "Thou Shalt" Lies a Deeper Word: The Theologian as Ethicist', in Heather Thomson (ed.), *Embracing Grace: The Theologian's Task* (Canberra: Barton Books, 2009), pp.103–118.

[36] Diamond, 'Losing Your Concepts', p.264.

[37] Rowan Williams, *Resurrection: Interpreting the Easter Gospel*, second edition (Cleveland, OH: The Pilgrim Press, 2002), p.45.

him whole was a costly process because it meant that he could no longer hide from the truth of his actions, who he had become in betraying his friend and teacher. Gaita writes that, if someone who has done evil were 'the beneficiary of a saint's love', it would be 'a severe love'. This is because 'it would not count as love unless it were lucid about the evil of his crimes, about the banality of his response to them and about his failures to be remorseful for them. But love it would be'.[38]

Early in *Dead Man Walking*, Poncelet seems incapable of facing what he has done with any lucidity: he claims he is innocent, that his partner in the crime is the only culprit. Sister Helen sees him whole and seeks to love him anyway, not in a sentimental way that allows him to evade or excuse his crime by, for example, focusing on the deprivations of his childhood, but in a way that holds open the possibility of truthfulness, repentance, forgiveness and restoration. Eventually, in the light of the way she sees him diminished by his crime yet called into wholeness, he is able to let go of his evasions, to be present to what he has done and become, and to seek and receive forgiveness. For the first time he calls his murdered victim by his name. Love of a certain purity reveals the reality of another, and it also reveals and restores us more fully to ourselves.

Finally, I suggest that Sister Helen's love revealed in a deeper way not only Poncelet to us and Poncelet to himself, but also what is morally at stake in the use of the death penalty. This is a subtle matter. Although the film is made from the point of view of those opposed to the death penalty, it does not directly argue that it is 'wrong' or morally indefensible or that it violates basic human 'rights'. It repeatedly focuses on the horror of the crimes for which this punishment was meted out, and on the ruined lives of the families of those murdered. Even so, in all that complexity and unremitting pain, the film shows us what we are doing when we execute a human being.

Through Sister Helen, we have come to know more deeply what a human life is because we see that even an evildoer is an unrepeatable particularity, has depth and a life to lead, is capable of being forgiven and loved. Through the remorse that her love makes possible for Poncelet, we have come to know more deeply what a terrible thing it is to harm another, to be a murderer. We have seen ourselves, however dimly, in his life and he has come to see himself in those he murdered, finally understanding what he has done in depriving them of *their* lives, their irrecoverable promise. And after all that, there is the execution. As Poncelet takes the terrible final walk from his cell to the death chamber, in the moments before he is deprived of his life inexorably and mercilessly, all of this is present to us. The film is not an argument about the pros and cons of the death penalty, but reveals what the death penalty is. This is what it means to execute someone. In the same way that Poncelet had to realise what it means to be a murderer, so the film asks us to realise what it means to be a society that executes. No serious moral reflection

---

[38]   Gaita, *Good and Evil*, p.xxx. Gaita refers particularly in this context to the crimes of Adolf Eichmann, and to Hannah Arendt's discussion of the 'banality' of the evil she witnessed in him at his trial.

about the death penalty is possible without it being revealed to us *what it is* that we are talking about. And, I am suggesting, it is only love that has the power to reveal that. Love and knowledge belong together in the moral domain.

I have already said that I do not claim that *only* moral life sourced in Christ has this revelatory capacity.[39] I do claim, however, that it is a necessary mark of an ethic from resurrection that it display this power, and I want now to recapitulate and expand my exploration of how the resurrection makes this kind of responsiveness possible.

In Chapter 1, I quoted Gaita commenting that love with this power of revelation is not 'something at the furthest limits of what is humanly achievable'.[40] He emphasised both its gift quality and its inseparable connection with humility. The love of saints is connected, to use Murdoch's term, to 'unselfing'. Speaking of the reality revealed in the light of Mother Theresa's love for the afflicted, for example, Gaita says that 'there is a sense in which *she* disappeared from consideration',[41] and Murdoch notes similarly the essential humility of the good person.[42] 'The chief enemy of excellence in morals (and also in art)', she writes,

> is personal fantasy: the tissue of self-aggrandizing and consoling wishes and dreams which prevents one from seeing what is there outside one. Rilke said of Cézanne that he did not paint 'I like it', he painted 'There it is'. This is not easy, and requires, in art or morals, a discipline ... We cease to be in order to attend to the existence of something else, a natural object, a person in need. We can see in mediocre art, where perhaps it is even more clearly seen than in mediocre conduct, the intrusion of fantasy, the assertion of self, the dimming of any reflection of the real world.[43]

This connection between pure love and unselfing is, however, liable to profound misunderstanding both within and outside the Christian tradition. The issue turns on what we understand love to be, and so on a significant distinction between two conceptions of unselfing.

---

[39]   Gaita, for example, discusses an instance of love with the power of revelation that was shown by one of the prisoners in Auschwitz for his fellow captive. Primo Levi tells of it in his book *If This is a Man* (trans. Stuart Woolf; London: Abacus, 1987), and Gaita uses it in part to show that works 'of saintly love' need not be performed 'by religious people'. *Good and Evil*, p.xv.

[40]   Gaita, *Good and Evil*, p.204.

[41]   Gaita, *Good and Evil*, p.205. James Alison notes that it is characteristic of Jesus in John's gospel that he consistently points away from himself towards the Father, that he is completely other related. He goes on to say that this 'was exactly the impact caused on a friend of mine by a recent series of conversations with Mother Theresa; he came away most struck by the evident way in which she is moved by another'. *Knowing Jesus* (Springfield, IL: Templegate Publishers, 1994), p.109.

[42]   Iris Murdoch, *The Sovereignty of Good* (London: Routledge, 1970), pp.103–104.

[43]   Murdoch, *Sovereignty of Good*, p.59.

What is the love that has the power of revelation? I would say, following Bonhoeffer, that it is not our love, but God's. Merton writes of his experience in Louisville that he saw the person each one is 'in God's eyes'. Just as God's Goodness lies beyond our conceptions of good and evil, so Bonhoeffer argues that God's love cannot be conceived in the first instance from the side of ordinary human love. Indeed, he writes, we 'must exclude any definitions that seek to understand the essence of love as human behavior, as disposition, dedication, sacrifice, will for community, as feeling, passion, service, or deed'.[44] Why is that so? Bonhoeffer says it is not 'because any human behavior always still contains a "remnant" of selfishness that completely obscures love. Instead, it is because love is something completely different from what these definitions imply'.[45]

A little later, Bonhoeffer implicitly concedes a certain hyperbole in this claim. God's love is not discontinuous with our natural thought about love: 'the choice of the term "love"' to describe God is not, he says, 'simply arbitrary, for even though this concept gains a completely new meaning through the New Testament message, nevertheless it is not entirely unrelated to what we mean when we say "love"'.[46] Even so, he maintains, we only rightly know what love is because of God's self-revelation *as* love: 'God is love (1 John 4.16). For the sake of clarity, this sentence must first be read with the emphasis on the word *God*, even though we have become accustomed to emphasize the word "love". *God* is love: that is, love is not a human behavior, sentiment, or deed, but it is God who is love'.[47]

The character of God's love is revealed to us as Jesus Christ. 'Only in Jesus Christ, and above all in his death for us, do we come to know what love is. "We have recognized love by this, that he laid down his life for us" (1 John 3.16)'.[48] We misunderstand this claim, says Bonhoeffer, if we derive a general concept of love from it, as if what mattered was giving up one's life for another, suffering in this kind of way. 'Love is not what Christ *does* and *suffers*, but what *Christ* does and suffers'.[49] Love consists in 'the reconciliation of human beings with God in Jesus Christ';[50] it 'denotes what God does to human beings to overcome the disunion in which they lived. This deed is called Christ, it is called reconciliation'.[51]

What practical difference does this discussion make? The basic issue concerns the logic of moral responsiveness. I argued in the previous chapter that no amount of trying to be good, to possess a goodness of our own, will take us to true Goodness. That is because the only true Goodness is God's. We are enabled to participate in it as we receive it as gift, letting go of our projects of self-making,

---

[44]   Bonhoeffer, *Ethics*, p.332.
[45]   Bonhoeffer, *Ethics*, pp.332–333.
[46]   Bonhoeffer, *Ethics*, p.335.
[47]   Bonhoeffer, *Ethics*, p.334.
[48]   Bonhoeffer, *Ethics*, p.334.
[49]   Bonhoeffer, *Ethics*, p.335.
[50]   Bonhoeffer, *Ethics*, p.335.
[51]   Bonhoeffer, *Ethics*, p.336.

our desire to secure our own righteousness. It is the same with love. No amount of trying to love from this side of our disunion with God, ourselves and each other will enable us to love God with our *whole* selves or our neighbours *as* ourselves (Matt. 22.37–40). We are set free to love in this way – *whole*-heartedly, pure in heart – only insofar as we are ourselves loved into wholeness. From the place of union with God, we love with God's own love. The 'relation between divine and human love' writes Bonhoeffer,

> must not be misunderstood as if the divine love indeed preceded human love, but only in order to activate it as an autonomous human doing ... independent and free from the divine love. On the contrary, for all that has to be said about *human* love, the premise still holds that *God* is love. Since there is no love that would be independent, autonomous, and free from God's love, it is this love of God and none other with which human beings love God and neighbor.[52]

This account of love may appear abstract and effectively irrelevant. How do I (or others) know whether I am loving with 'merely' human love or with God's own love, or some mixture of the two? What difference does it make? The reason I have laboured this distinction, between love sourced in being loved and reconciled to God and love that is a function of moral effort, is that it leads us towards distinguishing between two conceptions of unselfing, which I shall call respectively self-sacrifice and self-dispossession. The distinction between these two modes of unselfing is, I think, of the first importance for moral life and does indeed make a difference to the character and possibilities of our loving.

How is it that we love with God's love? Once we speak of this possibility in terms of getting the self 'out of the way' or unselfing, we are confronted immediately with the question of our understanding of the self. What is it that must be un-done? To put this in the idiom of the New Testament, what does it mean to be exhorted to 'deny oneself' or 'lose one's life' for Jesus' sake (Mark 8.34–35)?

In Chapter 3, I offered an account of the formation of the self, which assumed a necessarily relational dynamic. We learn to be selves through our imitation of and relationship with others, and in practical terms this process almost always involves coming to apprehend ourselves to some extent as 'over against' others or in rivalry with them. Following Alison, I claimed that our need for *being* is often felt as a lack,[53] requiring defence or building up, and making it difficult for us trustingly to receive our selves as gift. I also said that, paradoxically, it is as we learn to let go the felt need to grasp at our identity (our 'ego') for ourselves that we discover ourselves given being by 'God's free determination'.[54] In relationship with this

[52] Bonhoeffer, *Ethics*, p.337. Emphasis in original.
[53] James Alison, *The Joy of Being Wrong: Original Sin through Easter Eyes* (New York: The Crossroad Publishing Company, 1998), p.33.
[54] Rowan Williams, 'Interiority and Epiphany: A Reading in New Testament Ethics', in *On Christian Theology* (Oxford: Blackwell Publishers, 2000), pp.239–264, p.250. James

'gratuitous' other, the self can relax into the process of its own becoming without defensiveness or grasping, letting go the illusion of its essential separateness and autonomy, its need to establish itself in the face of threat and non-being. This has become possible with the revelation of God's love for us and the gift of the Spirit; it is part of the meaning of salvation. What does this account mean for our conception of 'unselfing' in moral life?

Let me start by way of contrast, considering the conception of unselfing that belongs with an understanding of the self as essentially separate and self-contained.[55] Mark McIntosh has noted that modernity's conception of the autonomous self is powerfully correlated with the Enlightenment view of deity. On this view,

> God is a particularly powerful and invisible subject who acts over against human subjects, and must then withdraw in order to permit their freedom to act autonomously … Likewise the human person comes to be understood as a human subject over against whom exists the range of objects for potential mastery or subordination.[56]

Starting here, it is easy to conceive of unselfing primarily in terms of the subordination of the autonomous self and its desires to God and other people. Surrender to God entails ultimately the obliteration of the self, or at least the excision of those parts of the self deemed wilful or non-compliant. Selflessness in human relations involves denial or negation of one's own self in favour of the other. This is unselfing as self-sacrifice. Such a conception has increasingly been recognised as having potentially serious social, moral and psychological costs. Feminist critics have noted that the calls to self-denial and self-abnegation in the Christian tradition have been 'usually calls that men seem to have issued and women … expected to heed',[57] and others have pointed to the cost of the often life-denying, moralistic and violent suppression of self seemingly enjoined here.[58]

Alison writes: 'It is only if I dare *not* to define myself over against the other that I can be nudged into learning how to trust that I will be given being over time'. *Undergoing God: Dispatches from the Scene of a Break-in* (London: Darton, Longman and Todd, 2006), p.6.

[55] I am indebted in what follows particularly to Mark McIntosh, *Mystical Theology: The Integrity of Spirituality and Theology* (Malden, MA: Blackwell Publishing, 1998), chapter 7, 'Love for the Other and Discovery of the Self'. See also Coakley, '*Kenosis* and Subversion', and Williams, 'Interiority and Epiphany'.

[56] McIntosh, *Mystical Theology*, p.211. McIntosh notes that the line of thought referred to as postmodernism, which runs from Nietzsche through Heidegger and poststructuralism, raises 'serious questions about the distinction of subject and object, and who gets to define them – about whether there is such a thing as a "subject" in the modern and Romantic sense at all'. McIntosh, *Mystical Theology*, p.212.

[57] McIntosh, *Mystical Theology*, p.235.

[58] The pathology of such self-suppression and the moralistic climate (the 'system of goodness') that often surrounds it is illustrated brilliantly by Alan Bennett's television

By contrast, the self that is necessarily 'dialogical and relational', fully itself in loving and being loved, is in a very different situation.[59] Unselfing, in this context, cannot mean the suppression or sacrifice of the self-sufficient individual, since the very existence of such an isolated individual is understood to be an illusion. What, then, does it mean? Essentially it means the process we have already noted: it means the willingness to yield that in us which maintains the illusion of separateness, the drive to possess or secure the self over against others. Mark McIntosh has elaborated on the relationship between this understanding of unselfing and the Christian doctrine of God, in ways that help to bring out its significance for moral life.

On the Christian understanding, far from being the powerful subject of the Enlightenment's understanding, God is being-in-relation. God is God as the Father giving himself unconditionally to the Son and the Son returning to the Father.[60] This 'trinitarian mutuality of self-dispossession' *is* the life of the God who is love. 'No Person of the Trinity can *be* except by giving the whole divine essence to the others, yet that absolute – indeed infinite – kenosis is not the termination of the divine life but its very basis and meaning'.[61] When God loves us, it is not as a self-contained entity bestowing charity from a safe distance. Rather, to be loved by God is to be drawn, through God's self-giving in the Son and Spirit, into God's infinitely relational life. According to this theological anthropology, to become fully myself is nothing other than to participate in this movement of yielding and receiving being from the divine other. Receiving one's self and giving one's self to God belong together. Drawing on Simone Weil, McIntosh writes:

> We cannot really *be* who we have the potential to be unless we give up trying to be this self-construed, autonomous, object-making subject. 'We have to die in order to liberate a *tied up* energy, in order to possess an energy which is free and capable of understanding the true relationship of things' ... [W]hat is sought is not the disability of the human person, but that self-dispossession which is empowering, which releases what had been constrained.[62]

---

monologue 'Bed Among the Lentils' (*Talking Heads* series, BBC, 1988), and its theological implications discussed in Graeme Garrett, *God Matters: Conversations in Theology* (Collegeville, MI: Liturgical Press, 1999), and my 'Beyond "Thou Shalt" Lies a Deeper Word'. I discuss this in more detail in Chapter 6. See also John Milbank, 'Can Morality Be Christian?', in *The Word Made Strange: Theology, Language, Culture* (Oxford: Blackwell Publishers, 1997), pp.219–232.

[59]   McIntosh, *Mystical Theology*, p.211.

[60]   Although there is no fully worked out *doctrine* of the Trinity in the New Testament, its sources can be found in (among other places) Jesus' teaching of his oneness with the Father and his absolute transparency to the Father's will. For example: 'Jesus said, "When you have lifted up the Son of Man, then you will realize that I am he [Gk: I am], and that I do nothing on my own, but I speak these things as the Father instructed me"' (John 8.28).

[61]   McIntosh, *Mystical Theology*, p.235.

[62]   McIntosh, *Mystical Theology*, p.230, citing Simone Weil, *Gravity and Grace*, trans. Emma Crauford (London: Routledge, 1963), p.30. Earlier McIntosh interprets remarks

How does this constitution of the self through yielding and receiving self from God make a difference to our conception of unselfing in moral life and hence to the possibilities of *our* loving? When unselfing is conceived in terms of the sacrifice of my autonomous self and its needs, desires and interests for the sake of another, it is still 'I' who am at the centre of the action. *I* decide what is needful; I exercise my will or virtue and heroically sacrifice myself in whole or in part. I remain other to the one in need, acting out of my own resources and self-sufficiency. When unselfing is conceived in terms of yielding myself wholly into God's life and love, however, then it is the very reality of my 'I' that has been transformed. I do not 'own' myself in the same way: the 'I' that I might heroically sacrifice is no longer, since my life has been yielded into God's life. 'It is no longer I who live, but Christ who lives in me' (Gal. 2.20).

When it comes to moral response, then, I am not striving to enact love as a norm but becoming more transparent to and receptive of that reality. And this is a reality that fulfils my deepest needs and desires as well as those of others. Bonhoeffer claims that the place

> that in all other ethics is marked by the antithesis between ought and is, idea and realization, motive and work, is occupied in Christian ethics by the relation between reality and becoming real ... the relation between Jesus Christ and the Holy Spirit. The question of the good becomes the question of participating in God's reality revealed in Christ.[63]

When my selfhood is constituted by its relation to God's giving life, I am not concerned with the *competition* between my needs and the needs of others. I am released to see others *as* myself existing in and through this same love of God. Attention to and love for the other then comes through me, as it were, from God's life. It is not at my *expense* since it comes out of and flows into fullness rather than

---

of Edith Stein to signify that, 'standing within the Trinitarian self-surrender, the soul participates in that infinite giving of God to God which is both the ultimate kenosis and the eternal constitution of the divine existence ... [T]he saintly self-abnegation is not an ultimate dissolution of personal being but the empowering of the human to effect new possibilities', p.229. This line of thought has been explored with seemingly remarkable consistency, on McIntosh's account, through Augustine, the mediaeval mystics Marguerite Porete and Meister Eckhart, and in the twentieth century through Edith Stein and Simone Weil. Concluding a discussion of Eckhart, McIntosh writes: 'the consummation of human personal identity ... is found in breaking through to this paradoxical Trinitarian life where one *is* only by being wholly for the other. So it would seem that "I" am not so much constituted by some mysterious inner self which lies behind my outgoing relationship with others; rather, I am who I am exactly *in virtue of* that outgoing relationality'. *Mystical Theology*, p.227.

[63]   Bonhoeffer, *Ethics*, pp.49–50.

self-sacrifice or self-mutilation; in the trinitarian paradox of unselfing as selfing, loving the other with this love finally fulfils me, as the passage from Merton shows.[64]

By contrast, love for the other that comes from self-sacrifice perpetuates 'the opaque, illusory self, the block between God's love and the creature. It ... [maintains] myself as a kindly giving subject for all those needy others, who exist sadly but conveniently as objects for my self-expression'.[65] So as Weil says, love for the other in affliction is not possible for the creaturely self per se. Indeed, 'the human self can only truly love when it has allowed itself ... to become a participant in this triune event of loving'.[66] Only this essentially self-forgetful love is capable of loving the afflicted without condescension or of moving beyond a reflex revulsion to see an evildoer whole.

Although I have distinguished between unselfing as self-sacrifice and as self-dispossession, it is true that the process of yielding ourselves wholly to God may be costly, painful and difficult, as we confront our own fear, our desire for control, and what we experience at times as the appalling silence of God. Think of Jesus in the Garden of Gethsemane. It is also true that consenting to participate in God's love may lead in the conditions of the human world to the choice to forgo one's own 'interests', to suffering and death. Hence the connection between the love of saints and martyrdom. McIntosh remarks: 'In the eternal play of the trinitarian life this absolute renunciation of the self on behalf of the other may be an infinite event of bliss and joy, but in the broken shards of human moral history the very same event may necessarily be enacted in painfully sacrificial terms'.[67] It is therefore natural to speak in both these contexts of 'sacrificial' love. What is at issue here, however, is not the suppression or mutilation of the self, but its fulfilment and restoration through coming into deeper and deeper relation with the dynamic of trinitarian life. This is the source of the love of saints, its joy and revelatory power.

Vulnerable

The second mark of moral life sourced in the eschatological reality of the risen Christ is its vulnerability. By 'vulnerability' in this context, I do not mean the vulnerability that accompanies the commitment to love in a violent world. Rather, I mean the *moral* vulnerability that is the corollary of obedient responsiveness to a living reality and of relinquishing the security of systems of goodness. Acceptance of this vulnerability shapes moral reflection and discernment in distinctive ways, as well as transforming the significance of law for moral life.

---

[64] McIntosh speaks of 'an invitation to a form of absolute self-gift to the other which is simultaneously the very energizing of the one who gives'. *Mystical Theology*, pp.238–239.

[65] McIntosh, *Mystical Theology*, p.235.

[66] McIntosh, *Mystical Theology*, p.235.

[67] McIntosh, *Mystical Theology*, p.239.

I have argued that participating in God's Goodness, loving with God's love, is a function of our being reconciled to God and ourselves, freed from the need to secure ourselves or our goodness through moral effort. Christian moral life flows from our being ever more open to the energy of God's life and is oriented towards the becoming real of God's self-dispossessing and reconciling love among us. The difficulty is in discerning what participating in that reality amounts to in particular circumstances or, as Bonhoeffer expresses it, the difficulty lies in discerning God's will.[68]

All serious moral reflection grapples with issues of interpretation and judgement. I hope to do good and not harm, but in complex situations of competing needs and interests, what counts as doing good and not harm? No amount of codifying laws and principles delivers us from having to be responsible for the quality of our moral thought and responsiveness or from the risks associated with it.[69] The difficulty of discerning God's will includes this feature of moral life, but goes beyond it. It refers also to the experience of being drawn into participating in a reality beyond our comprehension whose moral meaning may be obscure to us, and which therefore calls for discernment by faith rather than sight. In this section, I explore the particular character of this vulnerability in Christian moral life and begin by drawing on a distinction between rationalism and voluntarism in moral thought helpfully articulated by Oliver O'Donovan.

What gives me a reason to act in one way rather than another? On what basis do I discern what I must, morally speaking, do? In the political sphere, O'Donovan suggests, we ascribe moral authority to two kinds of reason for acting. On the one hand, the command of an authorised body or the requirements of law give me reason to obey them, independently of the content of their prescriptions. For example, 'if the law requires me to pay taxes to support government programs which I think are immoral, I may still be obliged to pay the taxes of which I disapprove. This is one of the paradoxes of political authority: its moral claim is to a degree independent of the moral claim of its particular demands taken on their own'.[70] But this kind of moral claim is not unlimited. We may conform to its requirements while still being critical of them, and there may come a point when it is morally necessary to resist the demands of such authority. So, although political

---

[68]   'Those who wish even to focus on the problem of a Christian ethic are faced with an outrageous demand – from the outset they must give up, as inappropriate to this topic, the very two questions that led them to deal with the ethical problem: "How can I be good?" and "How can I do something good?" Instead they must ask the wholly other, completely different question: what is the will of God?' Bonhoeffer, *Ethics*, p.47.

[69]   This is a theme particularly of Martha Nussbaum, who speaks of the cultivation of perception and virtue as necessary for serious moral engagement in *Love's Knowledge*. See also Raimond Gaita's discussion of the necessarily personal character of moral thought. 'The Personal in Ethics', in D.Z. Phillips and Peter Winch (eds), *Wittgenstein: Attention to Particulars* (London: Macmillan, 1989), pp.124–150.

[70]   Oliver O'Donovan, *Resurrection and Moral Order: An Outline for Evangelical Ethics*, second edition (Leicester: Apollos, 1994), p.131.

authority may command my conformity, it is itself ultimately subject to 'truth, for only a perception of the truth can lead us to whole-hearted action'.[71]

O'Donovan suggests that this relationship between command and truth in the sphere of political authority sheds light by analogy on the concept of divine authority that informs traditions of Christian moral discernment. Here, on the one hand, it is understood that the authority of God 'can transcend the judgement of our moral reason ... In the face of divine command our reason declares its own authority suspended'.[72] On the other hand, if divine authority is to command us 'as absolute authority, it must command us as supreme reality. Authority presupposes a foundation in being, and ... divine authority will prevail only because it belongs to that first reality in which truth is grounded'.[73] O'Donovan notes that the traditions of theological rationalism and voluntarism emphasise different poles of this relationship between command and truth, command and reality, both of which are to be found in the Scriptures.[74]

Rationalism emphasises the continuity between God and the created order, which includes human reason, holding that God speaks through the order that reason perceives. It upholds belief in the reliability and intelligibility of the world and of God's purposes, which means trusting that what God asks of us will not be fundamentally alien to our conscience, our moral reason or our experience of reality. This understanding of 'an ontological continuity' between creation and creator is the basis of natural law, but its inherent risk is of domesticating the radical otherness of God, assuming a falsifying transparency of reason's operations and perceptions to the divine will.[75]

Voluntarism, by contrast, emphasises the discontinuity between God and the created order, and is concerned to uphold the radical sovereignty of God and the call to radical obedience. The value of this emphasis is in its refusal to domesticate God or, in O'Donovan's words, 'in its perception that the dialectic between reason and revelation rests not on an accidental deficiency of human reason but on the aboriginal metaphysical fact that human reason is not transcendent. Thus human

---

[71]   O'Donovan, *Resurrection and Moral Order*, p.131.

[72]   Elaborating on this facet of divine authority, O'Donovan writes: 'To encounter divine command is to encounter that which is more fundamental than all reason: it is to encounter the ultimate *fiat* to which no questions may be put. Reason itself directs us to understand that all our rational perceptions of morality are hypothetical, dependent on the form in which it has pleased God to give this *fiat* to us. Standing before the burning bush, reason knows that it must take off its shoes'. O'Donovan, *Resurrection and Moral Order*, p.131.

[73]   O'Donovan, *Resurrection and Moral Order*, p.132.

[74]   For example, there is God's 'self-posited faithfulness' (2 Tim. 2.13) and the eternal establishment of the created order (Ps. 104.5), and there is possibility of God's doing a 'new thing' (Is. 43.19). In Jesus' ministry there are many instances of his doing God's will, but of that looking like disobedience to God's law in the eyes of the religious authorities (e.g. John 9). O'Donovan, *Resurrection and Moral Order*, pp.132, 136.

[75]   O'Donovan, *Resurrection and Moral Order*, pp.132–133.

judgements are always, and as such, susceptible to divine criticism'.[76] The danger
of voluntarism, however, is that the alleged command of God risks becoming
arbitrary and despotic and hence losing any authority to command our allegiance.
'If nothing that our minds can comprehend is in the slightest degree relevant to
recognizing the authority of God's will, how is that authority to be recognized?
An initial concern to isolate sheer authority and sheer obedience must end up
paradoxically by abolishing both authority and obedience in an immediate clash
of wills'.[77] For this reason, O'Donovan concludes,

> If obedience is to be 'trusting', it must be hopeful. The disciple who obeys the
> divine word in defiance of his own limited perceptions of right is genuinely
> trustful only if he believes that the paradox is not an ultimate contradiction in
> reality. He must hope to see the moment of critical confrontation finally resolved
> by the elevation of his reason to grasp God's action as a coherent whole.
> Otherwise he is acting not in faith but in cynical despair ... Rationalism was not
> wrong to promise an ultimate scrutability in the divine purpose; it was wrong
> only as it attempted to empty that promise of its eschatological character and
> hurry forward to premature fulfilment by the route of a reductive immanentism.[78]

In other words, O'Donovan argues that the traditions of rationalism and
voluntarism express the double aspect of the epistemological situation in which
we human beings find ourselves. Ultimately, God's purposes and promises
are sure; ontologically things cohere. Yet our access to knowing that reality is
necessarily partial, distorted as our understanding is by sin, limited as it is by our
creatureliness. 'Because reason knows the cosmos from within, as an embracing
mystery which surrounds it, it knows that it can never be uncritical of any of its
own perceptions ... and that it must always be open to the possibility of revelation
from the standpoint of transcendence'.[79]

This has consequences for Christian moral discernment and reveals, I
suggest, the extent to which the vulnerability that I am arguing is a critical mark
of Christian moral life is a double vulnerability. On the one hand, it partakes
of the vulnerability of all moral understanding to dullness of perception, the
incommensurability of goods, the difficulty of applying principles to particulars,
the dangers of self-deception and failures of moral sensibility in forms such as
sentimentality, bitterness or cynicism. But in seeking to be responsive and obedient

---

[76] O'Donovan, *Resurrection and Moral Order*, p.136. O'Donovan goes on to say that,
for this reason, 'the risk of Abraham cannot be avoided'. The reference is to God's command
to Abraham to sacrifice his son Isaac in Genesis 22. This episode is famously discussed
by Søren Kierkegaard in terms of the 'teleological suspension of the ethical' in *Fear and
Trembling*, trans. Walter Lowrie (Princeton, NJ: Princeton University Press, 1954).
[77] O'Donovan, *Resurrection and Moral Order*, p.134.
[78] O'Donovan, *Resurrection and Moral Order*, p.136.
[79] O'Donovan, *Resurrection and Moral Order*, p.133.

to a living and eschatological reality that transcends its grasp, in understanding itself as answerable to *another*, Christian moral life is vulnerable at another level too. There is no formula, no failsafe mechanism for ascertaining the will of God. It cannot be read off directly from the orders of creation, the deliverances of human reason, or the intuitions of the human heart; nor can it be received reliably as private revelation or translated directly from the written commands of law as if we could reduce the living word of God to rules of moral conduct. The clash of Jesus with the Pharisees is paradigmatic here. Bonhoeffer writes:

> This discernment of the will of God is such a serious matter precisely because it is no longer our own knowledge of good and evil that is at issue here, but the living will of God; because knowing the will of God is not at our human disposal, but dependent entirely on God's grace; and, indeed, because this grace is and wants to be new every morning. The will of God can now no longer be confused with the voice of the heart, nor with any kind of inspiration, nor with any kind of absolute principle, since it reveals itself anew only to those discerning it in each particular case.[80]

Putting the matter in these terms may appear to render Christian moral discernment impossible, even dangerous, tempting each to appeal to a secret knowledge to legitimate moral response. The Enlightenment appeal to the transparency of public reason as the only basis for a common morality becomes explicable in this context. How is discernment of God's will in relation to particular moral questions and contexts not only possible but able to be engaged with critically? How may we know ourselves responsibly and truthfully related to the living reality of the risen Christ?

This question of discernment is central to Christian spirituality in general and has given rise over time to several traditions for discerning the truth of 'spiritual stances', understandings and practices.[81] Such traditions are technically known as 'rules for the discernment of spirits'.[82] Mark McIntosh notes in relation to the Christian mystical tradition that, in the end, the truth of a given spirituality can be evaluated only 'by an assessment of the kind of life it leads one to embrace, the kind of reality it leads one to encounter', and that this assessment has involved in every era of Christian spirituality the development of particular 'critical tools'.[83] These are *public* criteria, but being able to employ them involves more than the

---

[80] Bonhoeffer, *Ethics*, p.321.

[81] McIntosh, *Mystical Theology*, p.144. See also McIntosh's comprehensive treatment of traditions of discernment in Christian spirituality and their relationship to conceptions of truth and knowledge in his *Discernment and Truth: The Spirituality and Theology of Knowledge* (New York: Crossroad Publishing Company, 2004).

[82] McIntosh, *Mystical Theology*, p.144.

[83] 'From the first desert hermits to Cassian's reformulations and on to Ignatius of Loyola and beyond, every era of Christian spirituality has developed critical tools for

capacity for ratiocination. In the context of theological ethics, the critical marks that I am elaborating may be conceived as tools by means of which evaluation of the truth of moral discernment and responsiveness may proceed.[84] I shall return to this claim, but I need first to say something about the conditions of the very possibility of truthful discernment.

I have already argued that the possibility of our goodness and love is dependent upon our being reconciled to God, participating in God's life such that we love with God's own love. The same dynamic applies to the possibility of truthful discernment. It too presupposes the process of being reconciled to God, coming to share in God's life through the paschal journey from self-possession to self-dispossession. Both Bonhoeffer and McIntosh emphasise this transformation of the knower as the 'decisive and clear prerequisite'[85] of coming to share 'the mind of Christ' (1 Cor. 2.16) and so being in any way capable of knowing as God knows, discerning God's will (cf. John 7.16–18). This is because as long as human beings are separate from God, bound by death, fear and the illusion of self-making, our vision and understanding are distorted.

Drawing on Paul's understanding that humanity 'could no longer recognize God's truth shining forth in creation because they were no longer rightly acquainted with God, "They became futile in their thinking and their senseless minds were darkened" (Romans 1.21)', McIntosh suggests that 'from the earliest Christian thought there has been a strong connection between humans' relationship with God and the capacity to discern reality truthfully'.[86] And in the same way that Jesus' crucifixion and resurrection opens the possibility of participating in God's Goodness and love, so it is by having Jesus' dying and rising worked within them that the disciples become capable of receiving truth. The gift of the Holy Spirit, the gift of the risen Christ, is called by Jesus the 'Spirit of truth' who will 'guide you into all the truth' (John 16.13).

> Now at last, says Jesus, the Spirit will 'take what is mine and declare it to you', because now my sharing life with you (which is the very life of the Father) has broken through all the bonds and fears that have hindered and distorted our communication with one another. It is this new life, this new grounding in belief, that will make true discernment possible.[87]

---

gauging the truthfulness of the spiritual stances proposed in given texts and saintly lives'. McIntosh, *Mystical Theology*, p.144.

[84]   McIntosh proposes that reintegrating Christian theology and spirituality will involve learning how to apply rules for spiritual discernment to *theological* argument; I am proposing something analogous in relation to Christian ethics and critical moral reflection. *Mystical Theology*, p.144.

[85]   Bonhoeffer, *Ethics*, p.322; McIntosh, *Discernment and Truth*, p.8.

[86]   McIntosh, *Discernment and Truth*, p.4.

[87]   McIntosh, *Discernment and Truth*, p.11. See similarly Bonhoeffer: 'Discerning the will of God is therefore not something one can do on one's own, from one's own knowledge

As Bonhoeffer insists, however, this necessary grounding of truthful discernment in relationship to God does not make human discernment redundant.[88] Our discernment presupposes and springs from this relationship, but since it is a living relationship it does not issue in a life or knowledge 'that is given once and for all, a static entity, something possessed. With every new day, therefore, the question arises, how, today, here, in this situation, can I remain and be preserved within this new life with God, with Jesus Christ?'[89] Thus discernment will call for the exercise of intellect and 'attentive perception' to context; it will be 'encompassed and pervaded by the commandment', and draw on understanding garnered from prior experience. 'Under no circumstances', warns Bonhoeffer, is one to count on 'unmediated inspirations' that may lead to self-deception; rather, a sober and watchful attitude should prevail, with 'possibilities and consequences' carefully considered. In short, 'in order to discern what the will of God may be, the entire array of human abilities will be employed'.[90] Yet none of this care and attention can protect us absolutely from moral vulnerability, since it remains always possible that we do not discern as deeply or truthfully as we might, that we are deceived or obtuse to some degree.

The claim that we are necessarily morally vulnerable is deeply unsettling. Modern moral philosophy has seemed at times obsessed with the quest for moral certainty, seeking universal rules and prescriptions by means of which we may justify our moral responses, ensure our innocence, and pass judgement on 'hard cases'.[91] Philosophy resists its own limits, seeking answers to moral questions that it presumes will have justificatory force for any rational agent.[92] In the Judaeo-Christian tradition, divine command expressed as law has sometimes been considered a bulwark against the kind of moral vulnerability that I am arguing

---

of good and evil. It is, on the contrary, possible only for people who have been stripped of the knowledge of good and evil, and who therefore completely refrain from knowing the will of God by their own means – for those who already live in the unity of the will of God because the will of God has already been carried out in their lives. Discerning the will of God is possible only on the basis of knowing the will of God in Jesus Christ'. *Ethics*, pp.322–323.

[88] Bonhoeffer, *Ethics*, p.323.

[89] Bonhoeffer, *Ethics*, p.323. Similarly Williams: 'The new life is not a possession. It is, simply, new life. That is to say, a new world of possibilities, a new future that is to be constructed day by day. Life, after all, implies movement and growth'. *Wound of Knowledge*, p.19.

[90] Bonhoeffer, *Ethics*, pp.323–324.

[91] The distorting effects of this anxiety on philosophical conceptions of morality has been noted by Rush Rhees in *Without Answers* (London: Routledge & Kegan Paul, 1969), and discussed by Gaita in 'The Personal in Ethics'.

[92] The philosopher Bernard Williams has ironically drawn attention to the 'note of urgency' among moral philosophers as they seek this moral certainty with its presumed justificatory force: 'What will the professor's justification do, when they break down the door, smash his spectacles, take him away?' *Ethics and the Limits of Philosophy*, pp.22–23.

is unavoidable if we are seeking to live in obedient responsiveness to a living reality. What are the implications of the claim that vulnerability is a critical mark of Christian ethics for our understanding of and relationship to law?

There are two issues to be distinguished here, both of which I have already touched on. First is the question of our relationship to law as law. We have already seen that, insofar as the law functions to define identity and goodness over and against a necessary badness, it is part a system of human identity formation that has little to do with God. James Dunn has argued that it is precisely this concern with the use of law as a social boundary marker and spiritual guarantee that animates Paul's inveighing against the 'works of the law' in his disputes with Jews and Jewish Christians.[93] The issue is not law *per se* but law functioning to secure righteousness and a standing of one's own, and this is indicated particularly by Paul's focus on those 'works of the law' that delineate social belonging, the practices of circumcision and dietary observance.[94] Williams, commenting on the Letter to the Ephesians, notes that for that writer also the law has become 'ambiguous': 'the Law and the covenant are matters of gift; but because they are expressed in terms of clear and identifiable demands, it is possible to think that, as a recipient of this gift, you gain some kind of secure control over your identity'.[95]

This is the context in which Paul seeks to overturn the assumption that belonging to the covenant and even fulfilling its requirements *of itself* secures one's standing before God and guarantees one's righteousness. The possibility of being reckoned righteous is God's gift given through the resurrection of Christ and the reconciliation wrought by it, and this underlies Paul's insistence that his status as a member of the covenant people, his 'righteousness under the law', counts for nothing (Phil. 3.4–6), and that it was Abraham's *faith* rather than his

---

[93]   James D.G. Dunn, *Jesus, Paul and the Law* (London: SPCK, 1990), pp.219ff. Dunn also argues that Paul's attitudes are continuous with Jesus' own teaching, on the basis of an analysis of the material relating to Jesus' attitude to law in Mark 2.1–3.6. *Jesus, Paul and the Law*, pp.10–36.

[94]   Dunn argues that scholars have tended too quickly to assimilate Paul's first-century concern with God's relationship respectively with the Jews and 'lawless' Gentiles with the Reformation concern with the relationship between works and grace. This assimilation gives rise to the problem of accounting for Paul's continuing respect for the law when it is not functioning socially to distinguish Jew from Gentile. 'The law as fixing a particular social identity, as encouraging a sense of national superiority and presumption of divine favour by virtue of membership of a particular people – that is what Paul is attacking ... Divorced from that perspective, as the law understood in terms of faith rather than in terms of works, it can continue to serve in a positive role'. *Jesus, Paul and the Law*, p.224. Philip Esler has disputed Dunn's thesis on this score, arguing that Paul's argument in Galatians is that the *whole* law, and not simply the 'works of the law', which fix social identity, is made redundant by Christ. If Esler is correct, this only adds to the case I am making. Philip F. Esler, *Galatians* (London: Routledge, 1998), pp.182–184.

[95]   Rowan Williams, 'Resurrection and Peace: More on New Testament Ethics', in *On Christian Theology*, pp.265–275, p.266.

reliance on 'works of the law' that was reckoned to him as righteousness (Gal. 3.6–9; Rom. 3.21–30).

If it is not law *per se* but only law as the assumed guarantor of one's righteousness that is problematic, then that leaves open the question of the possibility of a different relationship to the law. Here the law could be received and understood as gift and yet its specific commands still be binding on God's people, the content faithfully expressive of God's will and its prescriptions consistent always with ultimate human good. In other words, might it be possible that one could know oneself justified by God independently of successful performance of the law, dispossessed of one's own righteousness, and yet hold moral discernment in any particular case to be finally determined by what the law commands? Indeed, might this be understood as part of the meaning of one's self-dispossession, the willingness to live entirely at the disposal of God's Word as expressed by the law?

Philip Esler has argued against that interpretation of Paul's meaning in the Letter to the Galatians. By claiming that 'the whole law is summed up in a single commandment, "You shall love your neighbour as yourself"' (Gal. 5.14), Paul is not (says Esler) leaving the ethical component of the law standing.[96] Rather, he is acknowledging that love of one's neighbour is 'the best the law can provide', 'while insisting that such love is available within the congregations from an entirely different source – the Spirit'.[97] Such love is the first fruit of the Spirit (Gal. 5.22), and the 'law and the Spirit are stark alternatives: "If you are led by the Spirit, you are not under law" (Gal. 5.18)'. That is, Esler continues, 'Paul is speaking of the replacement of the law by the Spirit, not the continuance of the ethical aspect of the law in the new dispensation in Christ'.[98]

This reading of Paul's meaning in Galatians, the insistence that in Christ love involves responsiveness to a living reality rather than adherence to the fixed prescriptions of law, resonates with my earlier discussion of rationalism and voluntarism in moral thought. Recall O'Donovan's recognition of the paradox of divine authority expressed in Scripture. God may command as God wills, and yet God wills to be faithful to God's word, steadfast and true. Authority is rooted both in God's power to command and in God's truth, and it is God's truthfulness, God's ultimate Reality, that constitutes God's power and renders my obedience to it 'whole-hearted' rather than simply capitulation to a despot. It is what renders obedience capable of transforming God's people into truthfulness, becoming themselves progressively more real as they live in accordance with God's Word.

---

[96]   Note that by 'law' (*nomos*) here, Esler suggests that Paul does not mean simply the Mosaic code, although that is its primary meaning in Galatians. The word can, however, have wider meaning and Esler points to Paul's use of the word *nomos* in connection with passages from Genesis (Gal. 4.21), from the psalms and from the prophets (Rom. 3.10–18). Thus, the 'word in this second sense refers to the whole of Israel's sacred tradition ... and is probably the equivalent of "scripture" (*graphē*) at Gal. 3.22'. *Galatians*, p.181.

[97]   Esler, *Galatians*, p.203.

[98]   Esler, *Galatians*, p.203.

God's commands, then, are given in service of the becoming of God's people: God's law is in service of the covenant relationship and can only be understood rightly in that context. Even the Decalogue, so often excerpted as a stand-alone set of moral prescriptions, presupposes the covenant expressed in its prologue: 'I am the Lord your God, who brought you out of the land of Egypt, out of the house of slavery' (Deut. 5.6; Exod. 20.2). The prologue invokes the story of what God has done for God's people and the meaning of the decrees and statutes is located in that story.[99]

What is the significance of that recognition? American theologian Paul Lehmann insists that it means

> we should stop aiming to *keep* the Commandments and instead seek to *obey* the One who gave them. We keep the Commandments whenever we follow the letter of the law with little or no regard to the humanizing presence and activity of God in the world. In contrast, we obey the One who gave the Commandments by seeking to understand through them what God has done for us to make and keep human life human and what God now calls us to do for others as well as ourselves.[100]

This recalls the striking understanding of obedience expressed by the Benedictine Laurence Freeman: 'Obedience is not doing what you are told, but becoming the Word you hear'.[101]

Paul Lehmann is known for his 'contextual ethics' and this conception of the way we are to read the law and its moral commands may seem to commend nothing more than a situation ethic based on a general principle of freedom or neighbour love, refracted through contemporary liberal values.[102] If I believe, for

---

[99]   Nancy J. Duff, 'The Commandments and the Common Life – Reflections on Paul Lehmann's *The Decalogue and a Human Future*', in Philip G. Ziegler and Michelle J. Bartel (eds), *Explorations in Christian Theology and Ethics: Essays in Conversation with Paul L. Lehmann* (Farnham: Ashgate, 2009), pp.29–44, p.40.

[100]   Duff, 'The Commandments and the Common Life', pp.40–41.

[101]   Laurence Freeman, *First Sight: The Experience of Faith* (London: Continuum, 2011), p.87.

[102]   Nancy Duff rejects the conflation of Lehmann's 'contextual' ethic with Joseph Fletcher's 'situation ethic'. While both Lehmann and Fletcher argue against the 'absolute and universal nature of moral law', they do so (she argues) for different reasons. Fletcher is concerned that the blind application of absolute law can lead to cruel consequences and so derives from the gospel a principle of *agape* that he applies as an act utilitarian. Christians should seek to promote *agape* to the greatest possible extent in each moral action. Lehmann is likewise concerned with the issue of cruelty, but more importantly considered 'that abstract, absolute moral laws and principles are inconsistent with divine revelation even when revelation takes the form of divine command'. And, for Lehmann, the context in which discernment of the will of God occurs is threefold. It involves not simply the context of the moral question itself, but also the overarching context of God's saving activity and

example, that to act consistently with the 'presence and activity of God in the world ... to make and keep human life human' means in our context recasting or even disobeying certain commandments or scriptural prescriptions,[103] how do I know this is not simply a manifestation of self-will opposed to God's will? Where is O'Donovan's difficult claim that the divine word may justly command us against our inclination or moral reason, against our present sense of what constitutes our 'good' or the good of others?

I do not think that something like Lehmann's account need deny this difficult possibility as long as we recognise that it cuts both ways. The divine law is understood as the Word of God written. In Christian understanding, it is this same Word that became flesh and dwelt among us in the person of Jesus (John 1.14) and is active as and through the Holy Spirit (John 14.23–24; Acts 1.8). To 'hear' this Word means listening with our whole being, open to the whole of God's transforming presence and reality. Sometimes this hearing may involve the written word of Scripture challenging the counterfeit reality of the world given to our present understanding and perception; sometimes it may involve the commandment or the enfleshed and enspirited Word challenging a legalistic reading of Scripture that, rather than communicating God's liberation and love, only mires its sticklers deeper in a web of unreality.[104] The paradox of rationalism and voluntarism in relation to discerning God's will is not solved by appeal to the written commandment alone, just because this paradox is internal to our truthful reception of God's Word.

James Alison has given profound personal expression to the moral risk generated by this paradox in his quest to be accountable to the fullness of God's Word as a gay Catholic. Writing a public 'Letter to a Young Gay Catholic' originally published in the journal *Concilium*, Alison claims the authority of his experience of reality (including the reality of God in Christ attested by the Scriptures) in defiance of the authority of the commandment against homosexuality as heard traditionally by the church. This act of defiance is, he says a 'refusal to believe something'. It is voiced as an objection, a '"but" in the back of my voice':

> But the God who is revealed to us in Jesus could not possibly treat that small
> portion of humanity which is gay and lesbian to a double-bind in the way the
> Church has come to do. He could not possibly say 'I love you, but only if
> you become something else', or 'Love your neighbor, but in your case, not as

---

the *koinonia* of the community created by that activity. 'The Commandments and the Common Life', p.34.

[103]   I have in mind not simply the law of Israel but, for example, Pauline teaching concerning the role of women in church and the subjection of wives to their husbands.

[104]   Jesus' teaching, spoken and enacted, concerning the Sabbath is an instance of this kind of 'hearing' of the law.

yourself, but as if you were someone else', or 'Your love is too dangerous and destructive, find something else to do'.[105]

Alison acknowledges that this is a risky place to stand. For 'the story hasn't ended yet':[106] the full 'scrutability' of God's purposes is not clear and we live in the time before the fulfilment of the eschatological promise. 'Neither do I know, nor do you know', he writes, 'whether my refusal to believe that God could possibly treat gay and lesbian people in the way that the village elders and the local court say he does, is a refusal born of faith in a love which will turn out to be true, or is simply a sign of my delusional flight into unreality'. For this reason, 'to invite you into the place ... of vulnerability and uncertainty until the story is brought to an end, is not something I do easily. It is a frightening place. For I cannot offer you a resolution'.[107] Of course, although Alison does not say this, it is equally a corollary of the fact that 'the story hasn't ended yet' that those who take the opposite view are in just as risky and frightening a place.

I suggest that it is recognition and acceptance of this humanly inescapable moral risk and vulnerability in our discerning of God's reality and will that leads directly to the gospel's injunctions against judging. If moral life is not simply a matter of fulfilling written commands or doing good as humanly perceived, but being responsive to the Word and will of the living God, then there is no straightforwardly accessible or infallible criterion by which we may judge ourselves or others. This does not mean we are not *accountable* for our discernment. It is just that only God is capable of making this judgement truthfully and completely. Part of the necessary vulnerability of moral life is surrendering final self-assessment or assessment of others to God. Bonhoeffer writes:

> Our self-examination cannot provide us with this or that evidence of our reliability and faithfulness, for we no longer have at our disposal a criterion by which we can judge ourselves; or rather, our only criterion is the living Jesus Christ himself. Our self-examination will therefore always consist precisely in surrendering ourselves completely to the judgement of Jesus Christ.[108]

And he cites Paul: 'I do not even judge myself; for I am not aware of anything, but I am not thereby justified. It is the Lord who judges me' (1 Cor. 4.4). Williams too notes that concern with self-assessment is finally a refusal to surrender judgement to God. It evidences a concern for one's own moral performance that Matthew's gospel describes as 'hypocrisy':

---

[105]   Alison, 'Letter to a Young Gay Catholic', *Broken Hearts & New Creations: Intimations of a Great Reversal* (London: Darton, Longman and Todd, 2010), pp.176–185, p.179.

[106]   Alison, 'Letter to a Young Gay Catholic', p.179.

[107]   Alison, 'Letter to a Young Gay Catholic', p.180.

[108]   Bonhoeffer, *Ethics*, pp.325–326.

When Matthew's Jesus uses the word 'hypocrite', as he so freely does in the Sermon [on the Mount], we must not think immediately of disjunction between inner and outer, of a problem about *sincerity*, but of the moral or spiritual weakness of someone who expects to be judged on external performance ... The 'hypocrite' has not learned that the self is not a sort of possessed object, to be refined or matured by conscious practice; the 'hypocrite' has to recognize the uncomfortable truth that the self's standing, the self's adequacy or excellence or attunement to God ('blessedness'), is out of the agent's control.[109]

In a similar vein, if I must surrender self-judgement, so must I recognise that I lack the wherewithal to judge others. Williams again: 'There is no secure access to the inner life of another, and if you judge by external standards, you may expect to be open yourself to equally shallow and unmerciful judgement'.[110] Bonhoeffer argues that those who use the law as a yardstick to judge their brothers and sisters raise themselves above the law, thereby seeking to replace God as judge. He too considers this primarily a question of hypocrisy because insofar as they focus on assessing the moral performance of others, these self-appointed judges relate to law in their own case in terms of being 'seen by others' (Matt. 6.1). The 'only appropriate attitude of human beings toward God is doing God's will'[111] and the 'doers' of God's will 'remain strictly focused on the word itself, and do not derive a knowledge from it that lets them become judges of their brothers and sisters, of themselves, and finally even of the word of God'.[112] Any relationship to God's word that allows for a 'sidelong glance' at the sinning brother or sister, any 'remnant of a judging attitude, would completely spoil the doing and turn it into pseudo-doing, into hypocrisy'.[113]

Here, however, we seem to run into a significant problem for Christian ethics. If each must discern for themselves the living will of God, then what kind of common moral life is possible? Does this insistence on the inescapably personal vulnerability and risk of moral discernment, this insistence on not judging, imply the illegitimacy of moral debate, challenge, disagreement and persuasion in the life of a community? How might a Christian ethic so conceived be capable of

---

[109]   Williams, 'Interiority and Epiphany', p.260. Williams goes on to suggest that Matthew (and Paul) ask in relation to these themes, 'can the moral agent relinquish the centrality of an image of herself or himself *as* moral agent? So long as we are, so to speak, polishing the image of the agent, what our actions show is a successful will; the *meaning* of the action terminates in the will's success. If we let go that image, the meaning of what is done is grounded in God, the act shows more than the life of the agent: it shows the character of the creator. But to get to that point, the discipline that the agent has to undergo is attention not to performance but to an interiority that is not to be possessed. It is visible and judgeable only by God'. 'Interiority and Epiphany', p.261.

[110]   Williams, 'Interiority and Epiphany', p.260.

[111]   Bonhoeffer, *Ethics*, p.326.

[112]   Bonhoeffer, *Ethics*, p.330.

[113]   Bonhoeffer, *Ethics*, p.328.

contributing to the discernment of a *common* good, the formulation of *public* moral policies? With these questions in mind, I turn now to what I claim is the third critical mark of a Christian ethic.

Compassionate

Here is an astonishing thing. 'God so loved the world that he gave his only Son, so that everyone who believes in him may not perish but may have eternal life' (John 3.16). So that human beings might be reconciled to themselves and each other, might share in the divine life and love, *God* suffered alongside us and for our sake. That is the testimony from the cross and resurrection and, suggests Douglas John Hall, is what caused Luther to understand divinity first of all *not* in terms of 'sovereign omnipotence (as it was for Calvin) but astonishing *compassion*'.[114] Compassion, from the Latin *com* (with) and *passio* (suffering), is the nature of God and, says Simone Weil, 'the effect and the sign of being united to God by love'.[115]

I have already argued through the examples of the monks of Atlas and Sister Helen Prejean that the love of saints issues in compassionate action capable of *being with* others and loving with God's own love without pity or condescension. In this section, I claim there is a further sense in which compassion, 'suffering with', is a critical mark of Christian ethics that shapes not only action but also the character and possibilities of moral discourse itself. That is, I suggest that participating in the eschatological reality of reconciling love makes possible an essentially *compassionate* moral discourse. By this claim I do not mean to commend a wishy-washy niceness or a fear of radical and painful disagreement; I mean rather to point to the possibility of moral discourse in which we continue to be 'members one of another' (Rom. 12.5) through suffering, frustration and seemingly infinite distance.

As long as I am seeking to secure my identity through possessing a goodness and righteousness of my own, or needing to defend my rights and interests against yours, moral disagreement will occur as threat. If, on the other hand, we each know ourselves held in being 'by God's free determination',[116] not needing to be 'right' in order simply to be, then moral discourse can proceed disinterestedly and generously. As Williams writes,

> [A] commitment to what might be called ... the *labour* of ethics can emerge only
> as the social world is freed from the assumption of basic and non-negotiable
> collisions of human interest. To put it another way, the self is free to *grow*

---

[114]   Douglas John Hall, *The Cross in Our Context: Jesus and the Suffering World* (Minneapolis, MN: Fortress Press, 2003), p.22.

[115]   From Weil, *First and Last Notebooks*, cited by McIntosh, *Mystical Theology*, p.234.

[116]   Williams, 'Interiority and Epiphany', p.250.

ethically (that is, to assimilate what is strange, to be formed into intelligibility) only when it is not under obligation to defend itself above all else – or to *create* itself, to carve out its place in a potentially hostile environment.[117]

I have focused thus far on the sense in which Goodness, love, and truthful discernment all arise from our being reconciled to God, our sense of being accepted gratuitously and loved into fullness. With the words I have just quoted, Williams articulates how genuine ethical converse arises from this same ground. It is within the reality and against the horizon of reconciling love that moral disagreement and struggle become potentially fruitful, since it is through our labouring faithfully before and within this reality that we may journey together towards deeper understanding and a vision of common good.[118]

This understanding of the ground and possibilities of moral conversation helps to resolve an apparent tension in theological ethics between individual discernment and communal accountability. In the previous section, I emphasised the moral risk and responsibility inherent in our necessarily personal discernment of God's call and will. I noted that faithful discernment presupposes the progressive transformation of the knower, and emphasised the injunctions against finally passing judgement on others or even ourselves. Judgement belongs to Christ; our discernment and our moral action are surrendered into God, which seemingly raises a difficulty for critical moral discourse in community. If my life 'is hidden with Christ in God' only fully to be revealed 'in glory' (Col. 3.3–4), then on what basis do we engage critically with our own or others' moral understanding and action?

Furthermore, this account of personal discernment appears to be in some tension with the New Testament's insistence that the key criterion for discernment of the Spirit concerns the effect of my practice and action on the community. If Christian life is sourced in being reconciled with God and so with each other, then the truth of my life is necessarily realised in communion. There is no private good over against the good of others, because my good and the good of all belong together. We are *all* one in Christ; 'our life and death is with our neighbour', wrote one of the desert fathers.[119] It is for this reason that Paul understood the good of the community, the good of the neighbour, to be the essential criterion for critical moral discernment, the fruit of the Spirit evaluated primarily in relational terms (e.g. 1 Cor. 14; Gal. 5.22ff).[120] This seems to imply that, if the community disagrees with or is disrupted by a particular moral policy or action, then discernment is at fault or at least seriously suspect. There is danger, however, in drawing this conclusion too swiftly, and I suggest that conceiving of compassion as a critical mark of Christian ethics guides us in holding this tension appropriately.

---

[117]   Williams, 'Interiority and Epiphany', p.250.

[118]   This is the principal argument of Williams, 'Interiority and Epiphany'.

[119]   See Rowan Williams, *Silence and Honey Cakes: The Wisdom of the Desert* (Oxford: Lion Publishing plc, 2003), p.22.

[120]   McIntosh, *Discernment and Truth*, p.112.

Left open by the appeal to relational criteria of discernment is the question of what counts as the 'edification' of the community, the 'good' of the neighbour in any particular case. The risk of uncritically deploying criteria of peace (say) as opposed to strife, unity as opposed to disunity, is the suppression of struggle and novelty in moral life or the conflation of love with comfortable consensus and the status quo. Such suppression might show itself differently according to ecclesial context. In conservative circles, moral consensus may be enforced fairly rigidly with little hospitality displayed towards serious moral disagreement or perceived transgression; in liberal contexts, there may be greater tolerance of difference but little engagement with its significance, and thus harmony preserved through a policy of mutual non-disturbance. In either case, what Williams calls the 'labour' of ethics is avoided. 'They have treated the wound of my people carelessly, saying, "Peace, peace", when there is no peace', says the prophet (Jer. 6.14). In such cases, the price of peace and unity is the premature closure or avoidance of questions whose true weight and meaning has not been faced and whose honest engagement may lead to a deeper and more truthful reconciliation.

How does conceiving of ethical conversation as itself a practice of compassion, a fruit of being reconciled to God, help to hold this tension between individual responsibility and communal edification, between peace as a fruit of the Spirit and disagreement and disruption as stages in the Spirit's bringing to birth a deeper reality and truth?[121] The key is grasping the sharedness of our life in the reconciled and reconciling reality of the risen Christ. We do belong together; we are members one of another. That does not mean that all our relationships are healthy, or that an important movement in moral life might not be resistance or challenge to the way things are. There are 'new things' to be born. Our belonging does mean, however, that we can never ultimately dismiss or abandon one another without at the same time diminishing ourselves. To be true to the deepest reality of our own lives means the willingness to be with and bear with the reality of others despite, at times, the struggle and pain of it. Moral life is one of the arenas in which this compassionate relationship is expressed and made possible by the resurrection of Jesus.

This has a number of consequences for the character of Christian moral discourse. It does not mean that disagreement and struggle are to be avoided; on the contrary, they may be embarked on with a basic trust and confidence that all such conflict is held within a deeper reality of communion. Ethical struggle occurs within this framework of eschatological hope and we remain brothers and sisters even across sharp moral disagreement. We must not be facile about this. O'Donovan's strictures against emptying the promise 'of its eschatological character' and of hurrying forward to 'premature fulfilment' apply here. There is no guarantee of easy resolution, and painful moral choices may have to be made in the face of upset, uncertainty and dispute. Christian moral discourse will be

---

[121]   Jesus said, after all, 'Do not think that I have come to bring peace to the earth; I have not come to bring peace, but a sword' (Matt. 10.34).

marked by patience, the willingness to take time in the hope that those disagreeing may grow into the 'same mind' through their shared openness to the Spirit (Phil. 4.2), but this does not mean that the waiting is endless and action paralysed.[122] Compassion, bearing with one another, may also mean risking decisive and divisive action in the hope rather than certainty of some future possibility of deepening truthfulness, reconciliation or forgiveness.[123]

My claim, however, is that it is a mark of Christian ethics that it remains open to 'the other' even if we must act before agreement is reached, and this affects the *tone* of Christian moral discourse. Although an ethic sourced in the reconciling love of Christ will seek clearly to name and stand against injustice and oppression, it will hope to do so in a way that holds open the possibility of friendship, repentance and reconciliation.[124] It will be characterised by humility, the painful awareness of the partial nature of its grasp of truth and the imperfect transformation of its love. Only this tone of voice arises from and testifies to the compassionate reality that informs, shapes and animates Christian moral life.

Moral Practice and Critique

How does an understanding of ethics as sourced in and responsive to an eschatological reality of living and reconciling love shape our moral lives, or provide guidance for moral discernment and choice? In response to this question, I have claimed that there are three critical marks of Christian ethics: revelatory

---

[122] It is worth noting the etymological connectedness of 'patience' with 'passion' in the Latin word *passus*, meaning 'suffering', 'undergoing', 'bearing'. This is the demeanour commended by the writer to the Ephesians: 'I therefore, the prisoner in the Lord, beg you to lead a life worthy of the calling to which you have been called, with all humility and gentleness, with patience, bearing with one another in love, making every effort to maintain the unity of the Spirit in the bond of peace' (Eph. 4.1–3).

[123] The story of the twenty-year process of discernment undertaken by the Quaker community in eighteenth-century America in relation to internal disagreement over the practice of slavery is an instance of the kind of compassionate moral discourse I have in mind. Led by John Woolman, some began to act on their conviction that slavery was wrong in advance of others, but in a context where all were actively committed to holding the tension long enough (for example, not banishing Woolman from the community) until the truth could become clear. Parker J. Palmer, *Healing the Heart of Democracy: The Courage to Create a Politics Worthy of the Human Spirit* (San Francisco: Jossey-Bass, 2011), pp.20–23.

[124] An exemplary instance of such an approach is Martin Luther King's exhortations to those campaigning for the civil rights of black Americans to love their enemies and forgive those who persecuted them: 'With every ounce of our energy we must continue to rid this nation of the incubus of segregation. But we shall not in the process relinquish our privilege and our obligation to love. While abhorring segregation, we shall love the segregationist. This is the only way to create the beloved community'. Martin Luther King, *Strength to Love* (London and Glasgow: Collins Fontana Books, 1969), p.54.

power, moral vulnerability, and compassion in moral discourse as well as practice. I said at the outset that these marks do not offer a set of rules by which to measure moral outcomes nor a fixed procedure for moral decision making. They clearly affect what kinds of response we might entertain in relation to particular questions or contexts, but they do not of themselves generate specific answers to specific problems. Rather, they help constitute and colour our moral imagination: they indicate what approaching moral questions from the resurrection might look and feel like, they suggest its tone and concerns. Let me then conclude this chapter with some brief and preliminary remarks about how these marks might function in moral practice and moral critique.

First, they suggest that we should not be surprised if Christian moral debate and practice is at times messy, unsystematic and painful. The recent debates within the Anglican Communion over homosexuality are a case in point.[125] Here we have a protracted moral disagreement that occurs at a number of levels. It concerns not only the presenting question of the morality of homosexuality but also the very process of Christian moral reasoning including the function and status of law in moral discernment, the relationship between individual and communal discernment, and the normative weight of unity and reconciliation as constitutive of moral truth.[126] We face questions about the limits of patience in seeking 'one mind' in the light of prophetic imperatives to act on 'the truth' as understood by different sides of the debate. A resurrection ethic does not protect Christian moral life from such difficulty and vulnerability; indeed, it may be that it intensifies it.

Second, I believe that the critical marks I have identified do offer resources for criticising a certain kind of Christian moralising. What can never be consistent with an ethic from the resurrection of the crucified is the strident and self-confident tone of those who are sure of their righteousness and innocence, the forging of an assured moral rhetoric over the bodies of individuals or groups cast out of fellowship. In my judgement, the tone of voice as much as the content of any moral prescriptions gives such discourse away.

Third, the mark of 'revelation' strikes me as significant and neglected. Philosophical and theological moral debate alike can become mired in the weary rehearsal of standard sets of arguments. Discussions of moral questions concerning the environment, sexuality, medical ethics and the like often begin by assuming that we know what it is that we are talking about, what is at stake, and the terms in which it is best conceived. The examples of Gaita's nun and Sister Helen Prejean indicate that that may not be so. What might open up in our moral lives, as individuals and communities, if we were to hold ourselves accountable

---

[125]   Note too James Alison's understanding that the same debate in the Catholic Church will be slow and painful. 'The Pain and the Endgame: Reflections on a Whimper', in *Broken Hearts & New Creations*, pp.186–208.

[126]   An incisive and painful account of some of these elements is offered by Giles Fraser in his Foreword to Andrew Shanks, *Against Innocence: Gillian Rose's Reception and Gift of Faith* (London: SCM Press, 2008), pp.viii–x.

for deepening our perception of what is before us, being transformed through our relationship to the living Christ so as to be capable of being present to and revealing reality more truthfully? This may be an experience of acute moral vulnerability, since the reality of God's life tends to shake up the false security of our lives and the concepts through which we understand them. Yet this may turn out to be the deepest contribution of an ethic of resurrection to the life of the world.

Chapter 5
Mortality and Moral Meaning

Christian language ... risks being unserious about death when it speaks too glibly and confidently about eternal life; it can disguise the abiding reality of unhealed and meaningless suffering. So it is that some of those most serious about the renewal of a moral discourse reject formal Christian commitment as something that would weaken or corrupt their imagination.[1]

Remember that you are dust, and to dust you shall return.[2]

St Benedict includes the injunction 'to see death before one daily' among the monastic instruments of good works.[3] Iris Murdoch insists that 'Goodness is connected with the acceptance of real death and real chance and real transience'.[4] In these conceptions, mortality and morality seem internally related. More than that, mortality seems to be constitutive of moral meaning and responsiveness. Take away death and we lose something morally significant. By contrast, James Alison claims that the meaning of goodness must be disconnected from death if it is to be true to the post-resurrection perception of God as 'brilliantly alive': 'If ... God has nothing to do with death, then ... what is good is in no way defined by death, and you are free to act in a way which doesn't respect the limits of good and evil which are imposed by living in the shadow of death'.[5] How are we to make sense of these seemingly incompatible visions?

I argued in Chapter 3 that the resurrection affects not simply the content of particular moral norms or values, but the horizon against which moral life assumes its shape, force and meaning. The effect of the resurrection on the horizon of our moral lives becomes acute as we contemplate the question of whether death is *internal* to our conceptions of moral responsiveness and significance.[6] Moreover,

---

[1] Rowan Williams, 'The Judgement of the World', in *On Christian Theology* (Oxford: Blackwell Publishers, 2000), pp.29–43, pp.39–40.

[2] From Liturgy for Ash Wednesday.

[3] *The Rule of St Benedict*, trans. Anthony C. Meisel and M.L. del Mastro (New York: Image Books, 1975), chapter 4.47, p.53.

[4] Iris Murdoch, *The Sovereignty of Good* (London: Routledge, 1970), p.103.

[5] James Alison, *Raising Abel: The Recovery of the Eschatological Imagination* (New York: Crossroad Publishing Company, 1996), p.42.

[6] Alison argues that the resurrection not only made available a perception of God as 'completely without reference to death', but that it has revealed thereby 'that every form of moral life is inadequate, because it doesn't go beyond death'. *Raising Abel*, p.42. See also John Milbank, 'Can Morality Be Christian?', in *The Word Made Strange: Theology, Language, Culture* (Oxford: Blackwell Publishers, 1997), pp.219–232.

the fact of human mortality remains. What, then, in the light of the resurrection, is an authentic relationship to our mortality and its moral meaning?

Mortality and Morality

The philosopher R.F. Holland called our mortality one of the 'big facts' of human life.[7] It is the limit that bounds our earthly existence, gives it shape and urgency. 'Man that is born of a woman hath but a short time to live, and is full of misery', says the funeral service in the *Book of Common Prayer*. St Benedict's injunction fits here, as does the extent to which it may be the imminent prospect of death that leads someone to seek reconciliation with another, or to face up to the truth of her life.[8] In these examples, the prospect of death is morally motivating. There are also deeper, conceptual links between mortality and moral life. In this section, I aim to explore some of these links.

The work of the philosopher Raimond Gaita is important here, although the context of his discussion is different. The focus of Gaita's argument is the inadequacy of philosophical approaches to morality that fail to notice the embeddedness of moral understanding and responsiveness in the whole of human life. It is in this context that he emphasises the significance of our mortality as part of the deep and philosophically unacknowledged background to theoretical accounts of morality.[9] I need to bring out a number of features of his argument, before I can suggest how it bears on our concerns.

Contemporary moral theories of both Kantian and utilitarian stripes seek to account philosophically for what makes human beings worthy of moral respect. Their response to this question typically involves the search for properties or features of human beings in virtue of which they are justifiably deemed morally significant, indeed of higher moral significance than other forms of life. That is because if we are to treat human beings as deserving of greater moral respect than other living beings, without that being merely a prejudice in favour of our own kind, then we must be able to specify the features in virtue of which such preferential treatment is justified.[10] The candidate properties usually boil down

---

[7] Raimond Gaita, 'Common Understanding and Individual Voices', in Jane Adamson, Richard Freadman and David Parker (eds), *Renegotiating Ethics in Literature, Philosophy, and Theory* (Cambridge: Cambridge University Press, 1998), pp.269–288, p.269.

[8] It seemed, for example, to be the immediate prospect of his execution that led Matthew Poncelet in the film *Dead Man Walking* to face the meaning of his crimes (see Chapter 4).

[9] Not only mortality but other 'big facts' such as sexuality, suffering, grief and so on inform our sense of life's meaning, says Gaita, and it is in relation to our sense of life's meaning that moral rules or virtues have the significance that they do. 'Common Understanding and Individual Voices', pp.272–273.

[10] For a powerful critique of this whole model of moral justification see Cora Diamond, 'The Importance of Being Human', in David Cockburn (ed.), *Human Beings* (Cambridge: Cambridge University Press, 1991), pp.35–62.

to properties of the mind – consciousness, rationality, the capacity to form strong preferences, and so on. These are called the properties of 'personhood'. On these accounts, being human is 'merely' a biological or species-designating description, and it is as *persons*, not as human beings, that we are deemed morally significant.[11]

Corollaries of this argument include that any being possessing the properties of personhood is deserving of the same respect, and that human beings who lack such properties may not be deserving of the respect due to persons.[12] So, for example, in the literature of applied ethics, the concept of personhood is often deployed in arguments concerning the beginning and end of life. Foetuses or those suffering irreversible brain damage are human but not persons, and therefore morally no more or less deserving of consideration than (say) animals or other forms of life with equivalent mental capacities.

There is a range of possible moral objections to this account of human moral value,[13] but Gaita focuses also on its philosophical inadequacy. He argues that the attempt to source or justify our moral value in properties of mind abstracted from their embeddedness in our human form of life distorts how moral meaning actually works. It is in this context that the moral significance of our mortality, among other features of our experience, may be seen. There are two strands to Gaita's argument. The first concerns what shapes our sense of the moral value of human beings, our sense that human beings are a particular kind of limit to our will and so, relatedly, the seriousness of morality.

For Kant, our rational nature, which includes our capacity to reflect, to choose our own ends, to be free rather than blindly directed by brute inclination, is of

---

[11]   Note that 'person' here means simply one who possesses the relevant properties of mind (the contrast term is 'human being'). It is not related to the theological notion of personhood as relational (where the contrast term is 'individual').

[12]   At the root of this philosophical discussion are both moral and epistemological concerns. On the one hand there is a moral imperative to treat like cases alike, to insist on non-arbitrariness in our ascriptions of moral significance. Thus, philosophers concerned with 'species-ism' argue that human beings who lack morally relevant properties of rationality, consciousness and so on deserve no higher moral status than animals with equivalent capacities. On the other hand, there is the desire to secure the grounds on which moral status rests by rational argument, with reference to specifiable and objective properties.

[13]   An account of the moral status of human beings that makes marginal to the moral community some of the most vulnerable among us seems, at the least, to be at odds with ordinary moral thought. There is a strong tradition in that thought that it is especially heinous to wrong the especially vulnerable. Gaita has written many times of the need for moral theory to keep among us the ineradicably afflicted. He has criticised not only arguments from personhood on these grounds, but also neo-Aristotelian conceptions of ethics emphasising the ethical significance of 'flourishing'. That emphasis, he suggests, makes it difficult to see how we could consider those 'steeped in severe and ineradicable affliction – those who have no prospect of flourishing – as the intelligible objects of ... respect'. Raimond Gaita, *Good and Evil: An Absolute Conception*, second edition (London: Routledge, 2004), p.26.

a qualitatively different value and significance from our other characteristics. It raises us, he thought, above nature, gives us a different and higher place in the universe than belongs to any other earthly creature. Our rationality, for Kant, is our distinguishing essence and that about us which merits above all else our respect, whether in our own person or the person of others.[14] On Kant's account, when we do wrong it is the rational nature in us which is harmed,[15] and it is that same rational nature which we violate in another when we fail to respect them.

The problem with this account of the meaning of evil done or suffered, notes Gaita, is that it cannot be inserted into non-philosophical contexts without parody and that necessarily raises questions about its adequacy. Take, for example, the moral response of remorse:

> Remorse often presents itself in the accents of a horrified discovery of the significance of what we did but it is trivialised if we try to express a murderer's horrified realisation in anything like this way: 'My God, what have I done? I have been a traitor to reason. I have violated rational nature in another!'[16]

It is true, Gaita acknowledges, that the moral significance we ascribe to human beings is partly conditioned by the fact that we are rational creatures, capable of reflecting on our lives, capable of seeking and responding to the meaning we find there. But 'it does not follow, and is not true' that moral respect is essentially *for* our rational nature and 'extractable ... as a disposition of all rational beings to one another, unconditioned by the concrete form which life takes for them'.[17] Rather, Gaita argues, the significance of our rationality as that which 'justifies' our moral sense of one another is parasitic on a much deeper and untheorised recognition of what human beings may mean to one another, on the fact that human beings 'have a power to affect us in ways we cannot fathom',[18] that another person's absence can make our lives seem empty, or that someone we have wronged may haunt us. It is because we can affect one another in such ways

---

[14]   Immanuel Kant, *Groundwork of the Metaphysic of Morals*, trans. H.J. Paton (New York: Harper Torchbooks, 1964), pp.92–96.

[15]   This is because to act wrongly is necessarily irrational. An action is rational only if we could will that it become a universal law; we cannot rationally will that an act (say) of dishonesty becomes a universal law because universal dishonesty would undermine the very possibility of speech.

[16]   Gaita, *Good and Evil*, p.33. Gaita goes on to remark that it is not only Kantian accounts that invite such parody: '"My God, what have I done? I have violated my freely chosen and universally prescribed principle that one shouldn't kill people under circumstances such as these!"' A similar point could be made of utilitarian accounts of the essence of wrongdoing. See Cora Diamond, 'How Many Legs?', in Raimond Gaita (ed.), *Value and Understanding: Essays for Peter Winch* (London: Routledge, 1990), pp.149–178.

[17]   Gaita, *Good and Evil*, p.28.

[18]   Gaita, *Good and Evil*, p.155.

that we experience human beings as unique and irreplaceable, and that evils such as murder mean what they do.[19]

Relatedly, where philosophical accounts seek to secure the universality of our moral concern on the grounds of our possessing the same supposedly morally relevant properties, Gaita argues that the 'we' of moral fellowship emerges to the extent that we experience ourselves as sharers in the same human condition, sharers in a realm of meaning. Only this background of shared meaning gives our possession of properties such as rationality their assumed moral significance. Gaita notes, for example, that when a slave owner denies moral equivalence to his slaves it is not because they lack properties such as consciousness or rationality, but because the slave owner does not see them as sharing in life with him, such that their possession of these properties means in their lives what it means in his own life. 'For the slave owner, the slaves' humanity is epistemically impotent. But the kinds of properties that philosophers generally believe to be morally relevant are fully visible to him'.[20]

And here, Gaita suggests, a sense of our shared mortality and its meaning may be constitutive of this fellowship. This comes out in his reflection on some remarks of Falstaff in Shakespeare's *Henry IV Part 1* (Act 4). Falstaff has been conscripting troops for the Welsh wars and taking bribes for releasing the fit:

> 'A mad fellow met me on the way', he remarks, 'and told me, I had unloaded
> all the Gibbets and prest the dead bodyes'. But when the Prince complains, 'I
> never did see such pittifull Rascals', he retorts, 'Tut, tut, good enough to tosse

---

[19]   It may be objected that responses like remorse, grief or love cannot be the grounds upon which our sense of the moral significance of individuals rests because such responses may be withheld from particular people, and yet they must be held to possess the same moral worth as anyone else. According to this objection, the moral significance of individuals must be grounded in properties that they possess, and not in the way that people contingently happen to respond to them. This objection, however, mistakes a conceptual for an empirical claim. Gaita is not saying that, as a matter of fact, we reliably respond to one another in certain ways and that, because we do so, appropriate moral concern is guaranteed. Rather, he is claiming that the reality and individuality of another human being revealed in the shock of a lucid remorse or love form the subject of morality itself. We could not derive the sense of human uniqueness and irreplaceability that underlies our sense of the seriousness of moral harms like injustice, betrayal and murder, simply by registering the presence of properties like rationality or sentience. There is, in short, 'nothing reasonable in the fact that another person's absence can make our lives seem empty' (Gaita, *Good and Evil*, p.155), but it is that we can mean that to each other that conditions the meaning of the wrongs we can do each other and hence the meaning of morality.

[20]   Gaita, *Good and Evil*, p.162. For the slave owner to come to 'see' his slaves as his moral equals, in other words, as capable of being deeply wronged or himself as answerable for their suffering, it would not be sufficient to point out their possession of certain properties. He must be able to recognise sorrow in their faces or depth in their lives.

foode for Powder, foode for Powder: they'le fill a Pit, as well as better: tush man, mortall men, mortall men'.[21]

Comments Gaita: 'Falstaff reminds the Prince of his fellowship and equality with "such pittifull Rascals". They are his fellow mortals. To speak this way of "mortals" is to speak of death in an accent of pity, and this accent is both expressive and constitutive of a sense of human fellowship'.[22] This is the fellowship and pity expressed, as we saw earlier, by the *Book of Common Prayer*. Gaita goes on to say that when someone speaks in such ways of our shared mortality the '"we" is not merely enumerative of beings who belong to the same class because of some common characteristic. It is the "we" that expresses fellowship and is conceptually interdependent with pity'.[23] Gaita does not argue that it is only our shared mortality that gives rise to this kind of fellowship, but he does claim that fellowship of this kind is the necessary background to our moral life. When this sense of fellowship is lacking, then no amount of appealing to equivalent properties can lead us to see another as 'with' us in life, their suffering meaning what 'ours' does, and so on.[24]

Drawing on Gaita's account, then, the claim that our mortality is internal to conceptions of moral value, meaning and significance can be explored in a number of dimensions. Death seems at least partly constitutive of our sense of the seriousness of moral questions: death makes our lives finite, which means not only that murder is an irreparable harm, but also that the many other kinds of suffering or deprivation that may blight a life cannot readily be redeemed. Relatedly, death conditions our experience of the fragility of human life, our sense of the irreplaceability of individuals, and hence the value and moral significance of every person. Finally, it is to the extent that we see others as sharers of the same human condition, that we recognise them as 'with' us in life. This is the 'we' of moral fellowship. Our shared mortality is not the only thing that generates this fellowship, but it is a significant feature of it and, as in Falstaff's case, may inform the character of our compassion for one another, our sense of both the pathos and dignity of being human.

I noted earlier that the context of Gaita's discussion is different from ours. He is concerned to point out the connections between moral meaning and its embeddedness in our experience of human life in the face of philosophical theories that neglect this interdependence. Gaita is right to insist that human moral life is

---

[21]   Gaita discusses this example as part of his argument concerning the inadequacy of the philosophical focus on 'rationality' as morally the most salient feature of human beings. *Good and Evil*, pp.24–25. Gaita is here quoting from Alan Donagan's discussion of this passage.

[22]   Gaita, *Good and Evil*, p.27.

[23]   Gaita, *Good and Evil*, p.27.

[24]   On this point see also Gaita, 'Common Understanding and Individual Voices'; Diamond, 'How Many Legs?'; Sarah Bachelard, 'Response to Bernadette Tobin', in Winifred Wing Han Lamb and Ian Barns (eds), *God Down Under: Theology in the Antipodes* (Adelaide: ATF Press, 2003), pp.216–224.

formed by the meaning things can have for us. It seems also true that mortality is one of the features of being human that significantly conditions our sense of the tenor and shape of life, and thus also conditions our sense of the seriousness of moral good and ill, of moral meaning and fellowship. How, then, does the proclamation of resurrection life intersect with this conceptual conditioning of our moral life by our mortality?

Morality's Complicity with Death

It may be true that moral life as we know it is internally conditioned by our mortality. It may even be that responsiveness to the human experience of mortality generates features of moral life, such as a quality of compassion or fellowship in vulnerability, that seem to deepen our lives. Even so, if the ultimate horizon of our life is resurrection rather than death, then is morality that relates to death *as* ultimate to some extent distorted or false? This is the central question that concerns me in this chapter. Before I engage it directly, however, I am going to explore a number of further respects in which moral thought may be formed by death. By contrast with the aspects of the interdependence of moral responsiveness and mortality emphasised by Gaita, the following account draws out seemingly more problematic features of that relationship.

I have already touched on the claim that it is our finitude that renders evils such as murder and injustice so serious. What concerns me in this section is that in the background of our moral lives is the sense induced by our finitude that life is scarce. Death, John Milbank suggests, makes life to be in short supply, death threatens life.[25] For that reason, he argues, virtue is defined as that which keeps death at bay, that which 'holds death back, inhibits death, protects people from death'.[26] It is 'paradigmatically heroism' and it is for this very reason in some sense reliant upon or complicit with death; 'ethics must covertly celebrate death, for only our fragility elicits our virtue'.[27] I shall return to this argument. For now, let me elaborate two ways in which the death-induced experience of scarcity or threatenedness may enter moral life. The first concerns the shaping of moral concepts; the second the habits of mind that affect our moral thinking.

Here is the next part of my argument in a nutshell. Certain of our moral concepts are shaped by our making death mean that life is in 'short supply'. If death does not mean that, then our moral responsiveness is potentially distorted not only at the level of conclusions we might draw about moral questions, but at the level of the concepts with which we attempt to engage them. But this distortion will only become visible if we see how those concepts appear in the light of an experience of life not threatened in the same way by death. I propose to explore

---

[25] Milbank, 'Can Morality Be Christian?', p.224.

[26] Milbank, 'Can Morality Be Christian?', p.224.

[27] Milbank, 'Can Morality Be Christian?', pp.220, 223.

this suggestion with reference to concepts of dignity and human rights, and I begin by considering the source and gravity of the concepts themselves.

What is the source of the claim, prominent in contemporary moral discourse, that all human beings possess inherent dignity and inalienable human rights? If the argument of the previous section is on the mark, it derives not directly from particular properties or attributes of human beings but has to do with the meaning we ascribe to human life. To speak of the rights or the inherent dignity of another person is not to describe some 'fact' about them, so much as to recognise and seek to express how they matter. This acknowledgement has the character of revelation. It is not forced upon us by reasons whose meaning is just obvious to any rational agent, and it is a recognition not cancelled by the empirical facts of inequality and indignity in human existence.[28] Such deep seeing is, as we have already noted, the work of love and may also be the accomplishment of art.[29] In his own way, Falstaff sees what might be called the inalienable dignity of the 'pitiful rascals' he recruits for the wars, and the poet Czeslaw Milosz has expressed the wonder internal to this recognition by pointing to the radical singularity of each life:

> Just as a sparrow on the roof, a field mouse,
> And an infant that would be named John or Teresa
> Was born for long happiness or shame and suffering
> Once only, till the end of the world.[30]

Just as Kant's sense of the moral significance of our rationality was tacitly dependent upon a deeper, untheorised sense of the meaning and wonder of human life, so too, I am arguing, are our concepts of rights and dignity.

---

[28]   Cora Diamond has pointed out that precisely this dimension of recognition, of being struck by the meaning of being human, underlies Kant's attribution of moral significance to our rationality. 'From a naturalistic or Humean view, reason may be seen just precisely as reason and nothing more, part of the way in which our actions are determined, part of the way in which we are able to satisfy our desires, whatever they may be. Reason does not (on such a view) show something special about the kind of creature we are or our place in the universe'. But, she says, just as for Kant the 'starry skies above him were not just starry skies, but led him to thoughts about man's place in the universe', so contemplation of our rational nature led him to think of the relationship between freedom and the empirical world, of what it is like to be a being with such a nature and hence 'the appropriateness of acting towards fellow possessors of reason in certain ways'. 'How Many Legs?', pp.172–173.

[29]   We have noted this kind of 'seeing' in Gaita's account of the love of the nun for the psychiatric patients, for example, and in Thomas Merton's recognition of the humanity he shared with the 'ordinary' folk of Louisville. See Chapter 4.

[30]   'And Yet', in Czeslaw Milosz, *Provinces: Poems 1987–1991*, trans. Czeslaw Milosz and Robert Hass (New York: Ecco Press, 1993), p.13. Copyright © 1991 by Czeslaw Milosz Royalties, Inc. Reprinted by permission of Harper Collins Publishers.

In the modern period, the *language* of rights and human dignity has been profoundly significant in articulating this recognition.[31] It has empowered people and groups of people to name their own moral significance and value, and to resist the unilateral imposition of values or identity by those with greater power. To claim one's rights or one's inalienable dignity may be an important moment in a process of liberation, enabling a necessary distancing from another's definition of my identity and interests. 'I/we am/are not what you have taught us to be and believe; to be what *we* truly are, we must reject *your* account of reality and overturn what it privileges'.[32] Despite this acknowledgement, however, there is a question about whether this language is fully adequate to the work it seeks to do, capable of nourishing and evoking the sense of human life upon which it tacitly relies.[33] Does over-reliance on this language, in fact, risk dissociating us from the reality it purportedly names and so risk distorting our moral responsiveness?

In Chapter 1, I discussed Raimond Gaita's account of his experience working in a psychiatric hospital with patients who were deemed incurable and who 'appeared to have irretrievably lost everything which gives meaning to our lives'.[34] He contrasted the love of the nun that made visible the humanity of the patients with the psychiatrists' sincere profession of their 'inalienable dignity'.[35] I have focused till now on the revelatory significance of the nun's love, but Gaita remarks also on what this episode suggests about the concept of dignity:

> It probably didn't help their cause for the psychiatrists to speak of the inalienable dignity of the patients I described. Natural though it is to speak this way, and although it has an honoured place in our tradition, it is, I believe, a sign of our conceptual desperation ... To talk of inalienable dignity is rather like talking of the inalienable right to esteem. Both are alienable; esteem for obvious reasons, and dignity because it is essentially tied to appearance. Like the protestation of rights to which it is allied, it will survive only if one is spared the worst.[36]

Simone Weil makes an analogous point about the notion of rights, which she considers to be inadequate to express the depth of certain moral wrongs, the deepest of our cries for justice:

---

[31]   Rowan Williams, 'Human Rights and Religious Faith', Lecture delivered at the World Council of Churches Ecumenical Centre in Geneva, 28 February 2012 (accessed http://www.archbishopofcanterbury.org/articles.php/2370/human-rights-and-religious-faith, 7 October 2012).

[32]   Rowan Williams, 'Interiority and Epiphany: A Reading in New Testament Ethics', in *On Christian Theology*, pp.239–264, p.242.

[33]   See Sarah Bachelard, 'Rights as Industry', *Res Publica*, 11/1 (2002): 1–5, p.3.

[34]   Raimond Gaita, *A Common Humanity: Thinking about Love & Truth & Justice* (Melbourne: Text Publishing, 1999), p.17.

[35]   Gaita, *A Common Humanity*, p.17.

[36]   Gaita, *A Common Humanity*, p.18.

If someone tries to brow-beat a farmer to sell his eggs at a moderate price, the farmer can say: 'I have the right to keep my eggs if I don't get a good enough price'. But if a young girl is being forced into a brothel she will not talk about her rights. In such a situation the word would sound ludicrously inadequate.[37]

Just as the language of dignity could not, in Gaita's experience, make visible the full humanity of the psychiatric patients so, for Weil, the language of rights cannot express the full meaning of the violation suffered by a young girl being forced into a brothel. Such language gets little grip on the desecration this involves, its radical refusal of recognition, and that means that if the notion of rights is all we have as a conceptual resource with which to articulate the wrong done to such a girl, we do not have the capacity to name the depth of the injustice she suffers. Though claiming to be not 'religious' himself, Gaita avers that talk of dignity and rights is inadequate replacement for being able to speak of the sacred. They are 'ways of trying to say what we feel a need to say when we are estranged from the conceptual resources we need to say it'.[38] It is in giving a fuller account of this judgement that, I suggest, we also glimpse the ways in which our concepts of rights and dignity may come to be complicit with death.

How is it possible that language that seeks to articulate deep recognition, responsiveness and respect for the wonder and preciousness of human beings might fail adequately to do so? Gaita and Weil both imply that the problem lies with the resonance of the concepts themselves. Just as Kant's appeal to rationality mistook the real source of our moral significance, so the appeal to our possessing human rights or dignity mistakes the real source of our value. It is not because we possess rights or have dignity that we matter; it is because we matter that we can say that we possess rights and have dignity. But we matter in ways that go deeper than can be expressed in this language. When someone is afflicted with the manifest indignities and humiliations of dementia or catastrophic brain damage, for example, to keep insisting counter-factually on their 'dignity' does not name what really matters about them, and does not help us to encounter their humanity or indeed our shared humanity. In such contexts, the attempt to fortify or deepen the concepts adjectivally, speaking of *inalienable* dignity and *unconditional* rights, only smacks of the 'conceptual desperation' of which Gaita has spoken.

Is this merely a verbal quibble? What is the problem with using concepts of rights or dignity to gesture at our basic moral significance and fellowship even if there is a sense of strain in some cases? The central problem, I suggest, is that they tend to undermine the possibility of recognising and receiving our mattering in ways that keep alive our belonging to one another and to a shared human condition. They suggest that our moral value is a matter of possession rather than gift, and that affects and distorts moral responsiveness in a range of ways. To explore this

---

[37]   Simone Weil, 'Human Personality', in Sian Miles (ed.), *Simone Weil: An Anthology* (London: Virago, 1986), pp.69–98, p.83.

[38]   Gaita, *A Common Humanity*, p.23.

line of thought, I am going to contrast the ultimate expression of our moral value through the concepts of dignity and human rights with its expression through the concept of the sacred. My discussion here is intended not as a direct argument for the 'sanctity of human life', but as an illumination of the differing possibilities for moral life implicit in these conceptions of human moral significance.

To speak of human beings as sacred locates their moral value in relationship to God.[39] On this understanding, our moral status is secured not by anything about us nor by anything we do, but simply by the free and gracious determination of God enjoyed in the same way by all.[40] It is gift and evokes gratitude – how amazing that it should be so. A feature of this understanding of human moral value is that it encompasses the paradox of our essential contingency and dependence, and our infinite mattering. On the one hand, you are nothing in and of yourself; you exist only through conditions and circumstances utterly beyond your control; you are dust and to dust you will return. On the other hand, you are a beloved creature, made for relationship with God and called to realise your unique vocation and potential, which is 'once only till the end of the world'.

Against this background, I am empowered to know my moral equivalence with my fellows, and so to claim my human rights and ask that my inherent dignity be respected. I am created equal and I belong equally to God and to the human family. The language of rights and dignity, emerging from this experience of common and gratuitous belonging, reminds us what is due to each one of us, simply in virtue of our shared origins and life. It is part of a process of furthering mutual recognition, expressing (as Williams puts it) the 'assumption of a basic empathy between persons living out the same human condition'.[41]

When the concepts of rights and dignity are disconnected from this larger background of gratuitous belonging, however, they tend to develop a different resonance. They encourage us to conceive of them as possessions, attributes belonging to us as individuals in virtue of which we should be respected and which we in turn are entitled to protect, uphold or extend. Rather than our value resting first and unconditionally upon our being recipients of God's love and creative determination, it becomes a potentially threatened commodity for whose defence we are responsible.

One consequence of conceiving our moral value in this way is its tendency to constitute ethical discourse as largely a strategy for managing or defending individual claims about competing rights and interests.[42] This is the basis of

---

[39]   This relationship may be expressed variously by speaking of our being created, our being in God's image, our being beloved children. See Williams, 'Interiority and Epiphany', p.249; Williams, 'On Being Creatures', in *On Christian Theology*, pp.63–78, pp.74–75.

[40]   'We are here, then, we are real, because of God's "word"; our reality is not and cannot be either earned by us or eroded by others'. Williams, 'On Being Creatures', p.72.

[41]   Williams, 'Human Rights and Religious Faith'.

[42]   Williams, 'Interiority and Epiphany', p.243; Sarah Bachelard, 'Beyond "Thou Shalt" Lies a Deeper Word: The Theologian as Ethicist', in Heather Thomson (ed.), *Embracing*

contractual ethical theory and although, as Williams points out, 'there are worse accounts' of the space of ethics, a serious problem is its difficulty generating anything like a conception of the *common* good.[43] We have already seen that there is a qualitative difference between the attempt to establish moral universality on the grounds of the equality of agents possessing the same empirical features, and moral universality established by the 'we' of fellowship. The latter conception has relationship internal to it, the possibility of mutual belonging and so of a common world of meaning, whereas the former leaves us 'always liable' to apprehend others as 'threat or rival'.[44]

When our moral status is secured by our each being beloved of God, then human moral differences must be worked through against this background of shared belonging and responsiveness to a reality that transcends us, before which we are each 'vulnerable or responsible'. This creates a moral space where my individual interests and needs have a voice, but it is a space for 'human negotiation that is not immediately trapped in rivalry'.[45] It allows for the possibility of moral growth and transformation, generated through shared answerability to one 'apprehended as other *equally* to my own project and interest *and* to any specific other subject in the field of negotiation'.[46] But when what is morally most significant about us is that we are each separately bearers of rights or dignity, then this seems to leave us without much room to grow morally and locked into an essentially competitive relationship. The moral task is not so much the negotiation of a shared sense of the good, but ensuring that 'my/our' rights and 'my/our' dignity are not denied or diminished.

Relatedly, a conception of our moral value expressed in terms of our purported possession of unconditional rights and inalienable dignity tends to generate a similarly threatened relationship to basic features of the human condition. In the same way that other people constitute potential threats to the freest enjoyment of my rights, dignity and interests, so too does illness, suffering, ageing and death. In certain circumstances, it is then as if I am required to defend my moral value against my humanity.

Consider, for example, the appeal to dignity in arguments concerning voluntary euthanasia. On the one hand, to argue for the moral justifiability of euthanasia on the grounds that one's dignity is at risk from illness and death seems incompatible with the claim that our dignity is inalienable. On the other hand, to the extent that such appeals are concerned with the preservation of dignity that is alienable after all, connected to the maintenance of a certain appearance in the world, there is a real question about their moral seriousness. Some people have an exaggerated sense of their own dignity. They cannot concede anything to their human frailty;

Grace: The Theologian's Task (Canberra: Barton Books, 2009), pp.103–118, p.109.

[43]   Williams, 'Interiority and Epiphany', p.245.
[44]   Williams, 'Interiority and Epiphany', p.243.
[45]   Williams, 'Interiority and Epiphany', p.244.
[46]   Williams, 'Interiority and Epiphany', p.244.

they cannot laugh at themselves. Appeals to the 'right to die with dignity' typically make no distinctions between conceptions of the dignity to be preserved. But why, then, are they assumed to be necessarily morally serious appeals?

These remarks are not intended as a rebuttal of every argument in favour of voluntary euthanasia, nor do I wish to trivialise the suffering and sense of humiliation and powerlessness that may lead someone to speak of wishing to preserve her dignity in the face of debilitating illness. But there is confusion and slippage in the assumption that appeals to our inalienable dignity are self-evidently morally serious or even conceptually coherent, which does not serve our engagement with this difficult question. Indeed, to say that what matters most in our moral response to a dying person is the preservation of their *dignity* seems to me radically to misname what is at stake. It is our capacity to be present, responsive to their humanity and ours that seems the real question. For our purposes now, the point is that when our conception of dignity is disconnected from our belonging to the human condition, with all its absurdity, frailty and vulnerability, then its capacity to reflect and engage with the deepest meaning of our experience, the most serious of our moral questions, is attenuated.

I have been exploring whether over-reliance on the language of human rights and dignity risks dissociating us from the moral meaning it seeks to express and so risks distorting our moral responsiveness. I have argued that, at their deepest, the concepts of human rights and dignity are expressions of the wondering recognition that human life matters in the way that it does, and that each human life matters in the same way. I have also argued that, insofar as they become dissociated from a lively sense of the gratuity of our value and shaped without reference to a deeper sense of belonging to others and the human condition, then they lose touch with their own conceptual roots. When that happens, the insistent assertion of our rights or dignity in the face of threat can sound shrill or beside the point, a kind of whistling in the dark. Instead of 'serving an awareness of infinite human distinctiveness', it becomes no more than 'a catalogue of entitlements', 'a purely aspirational matter'.[47] But how is this tendency to dissociation connected to our relationship to death, particularly to a sense of life as threatened by death? What is the argument for my claim that, in their dissociated form, these moral concepts are complicit with death?

Notice that, once my essential moral significance is expressed in terms of my rights and my inherent dignity, and once these features of myself become possessions, things I am entitled to defend or extend in the face of threat, then my moral value begins to look encroached upon, something that I must author or defend in the face of the claims of others, in the face of the threatened indignities of illness and ageing, and, finally, in the face of death itself. Resistance to threat, and ultimately to scarcity and death, constitute not only the occasion of my resort

---

[47]   Williams, 'Human Rights and Religious Faith'. In this context, Williams refers only to rights; I have included (somewhat against the drift of his discussion) the concept of dignity as suffering from the same difficulties.

to my rights, my dignity, but are built into the concepts themselves insofar as these concepts are disconnected from the context of gift and belonging.[48] They express an experience of moral meaning as essentially contentious rather than gratuitous. That is the sense in which they are complicit with and formed in reaction to death. This can be brought out further by seeing how the concepts of rights and dignity show up in the light of moral responsiveness that is liberated from the threat of death.

In the Acts of the Apostles we are told the story of Stephen. Accused of blasphemy for preaching the gospel, he further offends the high priest and the council of elders by reinterpreting the meaning of the Hebrew scriptures in terms of Christ. The crowd becomes enraged, but Stephen, on the brink of being stoned to death by the mob, is filled with the Holy Spirit and sees a vision of the resurrected and ascended Jesus. 'Look,' he said, 'I see the heavens opened and the Son of Man standing at the right hand of God' (Acts 7.55–56). For Stephen, this is no slightly sentimental gazing into heaven and pretending that horror is not there. As James Alison puts it, 'It was not just that the last seconds of Stephen's life were bathed in this heavenly light, but that what enabled him to tell the story he told to the high priest and his colleagues was exactly the fact that he was already living this vision'.[49] That is, Stephen was witnessing *from* the resurrection, testifying that the power of death had been overcome and that nothing need separate humanity from the love of God in Christ. He was, continues Alison, 'able to tell the new story which the risen victim had made possible, and, furthermore, live out this story in an absolutely coherent way, as if death did not exist, and do it to the end'.[50]

As with the examples of Sister Helen Prejean and the monks of Atlas, Stephen's living free from the fear of death generates new possibilities for moral response, including radical solidarity with those at risk from the world's violence and judgement, and radical forgiveness of those whose actions are still determined by the systems of goodness that deal out death (Acts 7.60). Furthermore, in its light we see also the relative poverty of the concepts of rights and dignity, their dependence on death for their urgency and weight.

To claim one's rights or the acknowledgement of one's inherent dignity matters when their denial leads to diminishment and, ultimately, death. Since we are vulnerable and mortal, these *are* morally serious claims. But if our mortality does not signify that we are ultimately separated from the source of life and from the capacity for love that is its fulfilment, then these moral concepts are relativised. They are important, but not ultimate. It would not be wrong to say of Stephen that

---

[48]   Brian Johnstone has distinguished between ethics based on an ontology of violence and ethics that, in the light of resurrection, assumes an ontology of peace in ways that resonate with this point. 'Transformation Ethics: The Moral Implications of the Resurrection', in Stephen Davis, Daniel Kendall SJ and Gerald O'Collins SJ (eds), *The Resurrection: An Interdisciplinary Symposium on the Resurrection of Jesus* (Oxford: Oxford University Press, 1997), pp.339–360, pp.349–350.

[49]   Alison, *Raising Abel*, pp.79–80.

[50]   Alison, *Raising Abel*, p.80.

he faced his death with dignity, but that way of speaking seems too poor to express the power that clearly possessed him. It does not capture the human possibility that he realised – the living of *his* life out of the power of God's love, connected to the open heaven, utterly unconcerned with his being a victim of humiliation or death itself. In the light of that reality, what does dignity or indignity matter?

The Dutch Jew, Etty Hillesum, writing in 1943 from a transit camp on her way to death in Auschwitz, expressed her experience of the open heaven in these words:

> I shall try to convey to you how I feel, but I am not sure if my metaphor is right ... The main path of my life stretches like a long journey before me and already reaches into another world. It is just as if everything that happens here and that is still to happen were somehow discounted inside me. As if I had been through it already, and was now helping to build a new and different society. Life here hardly touches my deepest resources – physically, perhaps, you do decline a little, and sometimes you are infinitely sad – but fundamentally you keep getting stronger.[51]

As the camp empties with transport after transport, Etty's letters convey the all-but-unspeakable horror and suffering and insanity of the 'fatal mechanism' in which she and her 'brothers and sisters' have 'become enmeshed'.[52] They convey also her profound attentiveness, her care and compassion for the suffering around her combined with her freedom from the power of despair, her extraordinary joy in life and trust in God despite everything. In her final letter, she writes:

> How terribly young we were only a year ago on this heath, Maria! Now we've grown a little older. We hardly realize it ourselves: we have become marked by suffering for a whole lifetime. And yet life in its unfathomable depths is so wonderfully good, Maria – I have to come back to that time and again. And if we just care enough, God is in safe hands with us despite everything, Maria.

She goes on:

> I myself fail to measure up in every way, of course. I can't cope with the many people who want to involve me in their affairs; I am often much too tired. Please give Käthe a cheerful look from me – and press your cheek to Father Han's for me, too? And do you still get on well together?[53]

These few lines reveal a life being lived beyond the power of death and fear. There is realism about the depth of suffering and the limits of her capacity to respond,

[51]　Etty Hillesum, *Letters from Westerbork*, trans. Arnold J. Pomeranz (London: Grafton Books 1988), p.78.
[52]　Hillesum, *Letters from Westerbork*, p.126.
[53]　Hillesum, *Letters from Westerbork*, p.144.

humility and acceptance of her frailty. There is deep sadness, together with an astounding capacity attentively to engage with the lives of others – 'do you still get on well together?' In the face of the increasing certainty of her own death, here is a life not concerned with self-preservation but with love. From the standpoint of this kind of responsiveness to life, to be concerned for one's dignity or to claim one's rights, seems beside the point. This is not simply because, as with Weil's discussion of a young girl being forced into a brothel, to speak of the wrongs suffered by Etty and her fellow Jews in terms of the violation of their rights seems woefully inadequate. Nor is it because for Etty to have sought to claim her rights in such a situation would have been practically futile.[54] It is because from where she now lives, unbound by the fear of death, these are not the concepts that express what matters most deeply about her or about human life.

To be concerned for my dignity, to be concerned for my rights – these concerns have the weight they have in a realm of scarcity, life bound by death, a realm where I need to possess or author my life in the space before death. But when death is in some sense already accepted and behind me, when life stretches already into a new world, then they are revealed as having an assumption of scarcity built into them. In heaven love will remain, but no one will be claiming their rights or standing on their dignity. This should not be misunderstood as an argument for political passivity or quietism, an excuse for not confronting injustice or fighting for the preservation of life. It is simply an attempt to *place* these concepts rightly, and to recognise that only a culture enclosed by death and the fear of death would consider them the deepest expression of our human moral significance.

To say that certain of our moral concepts tend to complicity with death still leaves open the question of the difference resurrection makes. This will be the focus of the next section of the chapter. Before moving to that discussion, I need to sketch one further sense in which our moral lives and understanding may be shaped by our relationship to death, through the formation of our habits of thought and our rationality itself. I draw on Mark McIntosh's analysis of what it could mean to come to share the mind of Christ.[55]

McIntosh begins his discussion by noting that we readily grant the claim that aspects of reality are inaccessible to minds that 'have fallen into certain debilitating conditions', when we consider the distorting effect of prejudices such as racism or sexism on perception.[56] Drawing on both the New Testament and the writings of the desert fathers, McIntosh suggests that analogous forms

---

[54] Etty writes of the German guards: 'When I think of the faces of that squad of armed, green-uniformed guards – my God, those faces! I looked at them, each in turn, from behind the safety of a window, and I have never been so frightened of anything in my life. I sank to my knees with the words that preside over human life: And God made man after His likeness. That passage spent a difficult morning with me'. *Letters from Westerbork*, p.124.

[55] Mark A. McIntosh, *Discernment and Truth: The Spirituality and Theology of Knowledge* (New York: Crossroad Publishing Company, 2004), chapter 5.

[56] McIntosh, *Discernment and Truth*, p.127.

of cognitive distortion, false perception and judgement, can be identified by contrasting the thinking and responsiveness of those entrapped in habits of mind shaped by scarcity and fear of death as compared with minds operating out of the experience of plenitude and abundance.

What does our thinking and responsiveness look like when it is formed by assumptions of threatenedness and by anxiety about scarcity? McIntosh draws on Paul's Corinthian correspondence to suggest that it manifests as envy, rivalry, comparative judgement, and 'ceaseless sizing-up of one another'.[57] In the faction-ridden community at Corinth, for example, Paul identified various markers by which different groups sought to secure their own standing and identity, including appeals to their baptismal lineage, class status and cultural sophistication, and spiritual elitism.[58] The function of all these appeals is to secure status and validation according to the perceptions of others. This same pattern of rivalistic self-assertion is noted by the desert fathers, who, remarks McIntosh, 'provide a number of probing analyses of this mentality':

> What they uncover there is a toxic seepage among envy, anger, fearfulness about the frustration or loss of one's own desires, and a grimly deepening need to best others in order to restore one's own self-esteem.[59]

In the context of moral life, such a mentality issues readily enough in harsh judgement, resentment and grudge bearing, enjoyment of others' failure, gossip, miserliness, and so on.

A number of stories of the desert fathers illustrates the radical contrast between this mentality bound by fear and scarcity with a responsiveness that is learning to reflect the gratuity, self-dispossession and non-rivalistic love of God. One story tells, for example, of the complaints of the righteous brethren against others who 'irritatingly nod off during the liturgy'.[60] When they bring their complaints before Abba Poemen, expecting him to correct the slumberers, he remarks simply that, when he sees a brother sleeping, he puts his head on his knees and lets him rest. Comments McIntosh, 'Here the new reality begins to dawn, one suspects, in a very confused way upon the minds of the righteous brothers'.[61] There are many stories of the refusal of condemnation by the wisest of the monks, of abundant mercy and freedom from grasping at possessions and even at righteousness. There is the monk who offers to give thieves who have plundered his cell the goods they have overlooked, and others who undergo false condemnation or join in solidarity

---

[57] McIntosh, *Discernment and Truth*, p.133.
[58] McIntosh, *Discernment and Truth*, p.129. See 1 Cor. 1.12, 1.26, 2.14.
[59] McIntosh, *Discernment and Truth*, p.133.
[60] McIntosh, *Discernment and Truth*, p.141.
[61] McIntosh, *Discernment and Truth*, p.141.

with those under judgement.[62] 'In all these stories the old order of reality marked by need, condemnation, and rapacity is overtaken by an endless resource that not only grounds everything in mercy and forgiveness but makes an outpouring gift of the very thing which before could be perceived only as a scarce commodity to be grasped and possessed as one's own'.[63] Rather than being in thrall to the need for esteem and the approbation of others, there emerges the possibility of resting and living from confidence in the generosity of God's regard.

The point that McIntosh emphasises is not simply that a fearful and grasping approach to life issues in morally problematic behaviour towards others – envy, lack of generosity, impatience, fault finding, condemnation and so on. It is that such fear and grasping distort moral discernment and judgment itself. How we see others, whether we see them as they are at all, is affected by our freedom (or lack of it) from needing to compare ourselves and be approved of. What, however, does this have to do with our relationship to death? Suggests McIntosh, it is fear of death that lies behind it all.

When Paul preaches Christ crucified so insistently to the Corinthian community, he insists that Christ has nothing to do with their schemes for propping themselves up in the sight of each other and the world. Whereas they enviously proclaim or defend their credentials and standing, Christ on the cross has embraced 'the very status (slavery, humiliation, and death)' that they most fear. By accepting this status, Jesus reveals that it has nothing to do with God and so, suggests McIntosh, 'the cross becomes the basis of discernment because it grounds the mind in reality free from the distortions of fear, envy, and anger – all of which have as their ultimate bogey-totem the shame and humiliation of death itself'.[64] It is only a responsiveness grounded fearlessly in this reality that is capable of loving oneself and others truthfully, capable of the non-possessive and disinterested regard for others that knows them and allows them to be. So, he suggests, the 'paschal mystery seems to recreate human perception and understanding', such that rationality formed and complicit with death can be healed and awakened to partake of 'the limitless divine abundance that is the very ground of the mind's activity':[65]

> Persons whose entire existence has become attuned to this abundance no longer understand anything 'according to the flesh', as St Paul puts it; that is, they no longer understand reality in terms of a fundamental lack compelling all to anxious self-seeking but are instead awake to the endless mercy of God's giving life.[66]

---

[62]   McIntosh, *Discernment and Truth*, pp.141, 135. For example, there is the story of Abba Bessarion: 'A brother who had sinned was turned out of the church by the priest; Abba Bessarion got up and followed him out; he said, "I too am a sinner"'. Cited in Rowan Williams, *Silence and Honeycakes: The Wisdom of the Desert* (Oxford: Lion Publishing plc, 2003), p.29.

[63]   McIntosh, *Discernment and Truth*, p.141.

[64]   McIntosh, *Discernment and Truth*, p.136.

[65]   McIntosh, *Discernment and Truth*, p.127.

[66]   McIntosh, *Discernment and Truth*, p.127.

That is the sense in which freedom from the fear or threat of death is constitutive of truthful moral discernment.

Ethics Unbound by Death

I have been arguing that moral imagination is affected by the horizon of death. Consciousness of death strikes us in various ways, and the question of whether its formation of our moral responsiveness is actually a deformation is not easy to approach. I have argued that to the extent that death colonises life with a sense of scarcity, threatenedness or fear, it shapes our thinking and responsiveness to be less generous and open, more competitive and rivalistic than when responsiveness to life is free of that anxiety. The more we seek to secure or possess our lives in the face of threat, the more we are dissociated from our belonging to one another and to the human condition. This dissociation and consciousness of scarcity inflects the moral concepts through which we seek to express and secure our moral significance.

In reply to this argument, someone may agree that the fear of death[67] distorts our moral responsiveness (including some of our moral concepts), but that this says nothing about whether mortality itself falsely conditions our moral lives. Moral thought may indeed be distorted by fear of death in the same way that fear of death might distort moral choices on particular occasions, causing someone to betray their principles or run away in battle. But this does not mean that our mortality itself is a false and falsifying horizon. In other words, on this view, the problem for moral responsiveness is not death but the fear of death. If this is true, then belief in resurrection, eternal life, may be part of the problem. Instead of encouraging and empowering people courageously to accept the reality of human finitude, the doctrine of the resurrection becomes another way of avoiding truth.

Let us agree that fear or avoidance of mortality is liable to be morally corrupting. The question that remains concerns the relationship of our moral lives to the fact of death. At the beginning of the chapter, I contrasted the seemingly incompatible responses to that question offered by Iris Murdoch and James Alison. Where Murdoch insists that 'Goodness is connected with the acceptance of real death and real chance and real transience',[68] Alison claims that 'what is good is in no way defined by death' and that since God is 'completely without reference to death … every form of moral life is inadequate, because it doesn't go beyond death'.[69]

---

[67]   Noting that fear of death may be more or less conscious, and may show itself more in forms of evasion or avoidance than directly. Ernest Becker writes profoundly of the 'vital lie' that constitutes our identities and through which we seek to remain unconscious of our helplessness and vulnerability, including our vulnerability to death. *The Denial of Death* (New York: Free Press Paperbacks, 1997).

[68]   Murdoch, *Sovereignty of Good*, p.103.

[69]   Alison, *Raising Abel*, p.42.

It is important to clarify how these responses differ from each other, since a superficial reading might miss that they share the insight that Goodness (God) has nothing to do with death. Goodness (God) is beyond death. The difference between them is to do with their understanding of death, how their sense of what death is conditions their conceptions of what constitutes truthful moral responsiveness and imagination. For Murdoch, death is ultimate, the end of human life, and only in the light of our finitude do we see what Goodness really is. We see that Goodness has no purpose beyond itself and yet is the only thing that really matters. If we are to be Good, we must be good 'for nothing'. For Alison, death is not ultimate and in the light of eternal life we see what Goodness really is.[70] Goodness is endlessly alive, abundant, a giving, creative and transforming reality. If we are to be Good, we must be drawn into participating in this reality beyond the false horizon of death. For Murdoch, we recognise and love the Good for what it is, insofar as we are set free from the thrall of death. We are set free from the thrall of death by accepting absolutely the reality of our mortality and pointlessness, refusing fantasy and false consolation. For Alison, we recognise and participate in God's goodness, insofar as we are set free from the dominion of death. We are set free from the dominion of death by resurrection, the life of God breaking into human life and possibility, revealing and offering life without end.

As I have noted in previous chapters, neither of these visions of reality is straightforwardly susceptible of discursive proof. Murdoch recognises that her claim that life 'is self-enclosed and purposeless' is a view 'as difficult to argue as its opposite'.[71] I have insisted that our only access to resurrection is through testimony and the experience of life lived in response to that testimony, and Murdoch's account is similarly based. She testifies to an experience of reality, and invites us to share it: 'We are what we seem to be, transient mortal creatures subject to necessity and chance'.[72] What this means is that exploring and evaluating these different conceptions of the relationship between mortality and truthful moral responsiveness will involve exploring the effect of each on our moral imagination, their impact on the lived experience of moral life.[73]

---

[70]   Alison does not, of course, deny the biological fact of mortality, but he denies that it is the final fact about human life. Dying is an opening into greater life, rather than a dead end. That is what resurrection means. See also Milbank, 'Can Morality Be Christian?', p.224: 'moral law ... assumes and requires death's existence, since it always views death as an enemy to life rather than as the passage of life to further life'.

[71]   Murdoch, *Sovereignty of Good*, p.79. The difference between the imaginative worlds of a 'tragic' vision of basic purposelessness and an eschatological vision sourced in resurrection is well discussed in Robinette's reflection on Gerard Manly Hopkins's sonnet, 'That Nature is a Heraclitean Fire and of the Comfort of the Resurrection'. Brian D. Robinette, 'Heraclitean Nature and the Comfort of the Resurrection: Theology in an Open Space', *Logos*, 14/4 (Fall 2011): 13–38.

[72]   Murdoch, *Sovereignty of Good*, p.79.

[73]   This recalls my argument in Chapter 2 in which I endorsed Williams's contention that the claims to the truthfulness and universal significance of Christian theological statements

How is it, according to Murdoch, that in the light of our finitude we see what Goodness really is? It is because our finitude brings starkly into relief that Goodness transcends us and is not a function of our will or understanding. True virtue and love of the Good has nothing to do with my ego-driven needs and desires, my standing in the world, and nothing to do with securing life or identity or even meaning. Goodness transcends ego and transcends purpose: it is 'for nothing'.[74] If I am good in the hope of reward, or if I treat others well out of regard for my own reputation, then my virtue is counterfeit.[75] It is still enmeshed in what Murdoch would describe as the 'fat, relentless ego', and expressive at best of partial value and understanding, largely blind to the independent reality of others and of Goodness itself. So, she writes that it is 'a genuine sense of mortality' that 'enables us to see virtue as the only thing of worth',[76] and that Goodness is connected with the acceptance of death because the 'acceptance of death is an acceptance of our own nothingness which is an automatic spur to our concern with what is not ourselves. The good man is humble'.[77]

Murdoch's sense of Goodness transcending purpose and the ego's desire for identity and consolation resonates deeply with the Christian understanding of the Goodness of God. God's Goodness is distinct from any system of goodness that serves the need to be right and make others wrong, or to receive rewards for virtue. God's Goodness is not our possession. We are answerable to it infinitely, and no one is good but God alone (Mark 10.18). Murdoch's vision also echoes the theological understanding that, starting from ordinary human consciousness, all conceptions of the good, all moral vision and responsiveness, tend to distortion, simulacra of the real thing.[78] Her insistence on the connection between acceptance of mortality and the possibility of truthful living therefore reflects Jesus' understanding that the way to life and true goodness is to die to one's false self, to leave oneself

---

can only be made out by seeing if in fact the narrative of Jesus *can* offer resources for an ethic and anthropology that is liberating.

[74]   Murdoch, *Sovereignty of Good*, p.71.

[75]   This echoes Socrates' contention, in the face of his own death, that it is possible to enact the 'shadow' of virtue out of fear (for example, a courageous man may endure death but only because he fears to suffer greater evils, and is thus courageous because he is a coward). Only someone who loves virtue and wisdom without regard for death or reward is truly virtuous: '[I]s not all true virtue the companion of wisdom, no matter what fears or pleasures or other similar goods or evils may not attend her? But the virtue which is made up of these goods, when they are severed from wisdom and exchanged with one another, is a shadow of virtue only, nor is there any freedom or health or truth in her'. Plato, *Phaedo* 69b, trans. Benjamin Jowett (New York: Prometheus Books, 1988), p.82.

[76]   Murdoch, *Sovereignty of Good*, p.99.

[77]   Murdoch, *Sovereignty of Good*, p.103.

[78]   Recall Bonhoeffer's remark that Christian ethics opposes the knowledge of good and evil that is the concern of 'all other ethics'. Dietrich Bonhoeffer, *Ethics*, Dietrich Bonhoeffer Works, Volume 6, ed. Clifford J. Green, trans. Reinhard Krauss, Charles C. West and Douglas W. Stott (Minneapolis, MN: Fortress Press, 2009), p.299.

behind. Murdoch quotes Simone Weil saying that 'the exposure of the soul to God condemns the selfish part of it not to suffering but to death', and claims that only one who knows this death is likely 'to become good'.[79] Here is someone who is able to be good 'for nothing' or, in Meister Eckhart's striking phrase, to 'live without a why'.[80]

An essential difference between Murdoch's conception of the nature of goodness and the Goodness of God, however, is to do with how this self-dispossession, this death of the ego, is answered, by what reality it is met. The testimony from the resurrection is that death is not ultimate. There is death and there is burial, void and emptiness, but then, beyond reason or expectation, new life is given. This would be false, an illusory consolation, if we invented it or made it a reward for dispossession. It would be an evasion of death if it were assimilated into a natural and inevitable cycle of dying and rising. Sometimes life just does reassert itself 'naturally', but this is not what resurrection is about. Resurrection is gift, new life given from the future, life not on the same plane as death but larger life that redeems and renews what has died.[81] The testimony from the resurrection is that Jesus died, utterly dispossessed, and that Jesus was raised from death. He handed himself over to death, and the reality that embraced him was eternal life, life constituted as forgiving and reconciling love.

Murdoch recognises something like the possibility of resurrection *within* human life when she speaks of the void, the abyss into which we can be drawn by grief, despair, affliction, self-dispossession. When something in us has died and we refuse to fill the space, when we wait patiently on a truth that is not yet given to us, we may be met by a new and living reality as gift. She writes: 'The second best should be exchanged for void. (Try again. *Wait.*) We intuitively know about perfection. Art and high thought and difficult moral discernment appear as creation *ex nihilo*, as *grace*. The *Meno* concludes that virtue does not come by nature, nor is it teachable, but comes by divine dispensation'.[82] But for Murdoch, this gift of grace, truth, and new life is not the reality that meets us upon our physical death. It holds true as a possibility within life, but it is not the reality within which life itself is held. There is a fundamental discontinuity.[83]

[79] Murdoch, *Sovereignty of Good*, p.104.

[80] Bernard McGinn (ed.), *Meister Eckhart and the Beguine Mystics: Hadewijch of Brabant, Mechthild of Magdeburg, and Marguerite Porete* (New York: Continuum, 1997), p.13.

[81] See for example, Alison, *Raising Abel*, p.29. The themes of the 'surplus', the 'how much more' of resurrection and its coming from the future are elaborated helpfully in Devin Singh, 'Resurrection as Surplus and Possibility: Moltmann and Ricoeur', *Scottish Journal of Theology*, 61/3 (2008): 251–269.

[82] Iris Murdoch, *Metaphysics as a Guide to Morals* (London: Penguin, 1993), p.506.

[83] Laurence Freeman has written that faith cannot be certain of anything, including its testimony to the possibility of union with God experienced as progressive transformation during life and believed to continue after death. 'Maybe ... the light just goes out'. But, he continues, 'if the *logos* is the coherence of things and if the world has meaning, then there

From the point of view of moral imagination, what is the difference between these two conceptions of reality? If the possibility of transcendent Goodness can be conceived of and form moral responsiveness either by Murdoch's route of embracing our finitude or Alison's route of believing in the resurrection, what difference does resurrection make for moral life? What does it matter, in other words, *how* morality is freed from the corruption of the self-seeking, self-protective ego, as long as it does become free? How does it make a difference to moral imagination if void and death are the ultimate as opposed to penultimate realities of human life? This question is critical for my thesis that resurrection transforms moral imagination and possibility. To engage it, we need to remind ourselves of the content of the New Testament proclamation of resurrection.

It is possible to conceive of the resurrection of Jesus as communicating two distinct truths about reality. The first is that God loves us and forgives our sins; the second is that there is life beyond death, eternal life. This is right, but not if these truths are understood apart from each other. Sebastian Moore writes that, 'while scriptural exegesis distinguishes two great themes or motifs of redemption, namely expiation and passage out of this world to the Father, these are only two dimensions of one Christian experience. Endlessly they interpenetrate. For the way beyond this world – this human culture-defined world – to the Father is the way of forgiveness'.[84] We learn the relationship between these two 'motifs of redemption' by unpacking the meaning of forgiveness.

In Chapter 2, I emphasised that the New Testament shorthand 'forgiveness of sins' names a dense and transforming encounter. In the disciples' meetings with the risen Jesus, it entailed their realising the depth of their alienation from God and from themselves. Under pressure of Jesus' failure and crucifixion they had no longer recognised Jesus as revealing the truth of God, nor had they proved capable of remaining faithful to their own commitments. Whether through betrayal, denial or despair, they had been carried away from themselves, from one another and God. The risen Christ returning to them with loving acceptance revealed to them the extent of their blindness and fear, their inability to live truthfully or lovingly out of their own resources, *and* the answering, recreating love of God.

'Sin' in this connection, then, refers not primarily to particular moral transgressions but to the whole fear-driven and self-protective complex of human

---

is a continuation of this process [of transformation] beyond all horizons. It is conceivable that it is logical up to the very last minute and then it becomes illogical because something completely unimaginable happens. Perhaps there is nothing except meaningless expansion of space without *my* being in any way part of it. Yet as we grow in faith this seems less and less likely ... The reason is in how faith reveals love'. *First Sight: The Experience of Faith* (London: Continuum, 2011), p.95.

[84] Sebastian Moore, *The Crucified Is No Stranger* (London: Darton, Longman and Todd, 1977), p.60. This same theme is treated by James Alison, *The Joy of Being Wrong: Original Sin through Easter Eyes* (New York: Crossroad Publishing Company, 1998), chapter 4.

being and motivation, which issues in self-deception and violence in one form or another.[85] Jesus, the victim of this fear-driven complex at the heart of individual and common life, returns to his disciples in peace. Finally, they glimpse the truth of themselves and the death-dealing mechanisms internal to all human identity formation and sociality, and they see them in the context of being (despite everything) loved and forgiven. So, at the very same time as they are enabled to know who they really are and what they have been part of, they are invited to learn to live from a reality that has nothing to do with that through their relationship with Jesus.[86] Their forgiveness, then, is not simply an acquittal of wrongdoing, but an encounter that actively recreates them. They begin to understand that, all along, it has been God's intention to liberate them from captivity to fear and illusion, and to empower them for fullness of life. That is what forgiveness of sins means – it is the transforming expression of and encounter with God's love.

How is this forgiveness connected to the promise of eternal life, life (of some kind) beyond physical death? What does it mean to say, as Moore does, that 'the way beyond this world – this human culture-defined world – to the Father is the way of forgiveness'? It means *not* that eternal life is a reward for (imputed) good behaviour, but that death is constituted for us by sin. I shall try to spell out what this claim amounts to.

I have insisted already that sin wields death. Death can come figuratively, as when someone denies me, refuses to be with me, to see what life is like from my side, and so 'kills me off', oppresses or injures or judges me, holds a grievance, refuses relationship and solidarity. Death can come literally, as when the Good Friday crowds and authorities repudiate Jesus, casting him out and crucifying him. What softens the hardened and death-dealing heart is mercy or forgiveness, letting down a barrier, letting go self-righteousness, self-protection or self-assertion. What allows for that softening, that letting go into vulnerability and openness, is not having to secure my identity over against threat – the threat of being hurt, or being cast out and repudiated myself, or the threat of condemnation from myself or others. So what allows me to forgive, to show mercy, is being unthreatened, being loved, being forgiven, the experience of being accepted unconditionally.

When the crucified and risen Christ returns to his disciples as forgiving love, when he unmasks their hardness of heart and loves them anyway, they are offered release from having to maintain their righteousness or (its mirror opposite) from having to excoriate themselves and others. To the extent that they are willing to undergo this love and forgiveness, they are liberated from their imprisonment in guilt, shame, self-deception and desolation, and so released to forgive others their hardness of heart, their sin. In Chapter 2, I noted that this process of undergoing forgiveness is not without difficulty and pain: it involves acknowledging and

---

[85]   Recall that even what appears to be our 'goodness' and law-abidingness deal judgement and death through the systems of goodness that we construct to shore up identity.

[86]   See James Alison, *Knowing Jesus* (Springfield, IL: Templegate Publishers, 1994), p.16.

owning one's failure and fear so that one can be restored to wholeness without illusion. Recall Williams's remark that, for Peter to be restored to himself and called again, 'his failure must be assimilated, lived through again and brought to good and not to destructive issue'.[87] But to the extent that the disciples are enabled by the risen Christ to repent and be forgiven, they are liberated from the need to wield death or to protect themselves against death wielded by others. All forms of death, repudiation, humiliation, condemnation, are revealed by Jesus' resurrection from death to be limited, partial, not ultimate reality. What is ultimate is God's eternal love. So, as Moore says, Jesus breaks the power of death for us. 'But the *power* of death – as opposed to the fact of death – is due to sin, and so Jesus breaks this power by mediating the forgiveness of sin. There simply is no other way to break it'.[88]

What then of the *fact* of death? Its meaning is transformed:

> What a fuss we make about death! The way we think about death is the extreme case of the ego's habit of characterising a larger reality, of which it is part, by its effect on itself. 'Fog in the Channel. Continent Isolated.', a 19th century English headline read.[89]

According to Moore, our ego makes death what it is, lends it drama and significance. Death means the end of the ego's attempt to secure itself, to maintain its identity and self-possession, and that is why death is experienced by the ego as victorious over it. 'As though the water were to say, on reaching what *we* see simply as boiling-point, "the fire has conquered"'.[90] Death's meaning for us, in other words, is connected to our desire to constitute our own reality and hence to our isolation from the life process. It is in this way interdependent with sin, 'the constituting of our reality as *the* reality', the 'arrogation of divinity'.[91] And this is why is it *being forgiven* rather than acceptance of biological reality that brings us into true relationship with our mortality.

But why is it being forgiven, rather than, as Murdoch has it, simply undertaking the psychologically difficult work of 'accepting our death', that brings us into true relationship with our mortality?[92] I think it is because it is simply not possible for us to will the acceptance of our death such that its meaning is transformed. Any attempt we make to 'accept death' still relates to death as *the* reality, an 'event', a 'reification [which] reflects the illusory centrality of the ego'.[93] So the

---

[87]   Rowan Williams, *Resurrection: Interpreting the Easter Gospel*, second edition (Cleveland, OH: The Pilgrim Press, 2002), pp.28–29.

[88]   Moore, *The Crucified Is No Stranger*, p.54.

[89]   Moore, *The Crucified Is No Stranger*, p.56.

[90]   Moore, *The Crucified Is No Stranger*, p.56.

[91]   Moore, *The Crucified Is No Stranger*, pp.57, 56.

[92]   Murdoch, *Sovereignty of Good*, p.103.

[93]   Moore, *The Crucified Is No Stranger*, p.57.

meaning of death remains the same, and now we try to embrace rather than resist it. But it is the *meaning* of death as ultimate that is false and is revealed to be so by the forgiveness of sin which is the decentring of the ego. Remember that to know oneself forgiven in this way just means to know one's unredeemed self as largely illusory, constructed unavoidably by being 'over against' others. Moore writes that 'in Jesus we honour the man without sin … In contemplating his death we are forced to see human death in its primary meaning'. In Jesus there is no separate, defended self who needs to accept the 'reality' of his death. His death is not death (as we experience it) but 'return to the Father'. But we cannot share in that experience of human mortality without the decentring of the ego that comes through recognising and repenting of our attempts to possess our own security and our illusions of goodness and significance, and learning to let them go.[94]

The 'believer's eyes are opened to a world unclouded by culture-qualified ego-centred death *not* through some cosmic ideology but through the experience of forgiveness in its completed state. It is the deep, labyrinthine, complex and evil-complicated heart of man that has to be opened for the new world to appear'.[95] It is not, then, that through the resurrection we are forgiven our sins and also come to believe in life after death as a separate thing. Rather, we know eternal life, life not cut off by death, *as* our sins are forgiven, as we yield our meaning to God's meaning, receiving our lives as gift. 'And this is eternal life, that they may know you, the only true God, and Jesus Christ whom you have sent' (John 17.3). This is not a matter of a reward for believing something; it is the recreation or transformation of self through the dense encounter of forgiveness, being forgiven our being-towards-death and liberated into new life. So resurrection is not consolation for death, but a reality that we may enter now and that is beyond our ego-centred life *and* death.

To return, then, to my critical question: what difference does it make whether moral responsiveness and imagination are freed from the corruptions of the ego by embracing our mortality or by believing the resurrection? I have argued that it is being forgiven that recreates human being and transforms responsiveness, enabling us to let go that within us which wields death or seeks violently to defend ourselves from death (figurative and physical) wielded by others. This is the humility that transforms our relationship to others as our fellows and allows us to receive our own lives and meaning as gift. Murdoch also suggests that the good man is humble, but she connects his humility with his psychologically difficult acceptance of his own nothingness and mortality. I have argued, however, that we

---

[94]   This seems to have been the relationship to his physical death that St Francis of Assisi entered into during his life and expressed in his *Canticle of the Creatures*: 'Praised be You, my Lord, through our Sister Bodily Death, from whom no one living can escape'. Bodily death is part of our creaturehood, part of our belonging to creation and the human condition, and is to be embraced fraternally and in humility. But since our true life is in God, only the ego could think that this death is our end.

[95]   Moore, *The Crucified Is No Stranger*, p.60.

cannot simply *will* the acceptance of our death, and that the decentring of our egos that is the condition of an authentic relationship to our mortality is something we likewise undergo in the process of recognising and repenting of our sins, being reconciled to our alienated and illusion-ridden selves through forgiveness.[96] It comes from being drawn into a reality that we cannot assimilate, so that we are no longer at the centre of either our life or our death.[97] On this account, resurrection is not a consoling 'idea' by which we may evade the truth of our mortality, but is a reality encountered and entered through a kind of dying, the costly letting go of the illusory separate self and its death-dealing ways. We discover the truth of resurrection by living into it.

Moral Imagination and Mortal Beings

Where, then, does the proclamation of resurrection leave the moral imagination of mortal beings? For one thing, it places our thinking about death differently, and thus affects our sense of the seriousness of morality. This is a subtle matter. I noted at the beginning of the chapter Rowan Williams's concern that when Christians speak too glibly and confidently of eternal life, they risk not taking death seriously enough. At times, to my ear, both Milbank and Alison run this risk. Milbank, as we have already seen, claims that all customary morality covertly celebrates death, since virtue is defined as that which inhibits or holds death back. With the resurrection, something entirely different becomes possible:

> As resurrection cancels death, and appears to render murder non-serious, it restores no moral order, but absolutely ruins the possibility of *any* moral order whatsoever. That is to say, any reactive moral order, which presupposes the absoluteness of death.[98]

---

[96] Alison writes that forgiveness stretches into our human death: 'the forgiveness which flows from the resurrection affects not only such acts as we may have carried out, but, much more importantly, what we had hitherto imagined to be our very natures. If death is something that can be forgiven us, we were not only wrong about God, but we were fundamentally wrong about ourselves'. *Joy of Being Wrong*, p.118.

[97] Williams cites a passage from Iris Murdoch's novel, *The Red and the Green*, which expresses a recognition somewhat along these lines: 'The Christ who travels towards Jerusalem and suffers there can be made into a familiar. The risen Christ is something suddenly unknown'. The suffering Christ can be assimilated too easily into self-pity, the drama of the ego: 'This could not alter him a jot though he contemplated it forever. What was required of him was something which lay quite outside the deeply worked pattern of suffering, the plain possibility of change without drama and even without punishment. Perhaps after all that was the message of Easter. Absence not pain would be the rite of his salvation'. Quoted in Williams, *Resurrection*, pp.68–69.

[98] Milbank, 'Can Morality Be Christian?', p.229.

He goes on to assert that what makes murder wrong is not that it 'removes something irreplaceable', but that 'it repeats the Satanic founding act of *instituting* death, or the very possibility of irreplaceability, and absolute loss'.[99] In the resurrected order, however, there is no need to have a law against murder since all life partakes consciously of the creativity of God: 'the occasion for the exercise of death-presupposing virtue ... drops away, and only charity – gift and counter-gift – remain'.[100] In a related vein, Alison insists that, for God, death is 'nothing but a vacant form ... something whose reality has been utterly emptied out'.[101] 'Whatever death is, it is not something which has to structure every human life from within (as in fact it does), but rather it is an empty shell, a bark without a bite. None of us has any reason to fear being dead, something which will unquestionably happen to all of us, since that state cannot separate us effectively from the real source of life'.[102]

I agree that the resurrection transforms our sense of the meaning of death. In the light of resurrection, it is possible to face death not only with equanimity but even with joy (Heb. 12.2). But there remains in our human experience suffering associated with our mortality, and thus real harm inflicted by wrongs such as murder and injustice. Whatever resurrection life is, our death is really the end of *this* form of life and thus the end of certain ways of relating, certain ways of responding to our gifts and vocations. Death means our absence or the absence of those we love; it brings profound grief, loneliness and loss. Death might not be ultimate, but it is among the deepest of our sufferings. The loss of another, says Gaita, can make our lives seem empty. We do not honour the proclamation of resurrection by disguising that and this means that consciousness of mortality and human finitude rightly shapes our sense of the seriousness of morality, the gravity of moral harm, and the preciousness of human life.[103]

Nevertheless, if human life and death are held alike in a larger plenitude, if the resurrection reveals that 'neither death, nor life ... nor things present, nor things to come ... nor anything else in all creation' (Rom 8.38–39) can separate us from the love of God, then this makes a difference to our sense of the 'heaviness' of death in life. Moral responsiveness begins then to take on a different flavour, to

---

[99]   Milbank, 'Can Morality Be Christian?', p.229.
[100] Milbank, 'Can Morality Be Christian?', p.229.
[101] Alison, *Raising Abel*, p.29.
[102] Alison, *Raising Abel*, p.29.
[103] Timothy Radcliffe has protested against the Christian form of avoiding the reality of death by way of easy piety: 'If we do not endure sorrow and even anger, then we shall not be able to mourn. Faced with death, we should be desolate. There is a prayer for the dead, frequently and incorrectly attributed to Bede Jarrett OP, which claims that "death is only an horizon, and an horizon is nothing save the limit of our sight". And one wants to protest. It appears to trivialize death, as no more dramatic than a trip to London. Henry Scott Holland did not even think that he was going that far: "Death is nothing at all. I have only slipped into the next room"'. *What is the Point of Being a Christian?* (London: Burns & Oates, 2005), p.84.

have a different feel. Milbank speaks of the distinction between virtue that comes from plenitude rather than scarcity, from gift rather than reaction or sacrifice. For example, Luther, he says, understood stealing as a temptation not 'because there is a limited supply and we should allow others their share', but because it means we are acting from 'fear there will not be enough for us'.[104] The commandment not to steal is a commandment to trust God, to be generous: '[g]enerosity or true not stealing acts out of the assumption of plenitude, our confidence in God's power'.[105]

To the extent that our morality is heroic, dutiful and sacrificial, it is deformed by the assumption of death and scarcity. In the world we live in, still 'under the dispensation of death', it may yet be that what looks like self-sacrifice is required of us. But the true virtue comes from one who receives herself as gift and persists in giving, even in the midst of a world shot through with death. To act morally is to act out of plenitude, '*as if* there were plenitude, and no death'.[106] Milbank continues:

> Under the dispensation of death indeed, we only see gift via sacrifice, but the genuine sacrifice, supremely that of the cross, is only recognized as such in so far as it is the *sustaining* of joyful, non-reactive giving.[107]

Alison suggests that part of what this means is that God's goodness in the world shows up, not as a heavy moral programme that is always liable to turn into a system of goodness producing evil and exclusion as by-products, but in pointers, signs of grace.[108] I do not think this means we cannot attempt long-term and systematic moral reform (the abolition of slavery, working against unjust regimes or ideologies), but it transforms our being in relation to such projects. We can do this work with the *hilaritas* of the saint as opposed to the heavy virtue, the earnestness of the moralist. Self-giving is into life, not death, and there is thus a lightness, a freedom that becomes possible for the giver and is manifest in the world.

The resurrection means further that there is no radical discontinuity between human life and human death.[109] What happens on the other side of death is in some sense continuous with what is deepest in this life, and so being good 'for nothing' is not a kind of heroic or stoic *askesis* in the face of futility but the humble recognition that already my life and meaning does not belong to me as possession. 'So if you have been raised with Christ, seek the things that are above

---

[104] Milbank, 'Can Morality Be Christian?' p.225.

[105] Milbank, 'Can Morality Be Christian?' p.225.

[106] Milbank, 'Can Morality Be Christian?' p.229. This recalls, for me, Etty's demeanour in Westerbork.

[107] Milbank, 'Can Morality Be Christian?' p.228.

[108] Alison, *Joy of Being Wrong*, p.208.

[109] Alison remarks that the resurrection shows that, for God, death is not something that interrupts relationship, interrupts love. 'For God, death is as if it were not, which is why Abraham, Isaac, and Jacob live in God'. *Joy of Being Wrong*, p.116.

… for you have died, and your life is hidden with Christ in God' (Col. 3.1–3). Moral imagination shaped by resurrection rather than mortality is thus trusting and hopeful. It partakes of an openness and lightness, a sense of adventure and possibility, and these shape responsiveness even in the face of grave suffering and in the shadow of death.

Chapter 6

The Practice of Resurrection Ethics: Secularisation, Contemplation and the Church

> Now after John was arrested, Jesus came to Galilee, proclaiming the good news of God, and saying, 'The time is fulfilled, and the kingdom of God has come near; repent, and believe in the good news'. (Mark 1.14–15)

I have argued that the transforming event of resurrection affects the reality to which moral thought and life is responsive. In this respect, my argument shares the presuppositions of 'theological' or 'dogmatic' ethics. It claims there is no neutral account of being human or of reality in relation to which a timeless and universal rationality may develop a conception of the good or principles of right action. Rather, reality is a gift whose shape, meaning and purpose is revealed finally in the person and saving work of Christ. Paraphrasing Karl Barth, this means that Christian ethics is sourced in dogmatics, in our understanding of God and God's being towards us; and that dogmatics, our understanding of God, always implies ethics. Michael Banner elaborates on Barth's formulation as follows:

> [W]ith the insistence that dogmatics is ethics and ethics dogmatics, Barth asserts at one and the same time the essentially ethical significance of the subject matter of dogmatics, and the essentially dogmatic character of the presuppositions of a genuine ethics; he asserts, that is to say, that an account of the action of God is an account of an action to which certain human action properly and necessarily corresponds and by which it is evinced; and, conversely, that an account of good human action properly and necessarily makes reference to the action of God by which it is both evoked and warranted.[1]

---

[1]   Michael Banner, *Christian Ethics and Contemporary Moral Problems* (Cambridge: Cambridge University Press, 1999), p.3. Brian Johnstone distinguishes this 'dogmatic' approach to ethics as one of two main currents of reflection in Christian ethics. Represented by the work of Barth and Bonhoeffer, this approach holds that 'reality is defined in terms of the language of faith – Jesus Christ *is* reality'. 'Transformation Ethics: The Moral Implications of the Resurrection', in Stephen Davis, Daniel Kendall SJ and Gerald O'Collins SJ (eds), *The Resurrection: An Interdisciplinary Symposium on the Resurrection of Jesus* (Oxford: Oxford University Press, 1997), pp.339–360, pp.340–341. Oliver O'Donovan describes the principal orientations of his own work in similar terms: 'Purposeful action is determined by what is true about the world into which we act; this can be called the "realist" principle. That

A lazy complaint about this form of Christian ethical reflection is that it is incapable of engaging with those who do not share its presuppositions, and is thus irrelevant or unintelligible to those outside the community of Christian faith. The complaint is lazy because it implies, on the one hand, that there is the possibility of a neutral starting point for moral reflection and, on the other, that fruitful conversation between different moral 'worlds' is impossible. But all reflection begins somewhere; even secular liberalism presumes a background picture of reality for which it cannot provide full discursive justification. As for the possibility of conversation between persons inhabiting radically different conceptions of the world, we discover it in practice rather than guarantee it by translation from particularity to allegedly abstract universalism. Raimond Gaita has written:

> Great plays, poems and novels often have what is appropriately called a universal meaning (or truth), but they are not, thereby, suitable for translation into Esperanto. They are – and my point is that it is not accidental that they are – translated from one natural language to another.[2]

The suggestion that theological or dogmatic ethics is necessarily sectarian or applicable only to the community of believers is, therefore, simply false.[3]

---

truth is constituted by what God has done for his world and for humankind in Jesus Christ; this is the "evangelical" principle. The act of God which liberates our action is focused on the resurrection of Jesus from the dead, which restored and fulfilled the intelligible order of creation; this we can call the "Easter" principle'. *Resurrection and Moral Order: An Outline for Evangelical Ethics*, second edition (Leicester: Apollos, 1994), p.ix.

[2]   Raimond Gaita, *Good and Evil: An Absolute Conception*, second edition (London: Routledge, 2004), p.34.

[3]   Stanley Hauerwas has responded to the charge of sectarianism in relation to his work on a number of occasions, and along similar lines. See 'Why the "Sectarian Temptation" is a Misrepresentation: A Response to James Gustafson (1988)', in John Berkmann and Michael Cartwright (eds), *The Hauerwas Reader* (Durham, NC: Duke University Press, 2001), pp.90–110. See also Nigel Biggar, 'Is Stanley Hauerwas Sectarian?', in Mark Thiessen Nation and Samuel Wells (eds), *Faithfulness and Fortitude: In Conversation with the Theological Ethics of Stanley Hauerwas* (Edinburgh: T&T Clark, 2000), pp.141–160. Banner too responds to the charge of sectarianism levelled at dogmatic ethics. He counter-charges that, in fact, it is those who insist on the transparency of all moral thought to argumentative justification who are unable to speak universally or to the real situation of the world. That is because the 'world' whose reality needs to be engaged is not the limpid and rationally amenable world of modernity and Archdeacon Paley, but the opaque and much darker world of Dostoevsky, Conrad, and the 'genealogists' Freud, Nietzsche, Marx, and the like. In this world of painful obscurity and existential vulnerability, the suggestion that moral relativism must be 'overcome by the demonstration of the existence of an epistemological space in which rational ethics can make its way' requires the illusion that human knowledge of good and evil can, despite everything, be secured. Thus the insights of the 'genealogists' must to some extent be denied. But, says Banner, dogmatic ethics

I have also argued that resurrection transforms the subjectivity of those who undergo it. It thus transforms moral imagination not as an *idea*, but to the extent that it is *undergone* through experiences of forgiveness and re-membering, receiving one's life as gift on the other side of death and judgement.[4] This transformation liberates moral life and thought from the need to secure one's own righteousness and identity, and so from defensiveness in relation to others and even mortality itself. I have drawn on the example of the 'love of saints' displayed by Gaita's nun, the monks of Atlas, and Sister Helen Prejean to indicate the new possibilities for human solidarity and compassion, the habits of mind and deeper revelation of moral meaning made available because of this undergoing. In other words, I have emphasised that moral life sourced in the resurrection is not first a theory, but arises from live encounter with the risen Christ.[5] It is this live encounter that transforms subjectivity and so moral imagination, and it is with reference to what becomes possible through that encounter that the claims 'for the universal pertinence of the proclamation of Jesus' can be assessed.[6]

The church is the community that, in the post-apostolic period, is charged with communicating this encounter with the crucified and risen Jesus. This suggests

---

does not need to pretend that knowledge of good and evil can be humanly attained and 'hence does not require a repudiation of the genealogists in so far as their understanding of the world, in which claims to knowledge of the truly human are irredeemably insecure, is understood as precisely what it is – an account of the limits of a human understanding of the world. Humanly speaking the world is properly known as it is here represented. But dogmatic ethics does not know the world humanly speaking; the ground which the genealogists have taken away is not the ground on which it stands. It does not need to live in a world where there is a knowledge of the good and the right on which it can build, or to which it can appeal'. *Christian Ethics and Contemporary Moral Problems*, pp.43–44. This is because it proclaims wisdom from elsewhere, Jesus Christ, Goodness as grace.

[4]   Rowan Williams has said, 'resurrection is the transaction in human beings that brings about the sense of selfhood given not achieved'. 'Resurrection and Peace: More on New Testament Ethics', in *On Christian Theology* (Oxford: Blackwell Publishers, 2000), pp.265–275, p.271. See also my Chapter 2.

[5]   I have also drawn on the example of Etty Hillesum, who, though clearly undergoing a profound transformation of subjectivity connected to a process of letting go self-protection, did not convert to Christianity and did not use the language of encountering 'the risen Christ'. See the Introduction by J.G. Gaarlandt to *Etty: A Diary 1941–43*, trans. Arnold J. Pomeranz (London: Grafton Books, 1985). I have emphasised in other places that I do not claim that *only* life sourced in Christ can be present or responsive to the moral possibilities and meaning that are made available through the resurrection. However, I *have* argued that the necessary transformation is a much deeper matter than simply sharing certain values, and must involve something like the process of forgiveness, surrendering illusions of self-righteousness, and so on. The question of whether someone like Etty could be described as encountering Christ as one 'unknown' (Matt. 25) as a consequence of her fierce commitment to truth (for example) is a much larger one than I can address here – and of course, raises serious moral difficulties if any such re-description has supersessionist overtones.

[6]   Williams, 'Interiority and Epiphany', in *On Christian Theology*, pp.239–264, p.253.

that a theological discussion of the practice of resurrection ethics calls for some account of the role of the church in moral formation and in witnessing to the resurrection's transformation of moral imagination. This is right, I believe, and yet there are questions about how a form of life sourced in resurrection and embodied over time in the church may remain genuinely an *agent* of God's reconciling goodness and love rather than becoming simply another system of goodness.

In the first part of this chapter, I explore the claim that the church is integral to the practice of Christian ethics in the work of Stanley Hauerwas and Samuel Wells. There is much in their understanding of the interdependence of epistemological and moral formation, and the connection of these to ecclesial practice and the transformation of the self that resonates with the argument of this book. Nevertheless, I find myself uneasy at what feels like the suggestion of triumphalism in aspects of their writing. By exploring this unease, I engage the issue of the relationship between Christian ethics and a spirituality capable of calling and sustaining persons in community on the costly journey through cross and resurrection. Finally, this leads me to consider the relationship between resurrection and secularisation, resurrection as the definitive undoing of religion as a system of goodness, and its significance for the practice of theological ethics in the public world.

The Church

The centrality of the church for Christian ethics is emphasised by both Stanley Hauerwas and Samuel Wells.[7] Hauerwas writes that it is 'from the church that Christian ethics draws its ethical substance and it is to the church that Christian ethical reflection is first addressed'.[8] The church, Hauerwas notes, is the community both formed by and partly constitutive of the narrative of the God of Abraham, Isaac, Jacob and Jesus; it is answerable to this story and is part of the condition of there being a story to tell. He writes:

> The story of God as told through the experience of Israel and the church cannot
> be abstracted from those communities engaged in the telling and the hearing. As

---

[7]   Others also share this approach, but Hauerwas and Wells seem representative of it, evidenced in part by their joint editing of *The Blackwell Companion to Christian Ethics* in the Preface to which they express the hope that, 'years from now, this book will be seen as a milestone for Christians ... a new turn not only for Christian ethics, but also for the way Christians learn to live in that time often identified as "late modernity"'. (Malden, MA: Blackwell Publishing, 2004), [p.xiii].

[8]   Stanley Hauerwas, 'The Servant Community: Christian Social Ethics (1983)', in Berkmann and Cartwright (eds), *The Hauerwas Reader*, pp.371–391, p.373. See also Wells' claim that 'ethics is about the action of God embodied in the practices of the Church'. *God's Companions: Reimagining Christian Ethics* (Malden, MA: Blackwell Publishing, 2005), p.5.

a story it cannot exist without a community existing across time, for it requires telling and remembering. God has entrusted his presence to a historic and contingent community that must be renewed generation after generation.[9]

The telling of this story requires there to be people of virtue, 'specifically, the virtues necessary for remembering and telling the story of a crucified savior. They must be capable of being peaceable among themselves and with the world, so that the world sees what it means to hope for God's kingdom'.[10] On this account, Christian moral responsiveness is constituted in part by the formation of the habits of character and virtue that enable the narration of the story of God. Moreover, the 'story is not merely told but embodied in a people's habits that form and are formed in worship, governance and morality'.[11] In other words, the church is a community formed by a particular narrative and practice, and it embodies that narrative and practice in its worship and by its formation of persons whose lives testify to the truth of the story.[12]

According to Hauerwas, the first and most significant contribution of this community of character to common ethical discourse is that of 'being itself' and so showing the world 'what the world is meant to be as God's good creation'.[13] This follows from his famous dictum: '*the church does not have a social ethic; the church is a social ethic*'.[14]

> [T]he church must never cease from being a community of peace and truth in a world of mendacity and fear. The church does not let the world set its agenda about what constitutes a 'social ethic', but a church of peace and justice must set its own agenda. It does this first by having the patience amid the injustice and violence of this world to care for the widow, the poor, and the orphan. Such care, from the world's perspective, may seem to contribute little to the cause of justice, yet it is our conviction that unless we take the time for such care neither we nor the world can know what justice looks like.[15]

There are two important caveats or qualifiers to these claims. First, Hauerwas notes that the distinction he draws between 'church' and 'world' is not an ontological

---

[9]   Hauerwas, 'The Servant Community', p.373.

[10] Hauerwas, 'The Servant Community', p.378. See also Samuel Wells, *Transforming Fate into Destiny: The Theological Ethics of Stanley Hauerwas* (Carlisle: Paternoster Press, 1998), esp. chapter 6.

[11] Hauerwas, 'The Servant Community', p.373.

[12] 'Christians are people who remain convinced that the truthfulness of their beliefs must be demonstrated in their lives. There is a sense in which Christian convictions are self-referential, but the reference is not to propositions but to lives'. Hauerwas, 'Why the "Sectarian Temptation" is a Misrepresentation', p.100.

[13] Hauerwas, 'The Servant Community', p.375.

[14] Hauerwas, 'The Servant Community', p.374. Italics in original.

[15] Hauerwas, 'The Servant Community', p.375.

or institutional one. The 'world' is simply that realm which is unfaithful to its true nature as created and redeemed by God or which operates without reference to God's will. The distinction between church and world therefore 'runs through every agent' such that 'there is no basis for self-righteousness on the part of those who explicitly identify with the church'.[16] Second, Hauerwas does not deny that, as well as simply 'being itself', the church may contribute in other ways to public moral conversation and learn in turn from the wisdom of the 'world'. His claim remains, however, that Christian ethics must recover the 'integrity of the church as an alternative political community',[17] such that it is not simply seduced by a language or conception of 'reality' that does not reflect the revelation of reality to which it is called to bear witness. It is thus primarily through participation in the life and witness of the 'visible' church that people are formed in habits of virtue and character that reflect and manifest God's life.[18] And it is by making manifest and reflecting the character of life with God that Christians best serve the world, making visible its true destiny and revealing what is destructive or diminishing in much that passes for its dominant moral discourse and practice.[19]

Worship, the preaching of the word and the celebration of the sacraments, is the practice above all that forms this Christian community and enacts its service. Hauerwas speaks of baptism as the rite of initiation through which we do not simply learn the story of Jesus' death and resurrection, but become part of that story. Likewise, the eucharist is 'the eschatological meal of God's continuing presence that makes possible a peaceable people'.[20] In the eucharist, 'we become part of Christ's kingdom, as we learn there that death could not contain him', so that as we partake 'we become part of his sacrifice, God's sacrifice so that the world might be saved from sin and death'.[21] Thus baptism and eucharist, sacramental worship, are not simply religious things but 'the essential rituals of our politics', the way the church enacts what it is. 'These liturgies do not motivate us for effective social

---

[16]   Hauerwas, 'The Servant Community', p.376.

[17]   Hauerwas, 'Why the "Sectarian Temptation" is a Misrepresentation', p.102.

[18]   'There is no "ideal church", no "invisible church", no "mystically existing universal church" more real than the concrete church with parking lots and potluck dinners. It is the church of parking lots and potluck dinners that comprises the sanctified ones formed by and forming the continuing story of Jesus Christ in the world'. Hauerwas, 'The Servant Community', pp.382–383.

[19]   For example, Hauerwas introduces an essay on abortion, as follows: 'The church must address the abortion problem as church. Abortion is not fundamentally a question about law, but about what kind of people we are to be as the church and as Christians'. 'Abortion, Theologically Understood (1991)', in Berkmann and Cartwright (eds), *The Hauerwas Reader*, pp.603–622, p.608.

[20]   Hauerwas, 'The Servant Community', p.383.

[21]   Hauerwas, 'The Servant Community', pp.383–384.

work; rather, these liturgies are our effective social work. For if the church *is* rather than has a social ethic, these actions are our most important social witness'.[22]

These, as Duncan Forrester has said, are attractive notions, 'heady stuff'.[23] They resonate with my claim that moral imagination and moral selves transformed by the experience of resurrection reveal more perspicuously the true nature and possibilities of human life, empowering the witness to and practice of love beyond fear and violence. Yet, there are aspects of this identification of the practices of the church with the practice of Christian ethics that seem problematic.[24] In what follows, I elaborate on two aspects of my unease with this emphasis on 'ecclesial' ethics.[25]

An obvious problem for ecclesial ethics is the actual state of the church. In a poignant essay, Forrester has written of what appears to have been the damning failure of a particular church to 'be itself' such that it faithfully manifested God's 'peaceable kingdom' or proved capable of forming a community of subversive virtue. The church in question stands just outside the perimeter wire of the World War II German concentration camp at Dachau, 'a graceful little eighteenth century church, freshly painted and with a typical central European onion dome on the top of its tower'.[26] We do not know, Forrester notes, about the response of the wartime congregation of this church to the murderous operations in the camp next door, but some things are almost certain:

> The Bible would have been read, Sunday by Sunday, or day by day. There would, at least from time to time, have been preaching, expounding and

---

[22]   Hauerwas, 'The Servant Community', p.384. This theme is extensively explored in the essays comprising *The Blackwell Companion to Christian Ethics*. In the first chapter of this volume, Hauerwas and Wells explain 'why the authors of this volume have chosen to perceive the discipline of Christian ethics through the lens of Christian worship, most particularly the Eucharist'. 'Christian Ethics as Informed Prayer', pp.3–12, p.3.

[23]   Duncan B. Forrester, 'The Church and the Concentration Camp: Some Reflections on Moral Community', in Thiessen Nation and Wells (eds), *Faithfulness and Fortitude*, pp.189–207, p.206.

[24]   Oliver O'Donovan has remarked on the way in which Hauerwas turns to the practices of the church as the place where we learn what creation means through 'the new order' enacted by Christ's resurrection, as compared with his own turn to 'the Christ-event and the apostolic witness'. *Resurrection and Moral Order*, 'Prologue to the Second Edition', p.xv.

[25]   I take the phrase 'ecclesial ethics' from Wells. He sketches a threefold distinction 'in regard to the imagined location of Christian ethics': universal ethics based on common or universal principles; subversive ethics arising from the hermeneutics of suspicion and championing the cause of the oppressed; and ecclesial ethics, which shares the concern for the oppressed and which finds in 'the traditions and practices of the Church, its narrative, and its hope, a more subversive gospel than "subversive" ethics can ever articulate'. *God's Companions*, p.4.

[26]   Forrester, 'The Church and the Concentration Camp', p.192.

application of the message of Scripture. Bread would have been broken in the Lord's Supper, the Eucharist, the Mass, with the people receiving the Body and Blood of the Lord. From time to time children and even adults would have been received into the household of faith in baptism. God's praise would have been sung, and prayers offered for the Church and the world. All the ordinary central activities of a congregation of God's people within a hundred yards of Dachau concentration camp![27]

Forrester doubts that this congregation raised up prophets who dared to denounce the system of the camp and confront its evil: 'there is so little evidence of dissident voices from within the churches requiring to be silenced'.[28] Did it nevertheless strive to witness to the possibility of an alternative, non-violent reality to the prisoners, who could have seen it coming and going from worship? 'I hesitate', says Forrester, 'to press my questions towards an answer because I fear the truth about that little church would not be as I might wish it to be. In all probability it was just a quiet little congregation meeting in a much loved building, and carrying on as if nothing unusual was happening behind the wire close by'.[29] And by contrast, among the prisoners in the camp, an environment explicitly designed to be a context of moral *deformation*, 'goodness and love were found to be present, surviving and even flourishing in a hostile climate'.[30] John Milbank, Forrester remarks, 'makes a neat contrast between world and Church, the world represented by Aristotle's polis, ultimately founded on violence, and the Church, as the *civitas Dei*, the abode of peace. But when we turn to the world in which we live this contrast is shown to be dangerously facile'.[31] One is tempted, Forrester writes, 'to say that the church and the camp at Dachau provide an empirical refutation' of Hauerwas' claim that the church is a social ethic.[32]

Hauerwas knows, of course, that the church is not the kingdom of God, that it regularly fails to be faithful and remains subject to God's judgement. Indeed, it is precisely through worship, he says, that the church is required to 'be open to continual "reality checks"':

---

[27]   Forrester, 'The Church and the Concentration Camp', p.192.

[28]   Forrester, 'The Church and the Concentration Camp', p.194.

[29]   Forrester, 'The Church and the Concentration Camp', p.194.

[30]   Forrester draws on Tzvetan Todorov, *Facing the Extreme: Moral Life in the Concentration Camps* (London: Weidenfeld and Nicolson, 1999) for this discussion. Forrester, 'The Church and the Concentration Camp', p.200.

[31]   Forrester, 'The Church and the Concentration Camp', p.204.

[32]   Forrester, 'The Church and the Concentration Camp', pp.206, 195. 'For that church outside the perimeter fence at Dachau stands in a sense for every church although its locale is apparently so much more extreme and demanding. And if it is a church which neither has nor is a social ethic, its existence, and the existence of many another church just like it, raises awkward questions' for Hauerwas' epigram.

God comes to this community in the form of a stranger, challenging its smugness, exposing its temptations to false 'knowledge', denying its spurious claims to have domesticated God's grace.[33]

Forrester recognises that Hauerwas is 'perfectly aware' that 'the actual visible Church to which we belong falls far short of living up to its calling' and that 'the Church must be a community of forgiven sinners who have learned to live by grace rather than a fellowship of moral heroes and virtuous achievers'.[34] Yet that very acknowledgement raises the question of whether practices of ecclesial fellowship and liturgical worship are sufficient to constitute the church as a community that lives seriously from cross and resurrection, such that moral imagination and responsiveness is radically transformed. Christian life means not simply formation into a culture and its habits, but the transformation of what Sebastian Moore calls the 'labyrinthine, complex and evil-complicated heart of man',[35] the very identity of the desiring self. People can be baptised as infants and share the Eucharist for sixty years, and not undergo that kind of transformation.

Hauerwas recognises the need to distinguish between authentic and merely conventional versions of Christian virtue and character. For example, in an early essay on 'the challenge of Auschwitz for persons who intend to be Christian', he argued that Christian complicity with Auschwitz began with precisely this failure to distinguish between cultural and faithful formation:

> For the complicity of Christians with Auschwitz did not begin with their failure to object to the first slightly anti-Semitic laws and actions. It began rather when Christians assumed that they could be the heirs and carriers of the symbols of faith without sacrifice and suffering. It began when the very language of revelation became an expression of status rather than an instrument for bringing our lives gradually under the sway of 'the love that moves the sun and the other stars'. Persons had come to call themselves Christians and yet lived as though they could avoid suffering and death. So Christians allowed their language to idle without turning the engines of the soul, and in recompense, their lives were seized by powers that they no longer had the ability to know, much less to combat.[36]

---

[33]   Hauerwas, 'Why the "Sectarian Temptation" is a Misrepresentation', p.101. Wells also notes the empirical failure of the church to 'embody God's redeeming grace', and similarly notes that God's gift to the church of practices of forgiveness embodied in rites of truth-telling, reconciliation and so on provides everything that is needed for the church to be restored to itself. *God's Companions*, chapter 7.

[34]   Forrester, 'The Church and the Concentration Camp', p.206.

[35]   Sebastian Moore, *The Crucified Is No Stranger* (London: Darton, Longman and Todd, 1977), p.60.

[36]   Stanley Hauerwas, 'Self-deception and Autobiography: Reflections on Speer's *Inside the Third Reich*, with David Burrell (1974)', in Berkmann and Cartwright (eds), *The Hauerwas Reader*, pp.200–220, p.201.

In another essay, he speaks of the possibility and moral necessity of growth in Christian life, and the significance of 'attention to masters of that life'.[37] Even so, his discussion of how such growth in authentic Christian life might occur in practice lacks depth and real engagement with the endemic failure of the church.[38]

Relatedly, the evasion of the 'reality' of the church seems at times matched by evasion of the 'reality' of human life. This means that the appeal to liturgical meaning as the primary resource for Christian moral thought and practice may become ideological, addressing life as it 'should' be rather than engaging with what is. This is my second difficulty with features of the ecclesial ethics of Hauerwas and Wells. Wells, for example, discusses Christian marriage as an aspect of the sharing of life rooted in baptism and expressed most fully in the Eucharist.[39] It includes, he claims, friendship, finance, fun and food, and is 'the great proclamation of abundance'.[40] 'All is focused on a single other – but the truth is that, far from not being enough, that one person is more than enough'; thus marriage, he avers, is not 'a zero-sum game, where one person sacrifices their career, or their friends, or their creativity, or their deepest needs, so that the other can be the hero, or be the star, or never have to lose the argument'. This means that 'the end of a marriage … is a process of great sadness'.

> For an inability or lack of inclination to play together is a denial of the exuberance of creation. Meanwhile estrangement proclaims that this friendship has not sustained either pursuit of vocation or participation in community – or both. And adultery, so often a symptom rather than a cause, is not so much a defilement of the purity of the marriage bed as a proclamation of a message of scarcity – that this partner is not enough – that reduces everyone to poverty.[41]

---

[37]   Stanley Hauerwas, 'Character, Narrative, and Growth in the Christian Life (1980)', in Berkmann and Cartwright (eds), *The Hauerwas Reader*, pp.221–254, p.252.

[38]   Wells himself concedes that 'gaps in Hauerwas' work are most noticeable' in relation to the question of the formation of moral imagination in the Christian community, and that on this question his essays 'have never found the focus they require'. *Transforming Fate into Destiny*, p.121.

[39]   Wells, *God's Companions*, p.89.

[40]   Wells, *God's Companions*, pp.94, 96.

[41]   Wells, *God's Companions*, p.96. In a similar vein, Hauerwas speaks of 'Christian marriage' as between members of a community 'more determinative than marriage'. This means that 'we as church rightfully will hold you to promises you made when you did not and could not fully comprehend what you were promising … From the church's perspective the question is not whether you know what you are promising; rather, the question is whether you are the kind of person who can be held to a promise you made when you did not know what you were promising. We believe, of course, that baptism creates the condition that makes possible the presumption that we might just be such people'. 'The Radical Hope in the Annunciation: Why Both Single and Married Christians Welcome Children (2001)', in Berkmann and Cartwright (eds), *The Hauerwas Reader*, pp.505–518, p.517.

Ideally (eschatologically), of course, marriage is not a zero-sum game; ideally it is sustained by the abundance of God's gifts in the life of each person. But what if it isn't? A sharp challenge to this mode of moral engagement is offered by Alan Bennett's television play, 'Bed Among the Lentils'. Bennett creates the character of 'Susan', a vicar's wife, who tells her story by way of a monologue that the audience 'overhears'.[42] Susan is oppressed by the Christianity of her pious and ambitious husband Geoffrey, his pompous bishop (who calls her 'Mrs Vicar'), and the over-zealous ladies of the parish. For her, the marriage is empty. 'She bluntly avoids intimacy with her husband when at one point he awkwardly hints at it', but nevertheless 'tries to fill the role of dutiful vicar's wife', organising the church fête, visiting the sick, and joining ineptly in the intensely competitive flower arranging activities of Geoffrey's parish 'fan club'.[43] When she takes refuge from the deadly conformity required of her in drink and later in a brief but passionate affair with the Asian grocer, Mr Ramesh, for 'the first time in a long time – perhaps ever – she feels noticed, appreciated, and even loved'.[44]

This story, in one sense, proves nothing and it does not deny that 'the end of a marriage ... is a process of great sadness'. It does suggest, however, that waxing lyrical about the eucharistic abundance of the idea of marriage evades a great deal of the messy and painful reality of many marriages (including Christian ones). In this kind of context, doing Christian ethics liturgically, as if the question of whether to end a death-dealing marriage could be engaged adequately with reference to the promise of eschatological abundance enacted in the Eucharist, is untruthful and cruel.

I agree with Hauerwas and Wells that the church is called to make visible the eschatological kingdom of God and to communicate the difference that living from and in the light of this promise makes to human life and possibility. I agree that being formed by the practices of the church, particularly undergoing the embodying of its narrative in worship and common life, is potentially transforming of the self and so of moral imagination and practice. I realise that merely enumerating the failures of the actual church or actual Christians does not constitute a rebuttal of the claim that ecclesial ethics witnesses to and makes habitable a different moral reality.[45]

---

[42] Australian theologian, Graeme Garrett, discusses the play as part of a wonderful reflection on 'functional christology', the visions of Jesus that people actually live with. *God Matters: Conversations in Theology* (Collegeville, MI: Liturgical Press, 1999), pp.117ff. The play itself was first presented in 1987 on BBC television and subsequently published: Alan Bennett, *Talking Heads* (London: BBC Books, 1988).

[43] Garrett, *God Matters*, p.127.

[44] Garrett, *God Matters*, p.128.

[45] Philip Kenneson has rightly pointed out that the church learns to confess its own sin and idolatry in the light of its learning to praise and recognise the true God, and that in this way even its failure can become a source of revelation: 'The *ekklesia*, as an imperfect anticipation of what God desires for all of creation, seeks to conceal neither its faithfulness nor its unfaithfulness. For if the *ekklesia* exists for God's glory and not its own, then its

And yet, despite their acknowledgement of the fact of the church's failure, neither Hauerwas nor Wells engages seriously with the question of how such failure can so regularly occur in communities remembering and performing the rites that supposedly form Christians in holiness.[46] At issue is not simply that the church fails to live up to its own ideals. Perhaps even more disturbing is the fact that the church commonly becomes a 'system of goodness' as ruthless and vicious as anything in the 'world'. Rather than being an agent of God's healing and reconciling love, a Christian ideology may then be deployed against those whose lives 'fail' to conform to the alleged shape of eschatological promise.[47] Formation through liturgical worship may not only do little to prevent such reactions, but may actually be the means in part by which a solid ecclesial identity, over against what is not itself, comes to be shaped and defended.[48] Factions within Christian churches and disputes (often violent) between Christian groups have bedevilled Christian history and continue to do so. Given this, what is lacking in the accounts of the practice of Christian ethics by Hauerwas and Wells is a deep enough engagement with the distinction between conformation and transformation, the relationship between moral life, ecclesial practice and the costly spiritual process of repentance and conversion, questioning and stripping, which undoes any self-possessed identity and what Rowan Williams has called the 'fixed assumptions of religiosity'.[49]

---

willingness to name its own sinfulness – as well as have its sinfulness named by others – is itself a form of faithful witness to this God and this God's work'. 'Gathering: Worship, Imagination, and Formation', in Hauerwas and Wells (eds), *The Blackwell Companion to Christian Ethics*, pp.53–68, pp.63, 66.

[46] 'Holiness is the way Christians seek to imitate the character of God, and holiness is what Christians seek in worship ... The task of ethics is to assemble reminders from the training we receive in worship that enable us to rightly see the world and to perceive how we continue to be possessed by the world'. Wells, *Transforming Fate into Destiny*, pp.121–122.

[47] Noting the need for the church to live in continual penitence for its failure 'to *be* a community of gift and mutuality', Rowan Williams has asked: 'What kind of a gospel can plausibly be preached, for instance, by a Church which is unable to deal with the moral, emotional or psychological collapse of one of its ministers except by a mixture of frigid and embarrassed public silence and punitive internal discipline?' *Resurrection: Interpreting the Easter Gospel*, second edition (Cleveland, OH: The Pilgrim Press, 2002), p.49.

[48] I am thinking of the way in which the distinction between 'baptised' and 'unbaptised' can readily function in much the same way as the distinction between 'circumcision' and 'uncircumcision', or the way in which various criteria of eligibility to participate in the Eucharist become a badge of one's belonging (or not) to a community.

[49] Rowan Williams, *The Wound of Knowledge: Christian Spirituality from the New Testament to Saint John of the Cross*, second edition (Cambridge, MA: Cowley Publications, 1991), p.11.

Contemplation

All Christian prayer and worship is a response to, and an invitation to,participate in, Christ's life and love for the world. This participation necessarily includes undergoing the dynamic of death and resurrection, handing oneself over to God in trust, surrendering self-possession, and receiving one's life back as gift. Why? Because Christian prayer and worship is an invitation to be transformed into the likeness of Christ, able to love with the love of God, and involves letting go or being stripped of the illusory and self-dependent self. It is a process of healing that cannot be accomplished without some experience of wounding, of integration that goes very often by way of the experience of dis-integration. Writes Williams,

> Our healing lies in obedient acceptance of God's will; but this is no bland resignation. It is a change wrought by anguish, darkness and stripping. If we believe we can experience our healing without deepening our hurt, we have understood nothing of the roots of our faith. Jesus' obedience in the circumstances of his earthly life, in temptation and fear, 'with loud cries and tears' (Heb.5.7), is what opens the long-closed door between God and our hearts, and, although that door is now decisively open, all must still pass through it to make the reconciliation their own. They must now 'obey' Christ, surrender to the pattern of his sacrificial torment and death – not in some kind of constructed self-immolation, but in response to the trials encountered simply in living as a believer, in the insecurities of faith, 'the conviction of things not seen'. It is an acceptance of the hidden God and his strange work, the God who is attained only through stripping and the purgation of his 'consuming fire' (Heb.12.27).[50]

'All must still pass through it to make the reconciliation their own'. This is the meaning of baptism and Eucharist.[51] In terms of the formation of moral imagination, it is this same passage, this letting go of self-possession that makes possible responsiveness sourced in God's own love and Goodness, and characterised by the critical marks of revelation, vulnerability and compassion. The problem remains, however, the human tendency to co-opt the very practices and forms of life that are intended to enact this self-dispossession and union with God into further strategies for buttressing the defensive and self-justifying ego.

---

[50]   Williams, *Wound of Knowledge*, pp.20–21.

[51]   Wendy Mary Beckett writes that the essential act of prayer is to stand unprotected before God, who will take possession of us. In the strong 'objective prayer of the mass and the sacraments', 'we have Jesus giving himself totally to the Father and taking us with him. Then we can almost see, acted out before us, what the Spirit is trying to effect in our own depths. Let him effect it … Whatever the past or my fears of the future, here and now, O Holy Spirit, utter within me the total yes of Jesus to the Father'. Cited by Ruth Burrows, *Ascent to Love: The Spiritual Teaching of St John of the Cross* (London: Darton, Longman and Todd, 1987), pp.63, 68.

As the New Testament interprets it, this had happened in the relationship of the Jewish religious establishment to the Torah. For Paul, for example, the very gift of the law that had been given to Israel 'as the possibility of a pattern of behavior honoring God in every detail of individual and corporate behaviour', an expression of dependence, has turned into 'a matter of abstract demand, whose satisfaction can justify a sense of "claim" upon God's favour' and a 'means of oppressing self and others'.[52] Jesus, as Paul came to see, had stood against 'law' in this sense and, through his own radical dependence on God even through failure and death, made available to his followers a different source of identity, 'a different sort of standard for probity before God'.[53] But, in turn, the gifts given to the church to support its living in accord with this Christic standard are themselves all too readily co-opted to function as possessions and guarantors of security and status. Such a turn was evident already in the New Testament period, with Paul struggling to prise the Corinthian community from its self-satisfied assurance that it had 'entered securely upon an inheritance',[54] and with his repeated insistence that authentic Christian conversion and transformation means living through experiences of 'daily affliction, ... daily rejection, ... daily dying'.[55]

The question these reflections pose for resurrection ethics, then, is how in practice such an ethic might be learned and sustained. The history of Christianity amply demonstrates that no practice of worship, no form of religious life, can guarantee that it will not turn into a means of avoiding the very transformation it ostensibly invites and promises. When this happens, resurrection becomes empty dogma and moral imagination remains mired in the old dualistic oppositions. What, then, is a way forward? Anthony Kelly has remarked,

> Receptivity to the phenomenon of the resurrection, openness to the prodigality of its effect, must be both critically and contemplatively recognized as the ongoing and permanent condition for Christian thought and practice.[56]

---

[52]   Williams, *Wound of Knowledge*, p.16. See also Williams, 'Resurrection and Peace', p.266.

[53]   Not that he 'preached a programmatic disregard for the Torah as such', but he is remembered for 'defining the conditions for entering God's kingdom in terms of the readiness' to be like a child, to belong and trust, to make a simple commitment to follow his way, and so on. Williams, *Wound of Knowledge*, pp.16–17.

[54]   Williams, *Wound of Knowledge*, p.19. See also Mark McIntosh, *Discernment and Truth: The Spirituality and Theology of Knowledge* (New York: Crossroad Publishing Company, 2004), pp.128–133.

[55]   Being transformed by the Spirit into Christ's likeness, 'from one degree of glory to another' (2 Cor. 3.18) happens 'by means of the painful and inexorable experience of failure'. Williams, *Wound of Knowledge*, p.18.

[56]   Anthony J. Kelly, *The Resurrection Effect: Transforming Christian Life and Thought* (Maryknoll, NY: Orbis Books, 2008), p.175.

Beginning with this hint, I want now to suggest that the practice of contemplative prayer offers a way into the transforming dynamic of death and resurrection that is less vulnerable than other forms of prayer to being co-opted by the ego as a strategy of avoidance or self-protection.[57]

Two concerns may be raised immediately by this line of argument. Does it imply that encounter with the risen Christ or authentic Christian transformation is undergone only by those who practise contemplative prayer? Does it imply that contemplative practice is invulnerable to corruption by the religious ego? My answer to both these questions is 'no', and I shall expand on these matters shortly. I begin, however, with a fuller account of the practice and power of contemplative prayer.

Sarah Coakley has described contemplation as 'a regular and willed *practice* of ceding and responding to the divine', an '*askesis*' that is '"internalized" over time in a particularly demanding and transformative fashion'.[58] It is 'the defenceless prayer of silent waiting on God',[59] a wordless and focused attention. Such prayer is learned through a disciplined and intentional practice not only of silence but of laying aside thoughts, so that the silence gradually comes to be internal as well as external. This laying aside of thoughts is usually the work of years and 'may use a repeated phrase to ward off distractions, or be wholly silent; it may be simple Quaker attentiveness, or take a charismatic expression (such as the use of quiet rhythmic "tongues")'.[60] How is this prayer so profoundly transformative? It is to do with the way it both 'makes space' for the subtle and transforming presence of God and enacts the handing over (the 'death') of the self so as to grow into Christ. It is, writes Coakley, 'a feature of the *special* "self-effacement" of this gentle space-making ... that it marks one's willed engagement in the pattern of cross and resurrection, one's deeper rooting and grafting into the "body of Christ"'.[61]

Coakley is at pains to note that this 'self-effacement' is no violent expression of self-suppression or self-abnegation.[62] It is not the expression in prayer of what

[57]   Samuel Wells mentions a connection between Christian moral formation and contemplative prayer, but he does not develop this thought. *Improvisation: The Drama of Christian Ethics* (London: SPCK, 2004), pp.81, 84.

[58]   Sarah Coakley, '*Kenosis* and Subversion: On the Repression of "Vulnerability" in Christian Feminist Writing', in *Powers and Submissions: Spirituality, Philosophy and Gender* (Malden, MA: Blackwell Publishing, 2002), pp.3–39, p.34. For the purposes of this discussion, I am using the terms 'contemplation', 'contemplative prayer' and 'meditation' as synonymous.

[59]   Coakley, '*Kenosis* and Subversion', p.34.

[60]   Coakley, '*Kenosis* and Subversion', p.35. Christian teaching on contemplative prayer using the method of repeating a phrase or mantra to focus attention and let go of thoughts is sourced (among other places) in the *Conferences* of John Cassian and the anonymous fourteenth-century work *The Cloud of Unknowing*. In the twentieth century, the teaching of John Main OSB and Thomas Keating OSCO has generated movements teaching silent meditation to Christian laypeople, which have become respectively the World Community for Christian Meditation and Contemplative Outreach.

[61]   Coakley, '*Kenosis* and Subversion', p.35.

[62]   Coakley, '*Kenosis* and Subversion', p.36.

Williams has called 'constructed self-immolation'.[63] The basic contemplative insight, however, is that at a certain point we need to leave behind our thoughts and our self-consciousness, since these are the means by which we maintain our illusions of separateness and self-possession, the ego or 'false self', and avoid naked encounter with God. As the desert monastic tradition taught, 'Prayer is not perfect when the monk is conscious of himself and of the fact that he is actually praying'.[64] Coakley speaks of this practice in terms of 'self-emptying' and with reference to the 'hymn' of Philippians 2:

> 'Have *this* mind in you', wrote Paul, 'which was also in Christ Jesus'; the meaning of that elliptical phrase in Greek still remains obscure, but I am far from being the first to interpret it in this spiritual sense, as a 'hidden self-emptying of the heart'.[65]

Benedictine teacher of Christian meditation John Main acknowledged the difficulty we experience in leaving thoughts and self-consciousness behind, saying that

> [i]t requires nerve to become really quiet. To learn just to say the mantra and turn away from all thought requires courage … [M]editation is the prayer of faith, because we have to leave ourselves behind before the Other appears and with no prepackaged guarantee that he will appear. The essence of poverty consists in this risk of annihilation.[66]

There comes, he continues, 'a delicate moment in our progress when we begin to understand the totality of the commitment involved in self-surrendering prayer, when we see the total poverty involved in the mantra'.[67] This is the complete simplicity 'that demands not less than everything', but it is *this*, he says, that is

---

[63]   Williams, *Wound of Knowledge*, p.21. Such self-constructed immolation is one of the games the religious ego plays, as Ruth Burrows emphasises in her discussion of John of the Cross. *Ascent to Love*, pp.26–30.

[64]   John Cassian, *Conferences* IX.31, trans. Colm Luibheid (Mahwah, NY: Paulist Press, 1985), p.120.

[65]   Coakley, '*Kenosis* and Subversion', p.35.

[66]   John Main, *Word into Silence* (London: Darton, Longman and Todd, 1980), p.23.

[67]   Main, *Word into Silence*, p.23. Cassian speaks of rejecting and refusing the abundant riches of thought, 'grasping the poverty of this little verse', and 'saying it over and over again, … meditating upon it without pause', so as to come to the blessedness of true poverty of spirit. *Conferences* X.11, p.136. *The Cloud of Unknowing* likewise enjoins leaving behind all thoughts beneath a 'cloud of forgetting' since, no matter how good and holy they are, 'Thought cannot comprehend God'. To know God is not the work of thought but of love, and only insofar as thoughts are left behind can the darts of desire and love pierce 'the cloud of unknowing that lies between [us] and … God'. *The Cloud of Unknowing & The Book of Privy Counselling*, ed. William Johnston (New York: Image Books, 1996), chapters 6 and 7, pp.46–48.

the condition of entering with our whole beings into the movement of death and resurrection which is the great axis of Christian life.[68] It is not enough to think this movement, to imagine ourselves making it, or even to believe that this indeed is the ultimate axis of reality. We are invited to hand over our whole selves to God through letting go self-consciousness. The surrender of our thoughts in the silence of contemplative prayer is the means by which we hand ourselves over, and hold nothing back. 'Now perhaps this is the greatest thing that we can do as conscious human beings – to offer our consciousness to God. In offering it we become fully conscious'.[69]

The reason, I suggest, that contemplative prayer is less vulnerable than other forms of prayer to being co-opted by the religious ego is connected to this radical surrender of self-consciousness. Even 'good' thoughts, pious or religious thoughts are to be let go in its *askesis*. *As* thoughts they are not God, and so are less than perfect union with God, less than the prayer of God's own Spirit within us.[70] So then, says the anonymous English author of the fourteenth-century treatise on contemplation *The Cloud of Unknowing* 'you must reject all clear conceptualizations whenever they arise, as they inevitably will, during the blind work of contemplative love ... Be sure that if you are occupied with something less than God, you place it above you for the time being and create a barrier between yourself and God. Therefore, firmly reject all clear ideas however pious or delightful'.[71] Part of what this radical poverty means, then, is surrendering all grasping at feelings of consolation in prayer and the satisfactions of 'religious experience'.[72]

Of course, we can be deluded about the extent to which we have genuinely surrendered ourselves. John Cassian speaks of the temptations of the '*pax perniciosa*' (ruinous peace) and the '*sopor letalis*' (lethal sleep), both of which John Main considers aspects of 'the prayer of anaesthetized, floating piety'.[73] Cassian connects the false peace with the illusion that we have 'arrived' at a spiritual resting place that is now ours to possess and enjoy, and the 'sleep' with the failure even to notice that we have been carried away by our distracted

---

[68]   Main, *Word into Silence*, p.26.

[69]   John Main, *Moment of Christ: Prayer as the Way to God's Fullness*, ed. Laurence Freeman (Norwich: Canterbury Press, 2010), p.114.

[70]   'It is our conviction that the central message of the New Testament is that there is really only one prayer and that this prayer is the prayer of Christ. It is a prayer that continues in our hearts day and night. I can describe it only as the stream of love that flows constantly between Jesus and his Father. This stream of love is the Holy Spirit'. Main, *Moment of Christ*, p.x.

[71]   *The Cloud of Unknowing*, chapter 9, p.52.

[72]   I have discussed the issue of 'experience' in contemplative practice in 'John Main's Contribution to Contemplative Theology: "In meditation we verify the truths of faith in our own experience"', in Laurence Freeman and Stefan Reynolds (eds), *John Main: The Expanding Vision* (Norwich: Canterbury Press, 2009), pp.51–75.

[73]   John Main, *Christian Meditation: The Gethsemani Talks* (Tucson, AZ: Medio Media, 2000), p.37.

thoughts.[74] Both states constitute blockages in growth towards union with God. As by grace we recognise and leave behind these false resting places, however, the disciplined practice of silent contemplation constitutes a peculiarly direct yet profoundly subtle subversion of the ego. This is the significance of the insistence on faith in the hiddenness of God's work, and on trusting oneself to unknowing or darkness.[75] This is the inward and daily dying, without the felt reassurance that we are doing anything much transformative or holy, that draws us into the authentic dynamic of Christ's dereliction and faith-filled self-giving to God.

Yet if progress in contemplation is not to be measured by the felt experience of God in prayer, then how do we know that we are not simply lost altogether, wandering further from God rather than growing hiddenly into Christ-likeness? The only sure tests are our deepening personal integration and healing, and our love for the neighbour. 'We know that we have passed from death to life because we love one another. Whoever does not love abides in death' (1 John 3.14). 'The "unselfing" involved in union with Christ's death', writes Williams, 'is made real in the public and social world; the displacing of the ego becomes a giving "place" to others, as God has given "place" to all in his Son'.[76] In a similar vein, Douglas John Hall has written that faith 'is that trust in God [that] frees us sufficiently from *self* to make us cognizant of and compassionate in relation toward the other – in particular, the other who suffers, who is hungry and thirsty, who is imprisoned; the other who "fell among thieves"; the other who knocks at our door at midnight in need'.[77]

I have not claimed that contemplative prayer is the only means by which the self can be displaced from the centre of our life, and by which we may grow deeper into union with God. Other forms of prayer and worship invite the same radical 'handing over', as does authentic love and service of the neighbour.[78] Experiences of suffering, where 'the believer's self-protection and isolation are broken' and the

---

[74]   John Cassian, *The Conferences*, trans. Boniface Ramsey (New York: Newman Press, 1997), IV.7 and X.8.

[75]   In her discussion of John of the Cross, Ruth Burrows identifies the same essential dynamic: 'It seems we are asked to let prayer disappear, surrender our "spiritual life", have no control over it. Yes, this is what must happen. We have to give full space to the Spirit awaking within us, uttering his secret inarticulate prayer. This is true prayer. Even the best spiritual education cannot "do it for us". Each of us must choose to trust not our own subjectivity but the God of all goodness and fidelity as revealed in Jesus ... In all other areas of our human existence we can try to gain control, manage for ourselves; in this we must learn the opposite, learn to let go, let another take over, one we cannot see, feel or taste'. *Ascent to Love*, p.57.

[76]   Williams, *Wound of Knowledge*, p.23.

[77]   Douglas John Hall, *The Cross in our Context: Jesus and the Suffering World* (Minneapolis, MN: Fortress Press, 2003), p.152.

[78]   I use the qualifier 'authentic' because service of neighbour is another of the ostensibly self-dispossessing practices of Christian life that may in fact become the means of self-making and self-congratulation.

heart is cracked open 'so as to make space for others', are likewise occasions for the birth of 'a new humanness, "more capable both of pain and love"'.[79] Nor have I claimed that the practice of contemplative prayer is invulnerable to corruption by the religious ego. There are false resting places and there is always room for self-deception.[80] Cassian insists that whatever progress we make in prayer and in openness to God is God's work, and not ours. Even dedicated contemplatives do not control their own spiritual growth, and when they forget this they fall into pride and distortion. For this reason, the experience of spiritual dryness, being forsaken by God, can be a necessary grace, so that,

> seeing the frailty of our spirit, we may not become proud because of any previous purity of heart which has been granted us by his visitation; and so that, by proving to us that when we are forsaken by him we cannot regain that condition of joy and purity by any groans and efforts of our own, we may understand that even our previous joy of heart was conferred on us not by our own doing but by his condescension, and that present joy must be sought anew from his grace and illumination.[81]

Any spiritual practice, including the practice of contemplative prayer, is dependent for its efficacy on God's grace and initiative, and not on our accomplishment. What contemplative practice lays starkly and powerfully bare, however, is the necessarily cruciform passage to reconciliation or union with God, self and neighbour, its recognition of how narrow is the way that leads to life (Matt. 7.14). By attending to the theology and practical experience of this prayer, I have sought to articulate more fully the distinction between transformative and merely conforming habits of Christian life. Only the former sustains the practice of resurrection ethics.

How does this reflection make a difference to the way in which appeal to worship and ecclesial life might function in Christian ethics? It points to the falsifying triumphalism of any appeal to the liturgically enacted 'reality' of eschatological abundance that is detached from the compassion of the crucified Jesus and the cruciform way of discipleship. Earlier I criticised Wells's discussion of marriage. In the biblical tradition, marriage is an image of the final reconciliation of all things and the union of humanity with God. To reflect that reconciliation

---

[79]   Williams, *Wound of Knowledge*, p.21. See my *Experiencing God in a Time of Crisis* (Miami, FL: Convivium Press, 2012).

[80]   Coakley notes, 'no human, contemplative or otherwise, is beyond the reach of either self-deception or manipulation by others'. '*Kenosis* and Subversion', p.36. Recall in this context Iris Murdoch's sense of the significance for moral life of 'contemplation of the Good', but also her recognition of the difficulties and potential danger of this kind of prayer: it is, she says, 'the true mysticism, a kind of undogmatic prayer which is real and important, though perhaps also difficult and easily corrupted'. Iris Murdoch, *The Sovereignty of Good* (London: Routledge, 1970), pp.101–102.

[81]   Cassian, *The Conferences*, IV.4.

may be understood to be the vocation of Christian marriage and its sacramental gift to humanity. One of the prayers for marriage in *A Prayer Book for Australia* asks that 'their life together be a sign of your love to this broken world, so that unity may overcome estrangement, forgiveness heal guilt, and joy overcome despair'.[82] Yet to relate to every actual marriage as if it were already an instance of that image, or as if it could be if only everyone would try harder, is to deny the heartbreaking and crucifying work of the human journey, the truth that sometimes it is only in the failure of sincerely undertaken commitments and endeavours that we grow to maturity, or are able to name and repent of the deeper 'sins'[83] that have brought us to this point.

A former religious sister told me that, after years of struggling with her vows, she began to understand that she had undertaken them in the first place out of a need for security and the certainty of salvation. In the deeply frightening process of asking whether this was the life God wanted for her after all, she faced letting go of everything on which she had relied. At that moment, she said, she finally understood St Francis's divesting himself of everything to stand naked before the love of God. For her, the real poverty to which she realised she was being called was not the vowed poverty of religious life, but the deeper surrender and vulnerability of letting go her ecclesial strategy for self-protection. It may have been, of course, that through her struggle she could have remained a religious, although on an entirely different footing. It may have been that her maturing could have happened within the framework of the vows she had made. In fact, however, that was not how she discerned her situation. May not the same kind of struggle be undergone in the life of discipleship in the context of a marriage? As certain 'sins' are recognised and the call to deeper integration and reconciliation answered, there may be the possibility of transforming the basis of one's first commitment. But will it necessarily be so?

Resurrection ethics is sourced in the experienced reality of the reconciliation of all things in Christ, the re-integration and forgiveness of that which separates us from the source of life, from ourselves and each other, and so being transformed into Christ-likeness, apt to love with God's own love. The church is the sacramental sign of that reconciliation already realised, and exists (as Hauerwas says) to be and to witness to the alternative kingdom. It is equally, however, the community of those on the journey through the cruciform passage towards that reconciliation, a fellowship of people consenting to undergo encounter with the living God with all the risks of mess and unmaking that encounter entails. To the extent that an ecclesial ethic becomes a finished product over against the untransformed world, it begins to grasp at a righteousness of its own. It then ceases to be a gracious

---

[82]   *A Prayer Book for Australia*, The Anglican Church of Australia (Sydney: Broughton Books, 1999).

[83]   By 'sins' here I have in mind the deep defences that keep in place our self-possession and strategies for self-protection – fear and avoidance, patterns of inauthentic self-denial or self-hatred, and so on.

invitation into the company of those making God's reconciliation *their* own and risks becoming just another system of goodness, with standards of moral probity defined in advance and saving itself the vulnerability of discernment in particular cases.[84] This is, to say the least, in tension with its testimony that authentic encounter with resurrection is always a movement of dispossession as well as gift.

Secularisation

This argument, however, seemingly renders resurrection ethics severely limited in its capacity to engage in moral discourse with any purchase in the public or common sphere. If Hauerwas' ecclesial ethics have been criticised for being sectarian rather than universal, how much more an ethic calling for the transformation of subjectivity that goes by the demanding way of undergoing death and resurrection. There is another difficulty too. At the beginning of the chapter, I dismissed the assumption that an ethic sourced in resurrection is in principle incapable of engaging meaningfully in general moral discourse or of making visible new moral possibilities in pluralist and secular contexts.[85] Yet, there remains a serious issue for any theological ethics. It is that, despite everything I have said and argued, the language of faith has seemingly 'gone dead' for large parts of our culture.

In Chapter 1, I noted Iris Murdoch's remarks concerning the way in which it 'used' to be possible to believe that God exists,[86] and Raimond Gaita's reflection that, if the nun at the psychiatric hospital explained her behaviour with reference to her love of Jesus, he 'need not even understand what that means, let alone "believe it", in order to respond as [he has] described' to her example.[87] Charles Taylor has identified these expressions of our 'secular age' as reflecting the shift from a time in which 'it was virtually impossible not to believe in God', to one where for many

---

[84]   Note that this understanding of the practice of resurrection ethics is consonant with Douglas John Hall's understanding of an ethic of the cross: 'The people of the cross does not come to each new situation in the journey of humankind already armed with ready-made answers; rather it positions itself in such a way as to discover the appropriate "word from the Lord". On the one hand such positioning means divesting itself of foregone moral conclusions that only insulate the church from exposure to real moral questions; on the other hand it means trusting that the divine Spirit, by whom it is led into its contextual wilderness, will also illumine its understanding and provide direction for its response. The first requirement of the ethic of the cross, then, is that the disciple community must allow itself to be led as deeply as possible into the sphere of *the question*'. *The Cross in Our Context*, p.201.

[85]   In what follows, I assume the context of the largely secular, Western world. Some questions for the practice of resurrection ethics in relation to other faiths may also be relevantly addressed by these remarks, but not all.

[86]   For example, Murdoch, *Sovereignty of Good*, pp. 74, 79.

[87]   Gaita, *Good and Evil*, p.214.

people 'faith never even seems an eligible possibility', such that 'even for the staunchest believer' it may be difficult in some contexts 'to sustain one's faith'.[88]

By exploring theologically the moral terrain sketched by Murdoch and Gaita with their talk of 'non-dogmatic mysticism' and 'ethical other-worldliness', I have sought to breathe meaning into the language of faith, to communicate the reality to which it attests and so to keep alive the imaginative and conceptual resources necessary if we are to 'see' things in certain ways.[89] Yet can commending the significance of this theological understanding contribute to the moral life of a culture that flatly struggles to make anything of this framework or language? What effect on the *practice* of resurrection ethics might follow the recognition that its contributions to public discourse occur (more often than not) as an incursion of incomprehensibly foreign speech? I suggest that the beginnings of a response to these questions lie in considering the relationship between resurrection and secularity, resurrection and the process of secularisation.

'Secularisation' is a complex concept. The notion of the 'secular' derives from the New Testament concept '*saeculum*', which denotes that which belongs to this present age.[90] Although, for the New Testament writers, institutions and powers that do not fully acknowledge Christ's sovereignty will have no part in the age to come, they continue legitimately to play a role in the divine plan. Indeed they are the arena and object of the reconciling and transforming love of God that has broken into 'this' age in the persons of Christ and the Spirit. Thus for St Paul and subsequently for St Augustine, the secular realm exists in the charged eschatological space between Christ's resurrection and the *parousia* when Christ will be 'all in all'.[91] Christians must respect this realm, yet know that their ultimate allegiance lies beyond it (Rom. 13.1–7; Eph. 6.5–9). This allows for the possibility of criticism, hope and protest, while also making room for what Rowan Williams has recently called 'procedural' secularism. In moral and political discourse, this safeguards a space for conversation that is neither a theocracy certain of its own

---

[88]   Charles Taylor, *A Secular Age* (Cambridge, MA: Harvard University Press, 2007), p.3. Some commentators dispute the thesis that the Western world is becoming increasingly secular, pointing to the growth in religious practice particularly in non-mainline churches. I agree, however, with Douglas John Hall, who writes that the demise of 'Christendom' is not simply about numbers but about influence, 'including the influence of this faith among the intellectual, artistic, and critical elites'. It is not, he says, that Christianity needs to be endorsed by these elites, but it does hope to be 'sufficiently stimulating to such representatives of "high culture" to be taken with some measure of seriousness'. *The Cross in Our Context*, p.161.

[89]   Cf. Gaita, *Good and Evil*, p.xix.

[90]   Robert A. Markus, *Christianity and the Secular* (Notre Dame, IN: University of Notre Dame Press, 2006), p.14.

[91]   Markus, *Christianity and the Secular*, pp.14–15, 37. Markus's discussion traces a transition in Augustine's thinking on this matter from a triumphal proclamation of the Christian empire in the early 400s to his mature reflection in *The City of God* on the illegitimacy of identifying any earthly 'city' with the heavenly one.

infallibility (the *eschaton* pre-empted), nor a public sphere from which reference to the meaning and significance of God's revealed future may be 'programmatically' excluded.[92] I am assuming the desirability of such procedural secularism as the context for theological engagement in moral questions of general import.

In the light of this understanding of the secular, one account of *secularisation* refers to the widespread adoption or emergence of the view that the present age is the only age there is. There is no world but this one, no transcendent reality beyond the 'immanent frame',[93] no anticipated future to which the present time is answerable. Charles Taylor's monumental treatment of this theme traces the cultural loss of belief in transcendence through the history of ideas and social movements, seeking to explain the religious situation of the contemporary West where the goal of human life 'for masses of people' is understood entirely in this-worldly or humanistic terms. A 'secular age', he writes, 'is one in which the eclipse of all goals beyond human flourishing becomes conceivable ... This is the crucial link between secularity and a self-sufficing humanism'.[94] Note that it is secularisation in this sense, the inability or refusal to acknowledge some reality beyond or transcendent to a 'self-sufficing humanism', that both Murdoch and Gaita are resisting.

There is a second account of secularisation, however, that construes the terms by which it is delineated differently. Rather than equating it with the collapse of transcendence, James Alison understands secularisation to be associated with the collapse of the distinction between sacred and profane.[95] Secularisation in this sense, far from being inimical to Christianity, is at the heart of the gospel itself, the proper outworking of the catholicity or universality of resurrection faith. Becoming clearer about this form of secularisation and its relationship

---

[92]   Rowan Williams, 'Rome Lecture: "Secularism, Faith and Freedom"', delivered at the Pontifical Academy of Social Sciences, 23 November 2006 (accessed http://www.archbishopofcanterbury.org/articles.php/1175/rome-lecture-secularism-faith-and-freedom, 8 October 2012). Markus writes of Augustine's approach that '[t]o assert the autonomy of the secular was to resist any hostile takeover of this middle ground between sacred and profane from either side: either to include it in the sacred – by Christian or by pagan – or to repudiate it as irredeemably profane or demonic'. *Christianity and the Secular*, p.37.

[93]   The phrase is Charles Taylor's, *A Secular Age*.

[94]   Taylor, *A Secular Age*, pp.19–20. Taylor narrates the ecclesial and theological contributions to the demise of transcendence primarily with reference to the Reform movement in early modernity. This contrasts with the argument of the Radical Orthodoxy movement, which has attributed modern secularisation to the theological turn to nominalism in the work of Franciscans such as Duns Scotus and William of Ockham. Taylor's summary of his relationship to this argument appears in *A Secular Age*, pp.773–776. See also, Scott Cowdell, *Abiding Faith: Christianity beyond Certainty, Anxiety and Violence* (Eugene, OR: Cascade Books, 2009), chapter 2.

[95]   James Alison, 'Sacrifice, Law and the Catholic Faith: Is Secularity Really the Enemy?', in *Broken Hearts & New Creations: Intimations of a Great Reversal* (London: Darton, Longman and Todd, 2010), pp.73–91.

to secularisation in Taylor's sense is critical for engaging the question of how resurrection ethics might contribute to common moral discourse, and for reflecting again on the relationship between the appeal to transcendence in ethics and its theological elaboration.

When the sacred is defined in opposition to the profane, then, like goodness defined in opposition to badness, it is dependent for its meaning on that which it excludes. The sacred–profane axis, argues Alison, belongs to the domain of the false or violent 'sacred' that has been subverted from within by the death and resurrection of Jesus. As I argued in Chapters 3 and 4, the apostolic witness concerning the significance of this event was not simply that the religious judgement of Jesus which led to his being killed (a judgement of 'profanation' or blasphemy) was now seen to be mistaken because of his vindication by God. Rather, it was the religious mechanism itself that was seen to be mistaken, insofar as the whole system operated to secure the righteousness and identity and belonging of some at the expense of others. The self-giving of Jesus into this 'sacred' system of goodness and the revelation of its essentially death-dealing and godless dynamic opened the possibility of humanity being freed from the thrall of *any* such system, enabling the discovery of new ways of belonging to one another and to God, new forms of solidarity beyond judgement and the fear of death.

This means at least two things. First, as we see from the testimony of the New Testament, increasingly the distinction between 'sacred' and profane, maintained by notions of taboo, religious rules and ritual sacrifice, is subverted. This distinction is now seen to have much more to do with human identity formation and boundary maintenance than with the 'new' humanity being brought into 'one body', the body of Christ, in the church. We see the painful process of subverting the old distinction in various places, as, for example, when Peter learns in his vision of unclean animals being presented him to eat that '[w]hat God has made clean, you must not call profane' (Acts 10.19),[96] and as the early Christian community grapples with questions of ritual purity and identity in relation to circumcision and the eating of meat sacrificed to idols. Writes Alison,

> Phrases like, 'everything is permitted, but not everything is convenient', or 'to those who are pure, everything is pure', or 'the letter kills, but the spirit gives life', could be quoted by anybody, and sound the rankest of secularising remarks. And they are. They are all phrases by which St Paul sought to make the oddity of the un-religion which he was preaching available to people: the subversiveness

---

[96]   In a trance, Peter sees 'something like a large sheet' being lowered from above, and in it all kinds of animals. A voice tells him to 'kill and eat', and when Peter protests that he has never eaten anything profane or unclean, the voice tells him that he must not call profane what God has made clean. This episode is the immediate precursor to Peter's encounter with the Gentile Cornelius and his baptism by the Holy Spirit, leading to Peter's amazed confession that 'I truly understand that God shows no partiality, but in every nation anyone who fears him and does what is right is acceptable to him' (Acts 10.34–35).

of the pattern of desire, unleashed by the sacrificial death of Christ, proving God's goodness to us when faced with any 'sacred' religious observance.[97]

Henceforth, belonging to God has nothing to do with the maintenance of these forms of 'sacred' rite.

It follows, then, that the proclamation of Jesus' death and resurrection occurs *essentially* 'not by imposing a set of laws, texts or norms, not by making a particular set of words, or a particular language, sacred and thus normative'.[98] It is not about the replacement of one religious ideology by another, although undeniably the history of Christianity is replete with attempts at just such ideological replacement.[99] Rather, it means making it possible for people to enter into the dynamic of the undoing of any form of 'sacred' belonging. This occurs, writes Alison, 'through preaching, liturgy and example in such a way that whatever is "sacred", or taboo, or demanding of sacrifice in that culture, ceases to have a hold on people as they come to lose their fear of death'.[100] As I emphasised in the previous section, Christian conversion is essentially about transformation, not conformation, being enabled to let go the self-justifying, self-sufficing self or communal identity and to receive one's true self and belonging as gift, such that one begins to *participate* in God's 'indiscriminately welcoming'[101] and non-defensive way of being in the world.

Where does this leave the concept of the sacred in Christianity? With the subversion of the false 'sacred', it may no longer be defined over against the profane as though these were static or fixed categories. There is nothing by definition that is profane or unclean, no food, no person, no nation or disease. There are instead ways of being, patterns of desire, that are consistent or not with God's merciful and all-embracing love for the world. True holiness, true sanctity is to be conformed to this way of being and its growth is perhaps most starkly evident in the character of one's relationships to those who are victims of the world and its systems of goodness. This is why the criterion of God's final judgement in Matthew's gospel is in terms of relationship to those who are hungry and thirsty, alien and naked, sick and in prison (Matt. 25.31–46). The true sacred, on this account, is intrinsically connected to catholicity, universality: 'the whole point of Christianity is to bring down the sort of wall of protective sacredness which

---

[97]   Alison, 'Sacrifice, Law and the Catholic Faith', p.81.

[98]   Alison says this is why the Catholic faith is 'of its nature syncretistic'. When it is being itself (rather than being an ideology) it should operate to subvert that within any culture which tends to sacrifice, sacred violence, and the fear of death. Alison, 'Sacrifice, Law and the Catholic Faith', p.80.

[99]   Alison, 'Sacrifice, Law and the Catholic Faith', p.89. See also Rowan Williams, 'The Finality of Christ', in *On Christian Theology*, pp.93–106, p.102.

[100]   Alison, 'Sacrifice, Law and the Catholic Faith', p.80.

[101]   Cf. Williams, 'Interiority and Epiphany', in *On Christian Theology*, pp.239–264, p.250.

makes universality impossible by having a necessary "other" over against whom we make ourselves "good"'.[102]

This understanding of the true sacred returns us to the concept of the secular with which I began this discussion. The secular age is the time in which this secularising 'good news' about God, this subversion of the false 'sacred', may be proclaimed and the transformed shape of human being and belonging may gradually be lived into. The beginnings of new life in Christ intermingle with the old, in the lives of believers as much as in the institutions of the world, and this is the time given for the transformation of the ways that lead to death into life.[103] What, then, is the relationship between the interdependence of the collapse of the false 'sacred' and secularity in this sense, and Taylor's understanding of secularisation as the collapse of transcendence?

For Christians, the transcendence of God is connected with God's otherness to the default energy and pattern of human being and belonging, which St Paul calls 'the flesh' and which is the source of the false 'sacred'.[104] This transcendent otherness is not 'of' the world and yet is radically involved in it, so that God is also known as immanent, engaging and transforming human life and the whole creation from within. The kingdom of God is 'among you', says Jesus; the kingdom of God is 'within' (Luke 17.21). Doctrinally, this immanent otherness is expressed in terms of the Spirit of God indwelling human hearts and bringing about the transformation and reconciliation of creation, drawing everything into the life of God (Rom. 5.5, 8).

When Taylor speaks about secularisation in terms of the loss of transcendence, he rightly notes the loss of a sense of 'otherness' to which human life might be answerable or by whose grace it might be transformed. What is perhaps less clear in his discussion is the distinction between different conceptions of transcendence and the sacred, and thus the nature of the relevant 'otherness'.[105] To the extent that

---

[102]   Alison, 'Sacrifice, Law and the Catholic Faith', p.88.

[103]   This transformation takes time and is susceptible of backsliding. Paul reproves the Galatians on just this point: 'Formerly, when you did not know God, you were enslaved to beings that by nature are not gods. Now, however, that you have come to know God, or rather to be known by God, how can you turn back again to the weak and beggarly elemental spirits? How can you want to be enslaved to them again? You are observing special days, and months, and seasons, and years. I am afraid that my work for you may have been wasted' (Gal. 4.8–11).

[104]   Williams speaks of the significance of the traditional understanding of God as a 'concrete' other, resistant to being understood as a mere function of my identity and agenda. 'Interiority and Epiphany', pp.243–244, 249. See also, Alison, 'Monotheism and the Indispensability of Irrelevance', in *Undergoing God: Dispatches from the Scene of a Break-in* (London: Darton, Longman and Todd, 2006), pp.17–32.

[105]   This lack of distinction between conceptions of the 'transcendent' and the 'sacred' is evident in Peter E. Gordon's discussion of Taylor's argument, 'Must the Sacred be Transcendent?', *Inquiry*, 54/2 (2011): 126–139. Gordon objects to Taylor's identification of the sacred with the transcendent, suggesting that, in the 'pre-Axial' world, the sacred

Christianity under Christendom was enacted as a new form of the false 'sacred', then I would say that increasing cultural difficulty in taking it seriously represents a development that is, from a Christian point of view, both to be expected and welcomed.[106] It is expected, confessionally speaking, in the sense that precisely this secularising tendency, the undoing of the false 'sacred', is the dynamic that is operative in the world through the Spirit. The Carmelite Ruth Burrows has written, 'We should therefore welcome what is known as secularisation. In itself it is right, something God wants. It is a purification, a dark night of religion which allows a real and living faith to emerge. Only too often what we think of as faith is simply shutting our eyes to three-quarters of reality lest it disturb (if not destroy) our so-called "faith"'.[107] Where transcendence is connected to the false 'sacred', then its collapse is not to be mourned.

What does seem problematic, however, is the exclusive humanist or programmatic secularist assumption that the false 'sacred', bad 'religion', can be overcome simply by jettisoning relationship to transcending otherness altogether. The notion that we might bypass the various axes that sustain 'over against' or violent forms of human being and belonging (sacred–profane, good–bad, in–out), and that the possibility of authentically catholic or universal human community might be secured without passing through the subversion and transformation of these axes, is illusory. Being 'over against' is not caused by ideological religion, but expressed by it. Its real source is the default pattern of human desire and identity formation, which, I have been arguing, is undone only by passing through the place of unmaking and death, by the process the biblical tradition calls repentance, conversion, and forgiveness.

This, however, returns us to the question of the loss of language and forms of life by means of which this process might be communicated in our culture.[108] It returns us to the question of how the practice and discourse of ethics arising from this undergoing of death and resurrection might contribute to common moral life. Gaita and Murdoch suggest that the moral reality revealed by the love of saints can

---

was attached to places, entities and persons within the world. For this reason, he argues that the distinction between transcendence and immanence as constitutive of religion and of the possibility of a good 'beyond ordinary human flourishing' is historical and contingent, and risks obscuring other ways in which the experience of the 'sacred' or at least a non-flattened humanism might be possible. But Gordon likewise does not engage with the Christian transformation of the false 'sacred'. In other words, the centre of gravity of his discussion of Taylor concerns the legitimacy of the foundational distinction between transcendence (sacred) and immanence (secular), whereas my concern is with the distinction between false (ideological) and true sacred. The essential element of the true sacred, on this account, is its 'otherness' to the default patterns of human being and belonging, but this otherness can be experienced as both (even simultaneously) transcendent and immanent.

[106] Taylor, similarly, would agree that much of what has passed and passes for Christianity is a kind of 'idolatry'. *A Secular Age*, p.769.

[107] Burrows, *Ascent to Love*, p.100.

[108] By 'communicated' I mean not only 'talked about' but also 'given access'.

be recognised apart from shared Christian confession, and with this I agree. The questions that concern me are, first, can such love grow in us and its revelatory and transformative power be kept alive, apart from practices of Christian prayer and discipleship? And second, can moral responsiveness arising from this transformation of subjectivity be given expression independently of religious language, communicated in 'secular' terms, such that its seeing and imagining of the world may contribute to common moral discourse?

These are difficult questions. In response to the first, it seems to me that learning to love as the saints do requires there to be certain conceptual possibilities and practices kept alive, places where grace may be met and the invitation into the fearful and lifelong process of handing oneself over to death and receiving one's life back as gift may be issued and the journey supported. As I noted in Chapter 1, the community of the church is an embodying structure for learning to hand over one's life in trust to transcendent otherness, growing in self-dispossessing prayer and living responsively to grace in penitence and gratitude. Although this community often obscures more than it reveals or opens up, we should not be naive about what its total eclipse might humanly mean. Yet it is not the only place where such a journey may be begun or undertaken, and theologically there is no reason to suppose that the church is exclusively where God's Spirit is operative.[109] Indeed, many of those who find their way eventually towards forms of Christian life do so because they have encountered the authentic dynamic of repentance and conversion elsewhere, and so are now able to 'hear' Christian language afresh.[110] The church is called to witness to the new life given by its crucified and risen Lord, but this need not and does not mean that this reality is the church's exclusive possession. Perhaps part of this very witnessing will involve the church's readiness to recognise and encourage this undergoing of death and resurrection under other forms.

As for Christian contribution to common moral discourse, I have just argued that it is internal to the transforming encounter to which Christianity testifies that, while earthed in historical particularity, it is not confined to particular 'sacred' places, forms and cultural expressions. It is, as Alison puts it, a secularising kind of

---

[109]   For example, the Declaration on the Relation of the Church to Non-Christian Religions, *Nostra Aetate*, proclaimed by Pope Paul VI on 28 October 1965 states, 'the Catholic Church rejects nothing that is true and holy in these religions. She regards with sincere reverence those ways of conduct and of life, those precepts and teachings which, though differing in many aspects from the ones she holds and sets forth, nonetheless often reflect a ray of that Truth which enlightens all men' (accessed http://www.vatican.va/archive/hist_councils/ii_vatican_council/documents/vat-ii_decl_19651028_nostra-aetate_en.html, 8 July 2013).

[110]   Many of those who belong to the World Community for Christian Meditation report that they have found their way 'back' to Christianity via the Buddhist teaching of meditation. I think in this context also of twelve-step programmes, as well as the Center for Courage & Renewal, which gives expression in intentionally 'secular' language to an analogous journey of transformation offered with reference to the work of educationalist and Quaker Parker J. Palmer.

'un-religion'. John's gospel attributes this form of secularisation to Jesus himself: speaking to the Samaritan woman at the well, he teaches that 'the hour is coming when you will worship the Father neither on this mountain nor in Jerusalem … [T]he hour is coming, and is now here, when the true worshipers will worship the Father in spirit and truth' (John 4.21, 23).[111] Reflecting on the relationship of Christianity to other religious traditions, Rowan Williams has argued that, if the history of Jesus 'enacts a judgement of tribalized and self-protecting religion',[112] religion as ideology, then that has implications not only for our sense of God, but also for 'tribal' religious speech, our attachment to particular forms of religious articulation of God's meaning and work.

Just as we are transformed by 'our readiness for dispossession', he continues, our readiness to lose 'the God who is defined as belonging to us and our interests', so 'in passing through that dispossession, religious speech moves some little way closer to being a speech that human beings as human beings may share'.[113] It is in this context that Williams refers to Dietrich Bonhoeffer's remarks on 'religionless Christianity' as calling, not 'for the secular reduction of faith, but a vision of the language of faith enlarging itself to become the language of that unrestricted human community' given in Jesus.[114] God is not possessed in our religious language and transforming encounter with God is not guaranteed by any religious formula: 'God can only live in the grammar of religious talk when that talk expresses God's freedom from it'.[115]

In his imprisonment, Bonhoeffer wrestled with the question of how the realities entrusted to Christian witness might be spoken as living words, liberating events. Because of its self-preoccupation, the German church, he believed, had become 'incapable of taking the word of reconciliation and redemption to mankind and the world'. Its language had gone dead. In Bonhoeffer's view, any new power of Christian speech would be given on the other side of the church's own conversion and purification, and this was ultimately a matter for God:

> It is not for us to prophesy the day (though the day will come) when men will once more be called so to utter the word of God that the world will be changed and renewed by it. It will be a new language, perhaps quite non-religious, but liberating and redeeming – as was Jesus' language.[116]

---

[111] Alison notes that the Mass is a portable and 'flexible form of worship', given as a sign of the undergoing of the dynamic of death and resurrection and in order to draw us into that same dynamic. 'Sacrifice, Law and the Catholic Faith', p. 82.

[112] Williams, 'The Finality of Christ', p.104.

[113] Williams, 'The Finality of Christ', p.104.

[114] Williams, 'The Finality of Christ', p.104.

[115] Williams, 'The Finality of Christ', p.106.

[116] Dietrich Bonhoeffer, *Letters and Papers from Prison* (enlarged edition), ed. Eberhard Bethge (London: SCM Press, 1971), p.300.

Until that day, however, 'the Christian cause will be a silent and hidden affair'.[117] Williams too, drawing on these same reflections, has said that, 'constrained by the awareness of how easily the words of [Christian] proclamation become godless, powerless to transform', the urgency to speak 'must often be channelled into listening and waiting, and into the expansion of the Christian imagination itself into something that can cope with the seriousness of the world'.[118]

All this suggests that, in our context, the practice of resurrection ethics must be non-defensive and non-possessive about the language through which it seeks to communicate the reality in which it is sourced and in light of which it contributes to the moral discourse of our time. Our speech and action must seek to make present God's peace and love for the world,[119] but this does not (and probably should not) always mean using overtly religious language. Like Jesus' own language, Williams says, it may be 'non-religious' in the sense that it is 'not primarily concerned with securing a space within the world for a particular specialist discourse. Whether or not it uses the word "God", it effects faith, conversion, hope'.[120]

What might this look like in practice? Let me offer two suggestions. In the previous chapter, I noted that some of our deepest moral questions concern the treatment of those human beings whom modern moral philosophy renders marginal to the moral community. The unborn, many of the dying, and the mentally disabled lack features of 'personhood', defined in terms of the capacity for ratiocination, self-conscious expression of preferences, and so on. Against this view of the criteria for human 'mattering', theological ethics draws on the concept of the sacred, saying that human moral meaning is bound up with our belonging to God prior to any possession or attainment of our own. Whether a human being satisfies the philosophical criteria for being considered a 'person' or not has nothing to do with their moral status. Yet merely repeating a formula expressing sincere conviction *about* the sanctity of all human life will not 'effect' the conversion that is needed to keep such people morally among us. In our context, notions such as 'sanctity of life' themselves need life breathed into them. This is all the more so since the notion of 'sanctity' is deployed, in other contexts, as part of a conservative Christian rhetoric whose main purpose seems to be to keep certain people and relationships *outside* the bounds of full human fellowship.[121]

I have said that one of the marks of resurrection ethics is its revelatory power. Part of what this calls for in the context of common moral discourse is attunement to what words can mean, what freight they bear. Part of what it means is not relying on tired religious formulae, but discovering for ourselves and afresh what

---

[117]   Bonhoeffer, *Letters and Papers from Prison*, p.300.
[118]   Williams, 'The Judgement of the World', in *On Christian Theology*, pp.29–43, p.40.
[119]   Cf. Williams, 'The Judgement of the World', p.41.
[120]   Williams, 'The Judgement of the World', p.41.
[121]   I am thinking, for example, of the way appeal to the 'sanctity' of marriage and of family values is used in arguments against church blessing of same-sex partnerships and gay marriage.

it means (for example) to say that human beings are sacred. Practising ethics from resurrection means touching and deepening moral imagination, our active sense of how life is transformed by not having to be afraid, and not having to be 'over against' anything in order simply to be. It means speaking *from* this place and not simply *about* it, and then discovering where and how this reality is manifest in other places, in art and literature, philosophy and political reflection that likewise seek to touch the depths of human meaning and suffering. So the practice of resurrection ethics calls for the involvement of the whole person who is in the process of undergoing transformation, and not simply on our capacity to engage in reasoned argument or deploy the expressions of orthodoxy. And it calls, too, for a willingness to experiment with the forms in which that reality may be truthfully communicated as something living. Christian ethics that is non-defensive and non-possessive about its language will thus call for an ever-deepening involvement with the 'secular', willing to risk itself in the world's language in service of the world's transformation and its own.

Is this recommendation simply capitulating to the terms offered by the world? I do not think so. It has been said that, when Australians first began travelling to Asia to holiday or to do business, their assumption was that, if someone did not understand English, speaking loud English was sure to do the trick. When conversation partners as sensitive and sympathetic as Gaita and Murdoch report that they do not understand what Christians are saying, then simply saying it loudly or more insistently is not an appropriate response. Of course, this does not mean there should be no opportunities for anyone to learn 'English'. Communities living out of the reality that gives meaning to theological language, spiritual practices that lead to the transformation of bitterness into forgiveness, alienation into belonging, self-defensiveness into other-centredness, witness to the fact that Christian faith is not simply an idle wheel but is connected to what is deepest in the human condition. They testify to the possibility of an encounter that does not simply convey the *idea* of reconciliation but mysteriously performs it. But if this reality cannot also be encountered outside the walls of 'sacred' community and language, then it is not the truth of all that is. Ruth Burrows again:

> We can no longer confine God within the sacral and treat with him there. We must see him in all that is or not at all. If we are weak in faith we may find his seeming absence unendurable, the effort to seek him in the world with all its attendant risks unbearable, and so we retreat into a ghetto, building up for ourselves a little world of spiritual make-believe which is safe, comfortable, and unchallenged … It seems that *this* is the sphere of the holy where God really is, whereas secularity is unholy and must be shunned. If we would go forward, if we would surrender to God we must keep our doors wide open. We must trustingly deal with the world, love it, enjoy it.[122]

---

[122] Burrows, *Ascent to Love*, pp.100–101.

Christian ethics, then, will join common moral discourse by speaking in whatever way it can to particular issues, seeking to deepen moral imagination and enliven the available conceptual resources, from the standpoint of its experience of God's indiscriminate love for all. At other times, however, and this is my second example of what resurrection ethics might look like in practice, it may seek to encourage different possibilities in the very conduct of public moral debate. Paul's testimony from resurrection is that we know ourselves now to be 'members one of another' (Rom. 12.5), indefeasibly sharers in a common humanity. In some circumstances, then, practising resurrection ethics will involve seeking to broker mutual recognition among all participants in a debate, opening the space of conversation itself. This is a reflection of the vulnerability and compassion internal to living from this new reality, its alertness to the tendency of all human morality to become a system of goodness that renders 'us' good by making others 'bad'.

As I write, the Australian community is in the midst of a painful and contentious public debate about asylum seekers, and particularly the arrival of so-called 'unauthorised' boats run by people smugglers. It is a moral question of real complexity: its elements include the profound desperation and vulnerability of many of those seeking asylum; the question of the fairness of processing their claims ahead of others who remain waiting indefinitely in camps off shore; the risks of encouraging more hazardous and fatal voyages by too readily granting asylum to those who arrive by boat; the question of the legitimate integrity of national borders; and the community's capacity to absorb large numbers of unplanned new arrivals.

Since the church should have, as Williams has said, a 'quite disproportionate interest in how mechanisms of exclusion work in human societies',[123] there is much that Christians should have to say about the content of various arguments deployed in this debate and its final outcomes. What I want now to suggest, however, is that the practice of ethics from resurrection might also offer resources for reconfiguring the very conduct of this national conversation. At present, the political form of the debate is in terms of win and lose, with different parties seeking the moral high ground and the appearance of decisiveness, with little public acknowledgement of the complexity, ambiguity and moral hazard involved in any response at present conceivable. The entire conversation occurs inside a rhetorical space characterised by fear, threatenedness and judgement, with little room for people of good will to explore options, tease out the implications of different responses, or recognise that we, Australians of all political persuasions and asylum seekers alike, are 'members one of another'.

What would it be like, I wonder, if Christian leaders explicitly reminded our community that we might conduct this difficult conversation less aggressively and with less concern for who occupies the moral high ground? What might become possible if the church were able to invite all involved into a space of deeper listening, itself risking being misunderstood by seeking to hear into

---

[123]   Williams, 'Interiority and Epiphany', p.262.

speech the concerns of all and then to share in common the burden of moral responsibility for the choices that are made? I have argued that resurrection faith means not having to secure our own goodness and righteousness. Christian moral responsiveness and leadership sourced in that faith could seek to open up a space for public moral discourse that acts as a catalyst for a new kind of conversation and a new maturity, a deepening of our sense of mutual belonging and responsibility.[124] In this way, the church might imitate and 'give glory' to God, not by its explicit religious or devotional language, but by reflecting in the world something of God's life, the 'non-competitive other' before whom all alike are called to be vulnerable and responsible,[125] and in whom my good and the good of my neighbour cannot be pulled apart.

---

[124] Of course, it also opens up a space of risk for the church, not unlike that entered by Jesus – being not 'religious' enough for the devout and simply not understood by the rest.

[125] The theme of Christian ethics as concerned with glorifying God, reflecting who God is, is significant in the final part of Williams, 'Interiority and Epiphany'. The notion of God as a 'non-competitive other' is in the same essay, pp.242–247.

Conclusion

I am the resurrection and the life. Those who believe in me, even though they die, will live, and everyone who lives and believes in me will never die. (John 11.25–26)

What I have been calling resurrection ethics might also be described as a Christian contemplative or wisdom ethic. It is how moral life looks from the place of union with God, noting that union with God means being drawn into a living and relational reality that is endlessly generative, transforming and giving. Resurrection ethics issues from the lived experience of this underlying plenitude and love that, despite all appearances to the contrary, encompasses the brokenness and suffering and confusion of the world. It is thus an ethic that is essentially non-anxious and unthreatened, trusting that love is truly stronger than death and that all human life happens in time that is given and capable of being redeemed, transformed.[1]

In Christian understanding, coming into this place of union is not simply a matter of getting in touch with a pre-existing wholeness, finding our way back to an untainted 'essential' self and a lost paradise. Rather, it is a journey of cross and resurrection that transforms all that makes for disunion and fragmentation from within, such that even wounds and failures become sources of healing. Jesus undoes the power of death by undergoing it and revealing that for God death is not the ultimate reality. The resurrection does not simply cancel death, as if death were on the same plane as resurrection life. Death itself is taken up into the life of the risen Jesus. As James Alison has emphasised, Jesus is risen *as* dead and that is the significance of the marks of crucifixion still visible in his body.[2] Likewise the risen Jesus liberates Peter from his failure and self-diminishment, not by cancelling or denying what he has done but by empowering him to assimilate his betrayal in the context of forgiveness, enabling him to be restored wholly to himself.

It is this journey *through* death, failure, shame and woundedness, the reconciliation of all things by forgiving and gratuitous love, that the New Testament proclaims as making possible a new communion between God and humanity, Jew and Gentile. What formerly divided us from God, ourselves and each other need

---

[1]   Cf. Rowan Williams, 'Interiority and Epiphany: A Reading in New Testament Ethics', in *On Christian Theology* (Oxford: Blackwell Publishers, 2000), pp.239–264, p.249.

[2]   He writes that 'the resurrection life was the giving back of the whole human life, leading up to and including the death. It is this that is the sign that death has been conquered, that the resurrection life isn't on the same level as death … The resurrection life includes the human death of Jesus. He is always present after the resurrection simultaneously as crucified and as risen Lord'. *Knowing Jesus* (Springfield, IL: Templegate Publishers, 1994), p.20.

no longer do so, for there is no need to defend ourselves against our failures and inadequacies, no need to shore up our lives and identities against the threat of death or ignominy. The Letter to the Ephesians understands that for this reason Jesus Christ 'is our peace' and in him all belong to 'one new humanity' that has 'access in one Spirit to the Father' (Eph. 2.14–18).

I have argued that this transformation wrought by the resurrection in our concept of ultimate reality and in the possibilities of human subjectivity has radical implications for moral life. It changes our imaginative sense of the world, the horizon against which moral life assumes its shape, significance and meaning; it transforms the moral responsiveness, the understanding and vision, of those who undergo it. I have argued further that this transformation gives content to the conception of transcendence in ethics to which both Iris Murdoch and Raimond Gaita appeal as the proper background to moral life. Indeed, I have said that in the absence of this kind of theological elaboration and its embodiment in a community of practice, it is not clear how the 'love of saints' and the concept of Goodness interdependent with it, which are central to Murdoch's and Gaita's sense of moral depth and meaning, can be kept alive, critically engaged and practically available in human life.

Resurrection relativises the dualism between life and death by drawing both into the larger reality of the eternal life of God. Likewise, the experience of subjectivity transformed through forgiveness and union with God means that distorting dualisms in moral life between good and bad, law and lawlessness, self and other, also take on a different resonance. I have not claimed that these distinctions are meaningless or that they can be discarded glibly in the name of an ersatz Christian 'freedom'. I argued in Chapter 5, for example, that although resurrection transforms our sense of the *meaning* of death, the fact of death in human life remains a source of profound suffering and grief. Our mortality thus rightly conditions our sense of the seriousness of moral claims and harms, the irreplaceability of human life. If it were otherwise, resurrection ethics would indeed offer what Iris Murdoch dismissed as 'false consolation'. Nevertheless, if human life and death are held alike in a larger plenitude, then this makes a difference to our sense of the 'heaviness' of death in life. We begin to recognise the extent to which some of our moral concepts are distorted by the assumed dominion of death, and we become more capable of moral responsiveness characterised by gratuity and non-anxiousness, the lightness or *hilaritas* of the saint. Life, including moral life, is no longer defined by the horizon of death. An analogous point applies to other dualisms in moral life.

For example, I argued that the dualism between goodness defined by badness is ultimately defeating of moral life and shown to be so by Jesus. As many of his encounters with the Pharisees reveal, those seeking to be good by comparison with those who are bad *cannot* love their neighbours as themselves. Their conception of goodness necessarily involves defining themselves over against their neighbour, in ways that are utterly at odds with the healing and merciful Goodness of God. Similarly, the seeming distinction between the moral responsiveness of the lawful and lawless may conceal an important similarity, a shared and distorting assumption of competition in the background of the self's identity. In different ways, the law-abiding Pharisee and (for example) the lawless libertarian are seeking to secure their lives, their meaning for themselves, and so, as Rowan Williams notes, operate in recognisably comparable modes of acquisitiveness.[3] Those who rely for their identity on fulfilling the law seek to establish their own righteousness, securing their place in the world by their successful moral performance. For those outside law-structured patterns of common life, the self's meaning and identity is also defined by what the self does, this time in fulfilling whatever are its own desires or aspirations. In either case, the need to control the self's identity, to be the source of one's own life, is taken for granted and makes impossible the growth of a universal community of genuine neighbour love and 'a common future'.[4]

It is the process of coming into union with God and communion with one another that subverts the assumptions underlying this dualistic structuring of moral life. This is because when we are assured of a place, of belonging and of a self by God, our life and identity does not need to be secured against threat or over against others. We are given being by the gracious determination of God – we can neither earn nor be deprived of our belonging in the world. Undergoing this realisation, which often involves a painful journey of unmaking old patterns of identity, makes possible participation in Goodness of a different order, the Goodness of God that is grace. Where goodness and badness are interdependent with one another, deriving from and reinforcing alienated subjectivity, each in different ways leads to death. 'Badness' may do so in obvious ways, and 'goodness' more subtly in forms such as judgementalism and moralism. The Goodness of God, by contrast, is not 'over against' anything and does not cast out. Like the love of saints, it is a reconciling goodness, one that can make even evildoers whole and render visible the humanity of the afflicted.

Even the distinction between selflessness and selfishness, from outside the space of union with God, risks functioning as no more than the twin sides of the same essentially alienated coin. When the self is conceived as separate and self-contained, then 'unselfing' in human relations involves denial or negation of one's own self. It operates within the same picture of competitive relationship as 'selfish' orientation, differing only in that it enjoins the denial of the self in favour of the other, rather than the reverse. Such alienated selflessness leads ultimately to death, in the forms of destructive self-negation, resentment, and, often, a paradoxical kind of pride. In place of the humility, mutual belonging and solidarity of a genuinely shared and vulnerable humanity, the 'self-giving' of the alienated self is inevitably condescending. When, however, the self is allowed to be constituted by its belonging to the inexhaustible life of God, receiving its being as gift and without defensiveness, then 'unselfing' occurs very differently.

---

[3]   Rowan Williams, 'Resurrection and Peace: More on New Testament Ethics', in *On Christian Theology*, pp.265–275, p.269.

[4]   Williams, 'Resurrection and Peace', p.268.

There is no longer *competition* between myself and others, but I am released to see others *as* myself existing in and through the same impartial love of God. The more transparent my own identity to God's life, the more I have undergone the 'death' of my alienated self, the more attention to and love for the other comes *through* me from God. It is not at my *expense*, since it comes out of and flows into fullness rather than self-sacrifice.

My argument, then, is that, from the place of disunion with God, alienated humanity seeks to be the source of its own life, and so necessarily tends towards defensiveness, fear or aggression. Our relations with one another are structured by competition, which means that even our highest moral ideals and aspirations, our most sincere moral striving and desire to be good, are in thrall to death and deal death. Although his meaning is susceptible of various interpretations, this predicament seems not alien to Paul's agonised recognition of the ambiguity of the law:

> So I find it to be a law that when I want to do what is good, evil lies close at hand. For I delight in the law of God in my inmost self, but I see in my members another law at war with the law of my mind, making me captive to the law of sin that dwells in my members. Wretched man that I am! Who will rescue me from this body of death? Thanks be to God through Jesus Christ our Lord! (Rom. 7.21–25)

The life, death and resurrection of Jesus transform the possibilities of moral life and imagination, because through him we are freed to let go self-possession and all that goes with it, entrusting our very selves (including our fears and failures) to the love and mercy of God. We then discover that our moral responsiveness is no longer ours, but participates in and reflects God's own Goodness and love. Of course, this transformation does not make moral discernment in particular cases suddenly free of difficulty. It does not save us from experiencing particular moral questions as painful or ambiguous, and moral responsibility is not now cast onto God, as if there is no longer need to be accountable for the seriousness of our thought, the character of our actions, and the generosity of our imagination.

Rowan Williams has written that the new life made available in Christ is not a new possession or fixed pattern, and nor is it infused in 'all-conquering fullness in a single moment'.[5] It is learned and lived into through particular human experiences as 'a new world of possibilities, a new future that is to be constructed day by day. Life, after all, implies movement and growth'.[6] And, in the conditions of alienated humanity, this new life from resurrection may be experienced in practice as a way of the cross. Systems of goodness, with clearly defined boundaries between in

---

⁵   Rowan Williams, *The Wound of Knowledge: Christian Spirituality from the New Testament to St John of the Cross*, second edition (Cambridge, MA: Cowley Publications, 1991), p.18.

⁶   Williams, *Wound of Knowledge*, p.19.

and out, good and bad, do not take kindly to the subversion of the means of cheap identity formation. Jesus is recorded as having warned his disciples that, along with the paradoxical abundance of the life of discipleship and dispossession, they were to expect 'persecutions' (Mark 10.30).

Even so, moral life sourced in resurrection knows freedom, lightness and confidence born of the felt knowledge that it is part of the larger story of our life with God and God's life with us. It is our responsiveness in particular circumstances to being drawn to participate in the divine life and so to let go self-possessiveness, to share the mind of Christ, and so to see as God sees, to be *for* others in the ways that God is for us and the world. The imaginative horizon of an ethic from resurrection is the life of God, inexhaustibly forgiving and compassionate, which sets us free from preoccupation with our own goodness or innocence and invites us into the adventure of a future lived in and from God's life. This is the future revealed by the risen Christ as reconciling love, in whose company we are together invited to go in peace to love and serve the world.

Bibliography

A Prayer Book for Australia, The Anglican Church of Australia (Sydney: Broughton Books, 1999).

Alison, James, *Knowing Jesus* (Springfield, IL: Templegate Publishers, 1994).

Alison, James, *Raising Abel: The Recovery of the Eschatological Imagination* (New York: Crossroad Publishing Company, 1996).

Alison, James, *The Joy of Being Wrong: Original Sin through Easter Eyes* (New York: Crossroad Publishing Company, 1998).

Alison, James, *Undergoing God: Dispatches from the Scene of a Break-in* (London: Darton, Longman and Todd, 2006).

Alison, James, *Broken Hearts & New Creations: Intimations of a Great Reversal* (London: Darton, Longman and Todd, 2010).

Bachelard, Sarah, 'Rights as Industry', *Res Publica*, 11/1 (2002): 1–5.

Bachelard, Sarah, 'Response to Bernadette Tobin', in Winifred Wing Han Lamb and Ian Barns (eds), *God Down Under: Theology in the Antipodes* (Adelaide: ATF Press, 2003), pp.216–224.

Bachelard, Sarah, 'John Main's Contribution to Contemplative Theology: "In meditation we verify the truths of faith in our own experience"', in Laurence Freeman and Stefan Reynolds (eds), *John Main: The Expanding Vision* (Norwich: Canterbury Press, 2009), pp.51–75.

Bachelard, Sarah, 'Beyond "Thou Shalt" Lies a Deeper Word: The Theologian as Ethicist', in Heather Thomson (ed.), *Embracing Grace: The Theologian's Task* (Canberra: Barton Books, 2009), pp.103–118.

Bachelard, Sarah, *Experiencing God in a Time of Crisis* (Miami, FL: Convivium Press, 2012).

Banner, Michael, *Christian Ethics and Contemporary Moral Problems* (Cambridge: Cambridge University Press, 1999).

Becker, Ernest, *The Denial of Death* (New York: Free Press Paperbacks, 1997).

Biggar, Nigel, 'Is Stanley Hauerwas Sectarian?', in Mark Thiessen Nation and Samuel Wells (eds), *Faithfulness and Fortitude: In Conversation with the Theological Ethics of Stanley Hauerwas* (Edinburgh: T&T Clark, 2000), pp.141–160.

Bonhoeffer, Dietrich, *Letters and Papers from Prison* (enlarged edition), ed. Eberhard Bethge (London: SCM Press, 1971).

Bonhoeffer, Dietrich, *Ethics*, Dietrich Bonhoeffer Works, Volume 6, ed. Clifford J. Green, trans. Reinhard Krauss, Charles C. West and Douglas W. Stott (Minneapolis, MN: Fortress Press, 2009).

Burrows, Ruth, *Ascent to Love: The Spiritual Teaching of St John of the Cross* (London: Darton, Longman and Todd, 1987).

Carlisle, Joseph, James Carter and Daniel Whistler (eds), *Moral Powers, Fragile Beliefs: Essays in Moral and Religious Philosophy* (New York: Continuum, 2011).

Carnley, Peter, *The Structure of Resurrection Belief* (Oxford: Clarendon Press, 1987).

Cassian, John, *Conferences*, trans. Colm Luibheid (Mahwah, NJ: Paulist Press, 1985).

Cassian, John, *The Conferences*, trans. Boniface Ramsey (New York: Newman Press, 1997).

Coady, C.A.J., *Testimony: A Philosophical Study* (Oxford: Clarendon Press, 1992).

Coakley, Sarah, *Powers and Submissions: Spirituality, Philosophy and Gender* (Malden, MA: Blackwell Publishing, 2002).

Cordner, Christopher, 'Two Conceptions of Love in Philosophical Thought', *Sophia*, 50 (2011): 315–329.

Cordner, Christopher (ed.), *Philosophy, Ethics and a Common Humanity: Essays in Honour of Raimond Gaita* (London: Routledge, 2011).

Cowdell, Scott, *Abiding Faith: Christianity Beyond Certainty, Anxiety and Violence* (Eugene, OR: Cascade Books, 2009).

Davis, Stephen T., '"Seeing" the Risen Jesus', in Stephen T. Davis, Daniel Kendall SJ and Gerald O'Collins SJ (eds), *The Resurrection: An Interdisciplinary Symposium on the Resurrection of Jesus* (Oxford: Oxford University Press, 1997), pp.126–147.

de Chergé OCSO, Christian, 'Testament', *Monastic Interreligious Dialogue Bulletin*, 55 (May 1996).

Diamond, Cora, 'Losing Your Concepts', *Ethics*, 98 (1988): 255–277.

Diamond, Cora, 'How Many Legs?', in Raimond Gaita (ed.), *Value and Understanding: Essays for Peter Winch* (London: Routledge, 1990), pp.149–178.

Diamond, Cora, 'The Importance of Being Human', in David Cockburn (ed.), *Human Beings* (Cambridge: Cambridge University Press, 1991), pp.35–62.

Diamond, Cora, '"We Are Perpetually Moralists": Iris Murdoch, Fact, and Value', in Maria Antonaccio and William Schweiker (eds), *Iris Murdoch and the Search for Human Goodness* (Chicago, IL: University of Chicago Press, 1996), pp.79–109.

Duff, Nancy J., 'The Commandments and the Common Life – Reflections on Paul Lehmann's *The Decalogue and a Human Future*', in Philip G. Ziegler and Michelle J. Bartel (eds), *Explorations in Christian Theology and Ethics: Essays in Conversation with Paul L. Lehmann* (Farnham: Ashgate, 2009), pp.29–44.

Dunn, James D.G., *Jesus, Paul and the Law* (London: SPCK, 1990).

Esler, Philip F., *Galatians* (London: Routledge, 1998).

Evans, C.F., *Resurrection and the New Testament* (London: SCM Press, 1970).

Fletcher, Joseph, *Situation Ethics: The New Morality* (London: SCM Press, 1966).

Forrester, Duncan B., 'The Church and the Concentration Camp: Some Reflections on Moral Community', in Mark Thiessen Nation and Samuel Wells (eds), *Faithfulness and Fortitude: In Conversation with the Theological Ethics of Stanley Hauerwas* (Edinburgh: T&T Clark, 2000), pp.189–207.

Freeman, Laurence, *First Sight: The Experience of Faith* (London: Continuum, 2011).

Gaita, Raimond, 'The Personal in Ethics', in D.Z. Phillips and Peter Winch (eds), *Wittgenstein: Attention to Particulars* (London: Macmillan, 1989), pp.124–150.

Gaita, Raimond, 'Common Understanding and Individual Voices', in Jane Adamson, Richard Freadman and David Parker (eds), *Renegotiating Ethics in Literature, Philosophy, and Theory* (Cambridge: Cambridge University Press, 1998), pp.269–288.

Gaita, Raimond, *A Common Humanity: Thinking about Love & Truth & Justice* (Melbourne: Text Publishing, 1999).

Gaita, Raimond, *Good and Evil: An Absolute Conception*, second edition (London: Routledge, 2004).

Gaita, Raimond, 'Morality, Metaphysics and Religion', in Joseph Carlisle, James Carter and Daniel Webster (eds), *Moral Powers, Fragile Beliefs: Essays in Moral and Religious Philosophy* (New York: Continuum, 2011), pp.3–28.

Garrett, Graeme, *God Matters: Conversations in Theology* (Collegeville, MN: Liturgical Press, 1999).

Goodyer, Jennifer Spencer, 'The Blank Face of Love: The Possibility of Goodness in the Literary and Philosophical Work of Iris Murdoch', *Modern Theology*, 25/2 (2009): 217–237.

Gordon, Peter E., 'Must the Sacred be Transcendent?', *Inquiry*, 54/2 (2011): 126–139.

Gunton, Colin, *Enlightenment & Alienation: An Essay towards a Trinitarian Theology* (Basingstoke: Marshall Morgan & Scott, 1985).

Gunton, Colin, *The Actuality of Atonement: A Study of Metaphor, Rationality and the Christian Tradition* (London: T&T Clark, 1998).

Hall, Douglas John, *The Cross in Our Context: Jesus and the Suffering World* (Minneapolis, MN: Fortress Press, 2003).

Hamilton, Christopher, 'Raimond Gaita on Saints, Love and Human Preciousness', *Ethical Theory and Moral Practice*, 11 (2008): 181–195.

Hart, William David, 'Naturalizing Christian Ethics: A Critique of Charles Taylor's *A Secular Age*', *Journal of Religious Ethics*, 40/1 (2012): 149–170.

Hauerwas, Stanley, 'Murdochian Muddles: Can We Get Through Them If God Does Not Exist?', in Maria Antonaccio and William Schweiker (eds), *Iris Murdoch and the Search for Human Goodness* (Chicago, IL: University of Chicago Press, 1996), pp.190–208.

Hauerwas, Stanley, *The Hauerwas Reader*, eds John Berkmann and Michael Cartwright (Durham, NC: Duke University Press, 2001).

Hauerwas, Stanley and Samuel Wells (eds), *The Blackwell Companion to Christian Ethics* (Malden, MA: Blackwell Publishing, 2004).

Hillesum, Etty, *Etty: A Diary 1941–43*, trans. Arnold J. Pomeranz, intro. J.G. Gaarlandt (London: Grafton Books, 1985).

Hillesum, Etty, *Letters from Westerbork*, trans. Arnold J. Pomeranz (London: Grafton Books, 1988).

Johnstone, Brian, 'Transformation Ethics: The Moral Implications of the Resurrection', in Stephen Davis, Daniel Kendall SJ and Gerald Collins SJ (eds), *The Resurrection: An Interdisciplinary Symposium on the Resurrection of Jesus* (Oxford: Oxford University Press, 1997), pp.339–360.

Julian of Norwich, *Revelations of Divine Love*, trans. Clifton Wolters (Harmondsworth: Penguin, 1966).

Kant, Immanuel, *Groundwork of the Metaphysic of Morals*, trans. H.J. Paton (New York: Harper Torchbooks, 1964).

Kelly, Anthony J., *The Resurrection Effect: Transforming Christian Life and Thought* (Maryknoll, NY: Orbis Books, 2008).

Kenneson, Philip, 'Worship, Imagination, and Formation', in Stanley Hauerwas and Samuel Wells (eds), *The Blackwell Companion to Christian Ethics* (Malden, MA: Blackwell Publishing, 2004), pp.53–67.

Kerr, Fergus, *Immortal Longings: Versions of Transcending Humanity* (London: SPCK, 1997).

Kierkegaard, Søren, *Fear and Trembling*, trans. Walter Lowrie (Princeton, NJ: Princeton University Press, 1954).

King, Martin Luther, *Strength to Love* (London and Glasgow: Collins Fontana Books, 1969).

Levi, Primo, *If This is a Man*, trans. Stuart Woolf (London: Abacus, 1987).

Lorenzen, Thorwald, *Resurrection and Discipleship: Interpretive Models, Biblical Reflections, Theological Consequences* (Maryknoll, NY: Orbis Books, 1995).

Main, John, *Word into Silence* (London: Darton, Longman and Todd, 1980).

Main, John, *Christian Meditation: The Gethsemani Talks* (Tucson, AZ: Medio Media, 2000).

Main, John, *Moment of Christ: Prayer as the Way to God's Fullness*, ed. Laurence Freeman (Norwich: Canterbury Press, 2010).

Markus, Robert A., *Christianity and the Secular* (Notre Dame, IN: University of Notre Dame Press, 2006).

McGinn, Bernard (ed.), *Meister Eckhart and the Beguine Mystics: Hadewijch of Brabant, Mechthild of Magdeburg, and Marguerite Porete* (New York: Continuum, 1997).

McIntosh, Mark, *Mystical Theology: The Integrity of Spirituality and Theology* (Malden, MA: Blackwell Publishing, 1998).

McIntosh, Mark, *Discernment and Truth: The Spirituality and Theology of Knowledge* (New York: Crossroad Publishing Company, 2004).

Merton, Thomas, *Conjectures of a Guilty Bystander* (Tunbridge Wells: Burns & Oates, 1995).

Milbank, John, *The Word Made Strange: Theology, Language, Culture* (Oxford: Blackwell Publishers, 1997).

Milbank, John, *Being Reconciled: Ontology and Pardon* (London: Routledge, 2003).

Milosz, Czeslaw, *Provinces: Poems 1987–1991*, trans. Czeslaw Milosz and Robert Hass (New York: Ecco Press, 1993).

Moltmann, Jürgen, *The Way of Jesus Christ: Christology in Messianic Dimensions* (London: SCM Press, 1990).

Moltmann, Jürgen, *Theology of Hope: On the Ground and Implications of a Christian Eschatology* (Minneapolis, MN: Fortress Press, 1993).

Moore, Sebastian, *The Crucified Is No Stranger* (London: Darton, Longman and Todd, 1977).

Moore, Sebastian, *Let This Mind Be In You: The Quest for Identity through Oedipus to Christ* (London: Darton, Longman and Todd, 1985).

Mulhall, Stephen, 'The Work of Saintly Love: The Religious Impulse in Gaita's Writing', in Christopher Cordner (ed.), *Philosophy, Ethics and a Common Humanity: Essays in Honour of Raimond Gaita* (London: Routledge, 2011), pp.21–36.

Murdoch, Iris, 'Vision and Choice in Morality', *Proceedings of the Aristotelian Society*, supp. vol. 30 (1956): 32–58.

Murdoch, Iris, *The Sovereignty of Good* (London: Routledge, 1970).

Murdoch, Iris, *Metaphysics as a Guide to Morals* (London: Penguin, 1993).

Nussbaum, Martha, *Love's Knowledge: Essays on Philosophy and Literature* (New York: Oxford University Press, 1990).

O'Collins, Gerald, 'The Resurrection: The State of the Question', in Stephen T. Davis, Daniel Kendall SJ and Gerald O'Collins SJ (eds), *The Resurrection: An Interdisciplinary Symposium on the Resurrection of Jesus* (Oxford: Oxford University Press, 1997), pp.5–28.

O'Collins, Gerald, *Believing in the Resurrection: The Meaning and Promise of the Risen Jesus* (New York: Paulist Press, 2012).

O'Donovan, Oliver, *Resurrection and Moral Order: An Outline for Evangelical Ethics*, second edition (Leicester: Apollos, 1994).

Palmer, Parker J., *Healing the Heart of Democracy: The Courage to Create a Politics Worthy of the Human Spirit* (San Francisco: Jossey-Bass, 2011).

Perkins, Pheme, *Resurrection: New Testament Witness and Contemporary Reflection* (London: Geoffrey Chapman, 1984).

Plato, *Phaedo*, trans. Benjamin Jowett (New York: Prometheus Books, 1988).

Radcliffe, Timothy, *What is the Point of Being a Christian?* (London: Burns & Oates, 2005).

Rhees, Rush, *Without Answers* (London: Routledge & Kegan Paul, 1969).

Ricoeur, Paul 'The Hermeneutics of Testimony', in Lewis Mudge (ed.), *Essays in Biblical Interpretation* (London: SPCK, 1981), pp.119–154.

Robinette, Brian D., *Grammars of Resurrection: A Christian Theology of Presence and Absence* (New York: Crossroad Publishing Company, 2009).

Robinette, Brian D., 'Heraclitean Nature and the Comfort of the Resurrection: Theology in an Open Space', *Logos*, 14/4 (Fall 2011): 13–38.

Rosner, Brian S. (ed.), *Understanding Paul's Ethics: Twentieth Century Approaches* (Grand Rapids, MI: William B. Eerdmans Publishing Company, 1995).

Shanks, Andrew, *Against Innocence: Gillian Rose's Reception and Gift of Faith* (London: SCM Press, 2008).

Shults, F. LeRon, *Reforming Theological Anthropology: After the Philosophical Turn to Relationality* (Grand Rapids, MI: William B. Eerdmans Publishing Company, 2003).

Singh, Devin, 'Resurrection as Surplus and Possibility: Moltmann and Ricoeur', *Scottish Journal of Theology*, 61/3 (2008): 251–269.

Taylor, Charles, *Sources of the Self: The Making of Modern Identity* (Cambridge, MA: Harvard University Press, 1989).

Taylor, Charles, 'Iris Murdoch and Moral Philosophy', in Maria Antonaccio and William Schweiker (eds), *Iris Murdoch and the Search for Human Goodness* (Chicago, IL: University of Chicago Press, 1996), pp.3–28.

Taylor, Charles, *A Secular Age* (Cambridge, MA: Harvard University Press, 2007).

The Cloud of Unknowing & The Book of Privy Counselling, ed. William Johnston (New York: Image Books, 1996).

The Rule of St Benedict, trans. Anthony C. Meisel and M.L. del Mastro (New York: Image Books, 1975).

Warner, Martin, 'Love and Transcendence', in Joseph Carlisle, James Carter and Daniel Webster (eds), *Moral Powers, Fragile Beliefs: Essays in Moral and Religious Philosophy* (New York: Continuum, 2011), pp.157–183.

Webster, John, '"Where Christ Is": Christology and Ethics', in F. LeRon Shults and Brent Waters (eds), *Christology and Ethics* (Grand Rapids, MI: William B. Eerdmans Publishing Company, 2010), pp.32–55.

Weil, Simone, *Waiting on God*, trans. Emma Craufurd (London: Fontana Books, 1959).

Weil, Simone, *Gravity and Grace*, trans. Emma Crauford (London: Routledge, 1963).

Weil, Simone, *Simone Weil: An Anthology*, ed. Sian Miles (London: Virago, 1986).

Wells, Samuel, *Transforming Fate into Destiny: The Theological Ethics of Stanley Hauerwas* (Carlisle: Paternoster Press, 1998).

Wells, Samuel, *Improvisation: The Drama of Christian Ethics* (London: SPCK, 2004).

Wells, Samuel, *God's Companions: Reimagining Christian Ethics* (Malden, MA: Blackwell Publishing, 2005).

Williams, Bernard, *Ethics and the Limits of Philosophy* (Cambridge, MA: Harvard University Press, 1985).

Williams, Rowan, *The Wound of Knowledge: Christian Spirituality from the New Testament to Saint John of the Cross*, second edition (Cambridge, MA: Cowley Publications, 1991).

Williams, Rowan, *On Christian Theology* (Oxford: Blackwell Publishers, 2000).

Williams, Rowan, *Resurrection: Interpreting the Easter Gospel*, second edition (Cleveland, OH: The Pilgrim Press, 2002).

Williams, Rowan, *Silence and Honey Cakes: The Wisdom of the Desert* (Oxford: Lion Publishing plc, 2003).

Williams, Rowan, 'Rome Lecture: "Secularism, Faith and Freedom"', delivered at the Pontifical Academy of Social Sciences, 23 November 2006 (accessed http://www.archbishopofcanterbury.org/articles.php/1175/rome-lecture-secularism-faith-and-freedom, 8 October 2012).

Williams, Rowan, 'Human Rights and Religious Faith', Lecture delivered at the World Council of Churches Ecumenical Centre in Geneva, 28 February 2012 (accessed http://www.archbishopofcanterbury.org/articles.php/2370/human-rights-and-religious-faith, 7 October 2012).

Wittgenstein, Ludwig, 'Lecture on Ethics', *Philosophical Review*, 74/1 (1965): 3–12.

Wynn, Mark, 'Saintliness and the Moral Life: Gaita as a Source for Christian Ethics', *Journal of Religious Ethics*, 31 (2003): 463–485.

Wynn, Mark, *Emotional Experience and Religious Understanding: Integrating Perception, Conception and Feeling* (Cambridge: Cambridge University Press, 2005).

Index

Note: numbers preceded by n are footnote numbers.

Biblical References

Made in the USA
Middletown, DE
27 July 2019